THE
DADDY
ESSAYS

Perspectives from an Unexpected Journey

NEIL TURNER

LINGERING
HEREFORD
PRESS

Cover and interior formatting by KUHN Design Group | kuhndesigngroup.com

Copy Editing by Blair Parke

First edition 2026

ISBN: 979-8-9942544-0-0

For Usha, who made me a better man;
for Ella, who introduced me to the joys of fatherhood;
for Colby, who taught me to cherish every moment;
for Alex, who shows me wonder and determination.

You are the heart of every page.

Just a Dad That Doesn't Like Prefaces

I f a book has a preface, I skip it. I'm probably the lesser for it, but when I crack open a book, I am ready to dive right in. On a recent drive, I started a new audiobook, which included a preface, prologue, and introduction. I got to my destination, and Chapter 1 hadn't even started.

And though I have daydreamed of writing a book since the age of fifteen, I never thought I would actually do it. But I knew if I ever did write a book, I'd skip writing a preface.

Still, readers of this book would benefit from some background and an orientation to set the stage for what they are about to read and know about me. So, in this chapter, I want to give a brief foundation to three questions: What is this book? How did it come to be? And how is it organized?

WHAT IS THIS BOOK?

This question is best answered by starting with what this book isn't. Primarily, it is not a book by a parenting expert.

I have no special training or certifications in parenting, child education, or relationships. You will see references to faith, but if there is a category below layman in religious doctrine, that is the one I would occupy. I philosophize a lot and psychoanalyze a little, neither of which should be taken too seriously.

You'll read stories of loss, but I am not a counselor, and though I expect my fellow bereaved parents to find commonalities, the audience is for all parents, not just those dealing with loss. In some ways, it's especially for those without loss to help them benefit from the painful lessons without the personal heartache.

Any advice contained within should be weighed with those admissions in mind.

I am just a dad, and parts of my dad journey have been unexpected. I never expected the loss of a child. I never expected to parent an autistic child. I never expected to become a stay-at-home dad, and I certainly never expected to find joy in changing diapers!

Along this surprising journey, I've learned some unforeseen lessons and perspectives. In sharing them, I hope you enjoy some laughs and find cause to hug and cherish your own family a bit more and a bit tighter. And if some of the lessons I learned resonate with you and make you look at things a bit differently, well, that is just a bonus for both of us.

HOW DID THIS BOOK COME TO BE?

My middle daughter, Colby, passed away at the age of two. In the aftermath, we made donations to several places in her memory, and along with the check, I would include a story about why their mission had touched our lives and hearts.

Not too deep into that process, I was overcome with the need to preserve other precious memories of Colby and being her dad, and I began writing about those, too. Writing a story forces a deeper thought process, and I found myself not just recording memories but finding lessons in them; that evolved into an unintended therapy of sorts.

These self-therapy sessions were healing, but they also wrecked me. After an essay was done, I was emotionally spent, but somehow better off than I had been before writing. I'd look forward to visiting the memories but would have to steel myself for the effort. That meant the gap between writing them would sometimes be quite lengthy.

However, that didn't matter because they were never intended to be a book. Selfishly, they were for me, though I did share them with friends and family.

Two things started to happen while writing.

One was that I began writing about other aspects of my fatherhood journey. Sometimes it would yield an essay with memories of my youth and apply them to my life as a dad. Sometimes it was just a funny story that happened with my other children. Other times, it was reflections of someone else in my life who shaped my outlook as a dad.

The second thing was that I started getting asked to share these stories with others. Someone would read about my diaper-changing adventures and want to share that with a soon-to-be dad. Someone else would want a copy of a story for their kids, siblings, pastor, or friend. I was honored by these requests and always taken a little aback that they meant something to strangers who didn't know our family personally.

The "you should write a book" comments were at first laughed off by me. Then shrugged off. Then started gnawing at me. Eventually, I let the idea take root that maybe there are others who would enjoy and benefit from these essays. And then I told myself the worst outcome is that my kids would have a collection of the essays, even if no one else read them.

I opened my hard drive to see if I had enough to even fill a book and was shocked to see I had nearly one hundred pieces written. This book is a collection of just over half of those that I selected as the most meaningful and/or most entertaining.

How is the book organized?

It helps to be mindful that these are essays are capable of standing on their own as individual stories. While I would be honored for you to sit and read all the chapters straight through, you are also free to pick and choose and jump around as much as you'd like and can do so without fear of losing an entire book's plotline. I am just as honored by the reader who picks this book up on occasions of needing encouragement, inspiration, or reflection and selects a chapter or two at a time to ponder over.

After narrowing the number of essays down to what I wanted to share, I faced the challenge of deciding how to organize them.

Because they were written before contemplating the compilation of them into a book, the order in which they were written wasn't preserved, so chronological order by creation date was out. Similarly, chronological by events would not work, and even if it did, some of the sadder stories would be clumped together. That would not only make for an emotional mountain to climb, but it would give the impression that time was only filled with darkness—or that as time moved on, the sadness didn't linger.

Instead, I front-loaded the earlier essays to contain key parts of the overarching story and balanced the rest with a mix of tones, so that you will never be too far from a funny moment or a story of gratitude. But don't shy away from the poignant stories that are sprinkled in. Though they don't gloss over the tragic, those moments make the happy times that much sweeter. If the final arrangement achieves that, then I'll be quite pleased because that is a fundamental thread in all our lives.

The chosen approach means that in one chapter a particular person may be 11, the next chapter off to college, and a subsequent chapter back to being 6. My hope is that by making you aware of this structure, it won't be disorienting.

To help you navigate the time-jumping and people involved, I've added a brief introduction to each essay to orient you. These are short and share any particular points to help you appreciate each chapter's contents or placement in the book.

To further help set the stage, let me give a brief introduction to our family here.

My wife, Usha, grew up in the Caribbean, primarily in Trinidad. We met as she was finishing grad school at Texas A&M, and we married a few years after that. The first twelve years of our married life was in Rockwall, Texas. At the time of this writing, we have lived the last twelve years in Oklahoma.

Ella is our oldest child, though no longer a child herself. She had the tough task of breaking us in as parents. In the following stories, you'll find her to be funny, sweet, and full of determination. She was 3 when Colby was born and 5 when Colby passed away.

Colby was just over two when she passed away. The first year of her life, we had no clues that anything was wrong with her medically, though she was on the smaller side. A one-year check-up detected a heart murmur that started us down the path to eventually finding out she had Geleophysic Dysplasia, a very rare genetic condition.

That condition affects many parts of the body, the heart being the most vulnerable among them. Heart failure resulted in her death. Researchers classify a disease as rare if it affects 200,000 people or less just in the United States. Colby's case of Geleophysic Dysplasia was estimated to be the 47th case known *worldwide*.

Colby's death was caused by heart failure resulting from that condition. As explained earlier, many of these stories center on Colby, as the essays were first born out of dealing with her tragic loss. In those stories, you'll find that she was so much more than her illness. Colby was not a sick child; she was a child who happened to be sick. That may sound like a distinction without a difference, but I will attest to the difference in outlook being huge.

Alex is our son. Born in Oklahoma almost four years after Colby died, he never got to meet his sister, but he definitely knows her! Not only has he heard her stories all his life, but he is also heavily shaped by the same forces—one force in particular. Usha, Ella, and Colby are all redheads, and if your life is filled with redheads, you know that is truly a force. And we are better off for it.

Alex also has autism, but autistic is just one of many adjectives and nowhere near the most important one.

And me? I'm just a dad.

Here are some of my stories.

CHAPTER 1

Lessons from Colby

A lot of consternation was involved in deciding to lead with this essay. Our pastor read it on my behalf at Colby's memorial service in May of 2010.

It is inherently sad, but the heartbreak has to be introduced at some point, and it is a defining part of my story so it makes sense to deal with it right out of the gate. And ultimately, its core lesson is the thesis of this book: Enjoy every moment and find gratitude in everything.

We are all struggling with trying to make sense of Colby's death. I wish I had some special insight to help understand why such a beautiful and spirited life ended so soon, yet I don't have those answers.

But while I don't have any answers about her death, I do know about her life. It was full of love and laughs, sweetness and strength, and the kind of wonderment and awe that only a child is capable of inspiring. And I know that Colby's life had meaning.

For me, much of that meaning was in what she taught me. The

lessons were many and varied, and some, I am sure, are yet to be discovered. I could never find the words to do justice to what I learned from Colby, but I would like to share just a few examples that are particularly treasured by me.

The first lesson I'd like to share is about her older sister, Ella. Before Colby was born, one of my great fears was that I had spoiled Ella so much that she would resent having a little sister around. Would she love her sister, or would they always fight? Would they compete for attention from my wife and I? She was so accustomed to being an only child; could she handle being a big sister?

Well, of course, everyone who had ever seen the two of them together knew how unfounded my worries were. Ella is an awesome big sister. Ella's love for Colby is endless, and she was always so patient and kind to her during their time together. No one made Colby laugh harder than Ella could.

And none of this took any coaching or prodding on our part. Ella was a natural big sister from day one.

In fact, just a few weeks after Colby was born, Ella went with me to Target on an errand. As we were walking down the aisles, she looked up at me and said, "Daddy, I really like Colby."

This was such sweet music to my ears. I looked back at her and said, "That's good because you know what? I really like her, too."

Ella smiled at me in that way that a little girl does when she is about to get her way, and she excitedly asked, "Daddy, can we keep her?" Classic Ella.

Barely able to form the words because I was smiling so hard, I told her we would have Colby for a long, long time.

My dear, sweet Ella. I am so sorry. Daddy made a promise to you that wasn't mine to make.

Colby wasn't with us for long at all, but she will always be with us in our hearts, and she was here long enough to teach me something about you that I will never forget. Never underestimate Ella.

Colby taught me about love. I've lived a blessed life. I have known the love of a wonderful wife, of family and friends, and, of course, by the time Colby was born, I had already experienced the special love of a daughter. Even with all of that, Colby managed to teach me even more about love. None of those lessons about love were more powerful than watching Colby interact with her mom.

I know that most parents can relate when I tell you that date night for my wife Usha and me doesn't come around as often as it should. We could take all the ticket stubs from the movies we've seen in the last five years and fit them in a matchbook. So, when date night does come around for us, it's something we really look forward to. Back in March was one such date—a dinner to celebrate our ninth wedding anniversary.

Usha had gotten ready, looking very beautiful in her stylish black dress, heels, and some special occasion jewelry that had not seen the light of day in quite a while. She took over watching the girls while I headed off to get myself ready. When I came back, they were nowhere to be found in the house, but the loud giggles and squeals from the backyard gave them away. I stepped out the back door, and what did I see? There was Usha in full date night attire—including heels—going down the slide with Colby in her lap, laughing and asking for more.

Usha wasn't worried about wrinkling her clothes, muddying her shoes, looking silly, or anything else. She saw some extra minutes to spend with her daughters, and she was not going to leave them unfilled. She made the most of these moments with unabashed and unguarded love, the power of which was on full display with Colby's joyous smile and a matching smile on Usha. The lesson was clear: The freer you love, the sweeter it is. I have not yet mastered it the way both Usha and Colby practice it, but I hope to.

Colby taught me about my relationship with God. As her health issues mounted, I became a lot more focused on God. I have prayed to Him, have pleaded with Him, and have questioned Him. I have tried to bargain with God, cussed Him, and have even doubted Him. And as the end drew near, I was certain I could not bear to make peace with Him ever again.

But then, my fears came true, and my time with Colby here on Earth was gone. Our pastor, Cheryl, gave her up to the Lord, and with that, my grudge with the Lord ended. Colby is in Heaven and with God. Someday I can be there with her, too—in a place without fears and with unending kisses from me to my sweet baby girl. There will be no more angst about what the future holds, just love.

God, I'll never understand why the things happened the way they did, but I am not angry with You anymore. How could I be when I know that one day, You will reunite me with my beloved daughter? I pray to You that every time the pain of this day eats at my very being, You help me to remember my heavenly reward and guide me down the path that leads there to Colby's raised arms, waiting for me to pick her up and hold her once again.

I could go on for days and on many different topics about the things Colby has taught me and still not scratch the surface. But I do want to share just one more lesson that I hope each of you will find helpful.

Colby's condition was tragic, but not without some blessings. One of which was that I had known for a while that our time with her might be short. That is a heavy burden, but with it comes the ability to treat every day like the precious gift that it is.

When you are in the position of having a limited number of days with someone you love, the hugs last a little longer, and the kisses are more frequent. When you are in that position, you take more photographs. When you are in that position, patience comes easier, and the humorous side of life is more apparent. When you are in that position, you take more time to smell the flowers, and playing just a little bit more together is an easily granted request. When you are in that position, life is richer, and the memories are so much sweeter; the I Love Yous are said much more.

Colby's lesson to you is that you are in that position.

My hope for you is that you realize it and that you can be more like Colby, making the most of every precious day with your loved ones.

Colby, thank you for the lessons and all the joy and richness you gave our lives. We love you.

CHAPTER 2

Daddies and Weathermen: Father's Day Thoughts

I wrote this essay prior to our son Alex being born, but the sentiments apply just as much.

It's hard for a father to know if he is doing a good job. In some regards, the bar is set quite modestly. Comparisons with others is a dangerous game done on a superficial level and yields faulty conclusions. Many times, the signals for course correction come a good deal after traveling the wrong path.

This piece tries to make sense of all that and find a Father's Day lesson in what it means to be a good dad.

Growing up in the Texas Panhandle, you quickly learn the expression, "If you don't like the weather, stick around for thirty minutes, and it will change." In my travels, I have learned that saying isn't unique to the Panhandle; many of you know exactly what I am talking about. For those of you who are acclimated to more consistent and predictable temperatures, let me offer a couple of examples to help illustrate the concept.

Here in Oklahoma, where I live now, earlier this spring, the weatherman announced we set a record high in the upper eighties for the day. In his next breath, he issued a freeze warning for the very next day.

I find a lot of humor in that alone, but the fact that I had recently installed one of those smart-learning thermostats made it that much funnier. It is supposed to use the outside weather and learn your normal preferences and habits to automatically create a programmed thermostat schedule. It's a neat device; it's blue when it's cooling, orange when it's heating. I discovered that when it's thoroughly confused, it stays pitch-black and won't come on.

Several years ago, I was traveling in Australia with a guy who grew up about an hour from my childhood hometown. Sitting around with the locals, we exchanged information about our respective home areas. Agricultural types dominated the conversation, so naturally the question of rainfall came up.

"How much rain do you get in Texas?"

My friend answered, "In our part of Texas, we get about fourteen inches of rain a year. And you ought to be there the night it comes."

An exaggeration, to be sure, but not by much. Just over a week ago, parts of our area received up to 13 inches of rain in about 12 hours. A week after that rain, the weatherman announced that official drought conditions were about three weeks away. If you do the math, that takes you from devastating floods to drought in one month.

Hopefully, you are getting a feel for the unpredictable weather I grew up with, which continues to be my normal. Add to that what I am about to say was from an era of meteorology from the dark ages, compared to the technology bonanza of today. But when I was a kid,

I dreamed of being a weatherman because I knew of no other job where you could be wrong by so much, so often, and not get fired.

In my travels, I've learned that joke isn't as unique to me as I originally thought either. But maybe in its overuse, there is a bit of truth there.

What other job can you have where you so often miss the mark, yet you're not only not fired, but you're also put on billboards, coffee mugs, and sent to schools to talk to kids, all while treated like a rockstar?

Well, I am glad you asked, because there is at least one other such job—being a dad.

Consider the number of dads there are in the world at any given moment. Let's call it two billion dads plus or minus a billion. (Disputes of that estimate can be emailed to googledidn'thaveagoodanswerinthetopthreeresults@justguessed.com.)

Now consider the number of "World's Greatest Dad" T-shirts, caps, bumper stickers, ties, coffee mugs, iPhone covers, tape measures, suspenders, ice cream bowls, license plate holders, and other such items. That number is about five billion.

I'll grant you that a great many of those items are on the shelves of Stuckey's gathering dust and that some dads have three or maybe four of such items. But no matter how you slice it, there are a lot of dads out there laying claim to the top title who have no business doing so.

Or do they?

This phenomenon has always intrigued me. But like most things about fatherhood worth knowing, I learned about this one from one of my daughters–this time from Ella.

During one car ride, Ella unexpectedly announced to me, "You are the best dad in the whole world."

With those billions of T-shirts in mind, I replied, "There are a whole lot of dads in this world."

She pondered that for a very short time and rephrased it slightly, "Well. You are the best dad in the whole world *for me.*"

The addition of those two words at the end added a lot of meaning. Of course, I appreciated the compliment, but beyond that, it drew everything into focus. It's not about being the number one dad of all the dads. It's about being—or trying to be—the best dad for *your* kids.

Maybe all those shirts are exactly right. Maybe they just need a little asterisk on them to indicate "for my kids." You don't have to actually be the best dad in the world for *your* kids to think you are. And that is a good thing, at least in my case.

Sometimes, I expect too much from my kids and sometimes too little. I let things that should be low priority interfere with quality time. My lectures are too long, and too often; my hugs are too short. And yes, I plead guilty to having, on at least one occasion, yelled, "Answer me!" only to interrupt my daughter's answer within the first syllable with "Be quiet when I am talking to you!"

Too often, my work or other life's frustrations erode my patience, and Ella bears the brunt. Too often, I say "no," not to protect or to teach but to make things more convenient for me. Too often, I am lost in the past or worried about the future and missing the now, or I append my praise with unneeded critiques for further improvement.

But despite all those flaws and many more, I am rewarded with my daughter's love and adoration every day.

Sure, I also think there are a lot of things I do pretty well as a dad. But like the weatherman, we dads are afforded a lot of mistakes and latitude along the way.

Compare expectations for dads to expectations for moms. I can volunteer at school for one of Ella's events, and I get tons of comments about "It's great to see a dad get involved"; I get that praise just for being there. Meanwhile, if a mom shows up with store-bought cookies for the whole class, she gets made to feel bad because they weren't homemade … with eggs from her own hens … with options for gluten-free … served with organic milk … from the free-range dairy three counties over … and still warm from the oven.

Another exaggeration? Sure. But again, not by much.

Yep. Thank goodness the bar for dads isn't as high as what moms get subjected to. Of course, that isn't pressure put on the moms by the kids; it's by other moms. I've seen how tough some moms can be on each other and suspect the makers of Valium have a major stake in Pinterest.

Maybe some moms could feel a bit better hearing Ella's "best for me" lesson, too.

I need to be clear here. I'm not saying the job of being a dad is unimportant. Clearly, the impact a dad has on a child is enormous.

And I'm not saying being a dad is a piece of cake, not the least of all for the reasons cited above. We share the weighty burden of helping grow and guide our children's spiritual, physical, emotional, and educational lives with our wives. We become overnight role models, which isn't an easy transition for most of us who have plenty of kid-like behavior in us.

We often fall into the role of referee and, with that, the associated treatment. Dads regularly get underestimated (which is also why we so easily get credit). And when we do tread into children's activities involving only moms, we have to navigate gender issues and associated complications. That is a whole book unto itself.

And it's hard finding and trying to keep things in balance, like knowing when to push and when to protect, or knowing when to fix and when to let them solve.

Is there anything that makes a dad instantly feel more like a hero than protecting their child or fixing something for them? Maybe not. Is there anything that can make a dad feel more helpless and ineffective than not being able to protect their child, or fix something when it is most needed? Certainly not.

And because of that, Father's Day will always be bittersweet for me. For all the joy I take from being a dad, and as much as I like to envision myself wearing a SuperDad cape, the memories of watching Colby battle and later succumb to her disease remind me how helpless I can be. For all the smiles created from the cherished memories accumulated so far, missing the memories that should have been causes pangs. Being a dad has brought me the greatest joys in my life and the deepest sorrow, and Father's Day is and will always be a reminder of both.

But more than the bittersweet, the biggest emotion Father's Day brings me is appreciation. I hear Usha and Ella whispering plans and gift ideas to make sure I feel special on Father's Day. They put in a lot of effort in figuring out what to get me—an admittedly tough person to get presents for.

But they should rest easy. They can't top what they, along with Colby, have already given me—the gift of fatherhood itself and the wisdom to cherish it. They have given me the opportunity to try and be the world's best dad.* That not only makes Father's Day special; it makes every day special.

Thank you, girls.

---

* *...for my kids*

CHAPTER 3

Chicken Pot Pie, Elevator Rides, and Other Thoughts From the Maternity Ward

This essay introduces the arrival of Alex into the family, while offering a look at the humor of those earliest days of fatherhood. A man's world changes the moment they put his baby in his arms. It's like a showing up for a test that you are totally unprepared for. It's scary as can be but yields great lessons and stories.

You don't have to try to spot the first-time dads at the hospital because they will tell you their good news before you have time to give them a second thought. They are running around all over the maternity ward with an odd mix of excitement, fear, and delirium that is usually only attainable through illegal drugs.

"Here, let me hold that door for you," and as you walk through, they share all the details about their new baby that they can cram in those five seconds. And if you pause to hear more, look out for a hug. We are in the bonding phase, and we are trying to bond with anyone who shows the slightest interest in our creation. Lord help you if you are the first nurse on duty, though, in my defense, I did quit sending her Christmas cards when she started marking them "return to sender."

Yes, day one of fatherhood is glorious, and we want to share that glory with all! Even if you're the cashier at the cafeteria and see a couple of thousand dads a year go through your line, we want to make your day by showing you iPhone pics of our baby. If I were a hospital worker, I would strike until new dads were banned from the cafeteria altogether or at least give them their food for free so nobody has to be in line behind them.

And if any of that sounds mean or like I'm poking too much fun at new dads, I'm allowed because not only was I that "new dad" once, when Ella was born, I played it to the hilt.

My favorite spot was the elevator ride. It's a captive audience, and no one else speaks.

"Hey, everybody! I'm a new dad! Let me tell you all about it! It's a girl! She has red hair! Her mom has red hair, too! When we saw the sonogram, we saw her hair, and we hoped it would be red! We wanted to ask the sonographer if it was red, but of course, you can't tell on a sonogram! But we asked anyway! And now it's red!

"Six? No. She was seven pounds! Seven pounds and two ounces!

"Oh! Floor six? No. She was born downstairs!

"Oh? You want me to push the button for floor six? Should I go with you to tell your friends up there? No, of course not; that would be silly. Of course. I don't need to be there. You can tell them! What's your e-mail? I'll send you pics!"

In the outside world, people are sometimes genuinely surprised and excited to hear this unanticipated news. No one whose elevator stops on the maternity floor is surprised, but that doesn't dampen our enthusiasm. To contemplate the ridiculousness of this, imagine if we were leaving the donut shop and doing such a thing. Walking out the door, we told the people passing by on the sidewalk, "Just got a maple bar—get this—with cream filling! High five! Don't leave me hanging!"

You thought staff elevators were for emergency cases or to help get doctors to their destinations quickly. No, they got them to avoid first-time dads. They went on strike to make it happen.

When Colby was born, things were a bit different. The day she was born started like the day Ella was born. That is to say, in the wee hours of the morning, Usha woke me up and whispered, "It's time." Both times, I wiped away drool from my face and tried to figure out what was happening while Usha giggled at my disorientation.

Once at the hospital, the day began as it had with Ella but several hours into labor with Colby, the doctors grew apprehensive. Then suddenly, their concern spiked, and we were told Usha needed a C-section, and she needed it now. Orders were shouted, staff were flying, and activity went into all-hands-on-deck mode. No one was saying, "Don't worry"; instead, they were saying, "We will do all we can."

Soon, they whisked Usha away to the operating room, leaving me waiting in the once bustling room by myself to wait for about twenty minutes until they could take me in, too. Those 20 minutes felt like 20 hours: I paced, prayed, and cried, all at the same time. I was worried about them both, trying my best not to contemplate either one of them not making it but being completely unsuccessful at it.

Finally, a nurse came to get me. When I walked into the room, a curtain was up, covering Usha from the chest down. She was concerned but calm; that calmed me some as well. I sat, stroked her hair, and braced myself for whatever was about to come.

The doctors mostly worked silently. When there was talk, it was laden with technical, medical terms, and their voices were tense. Then the doctor spoke to me, "Dad, I'm about to lift her up if you want to see."

I peeked over the curtain to see Colby for the first time. She was a deep shade of purple that I was not expecting. I couldn't see any movement. Usha studied my face for a reaction. "What does she look like?"

Nobody spoke; I didn't know what to say. Once again, time slowed.

Then, Colby let out a little roar/growl. Usha said, "She sounds like Baby Jaguar from *Go Diego Go*," referring to a cartoon popular with toddlers. The sounds of life and Usha's joke broke through the thick tension in the room. The medical staff chuckled, took a brief sigh of relief, and then quickly split into two groups: one taking care of Usha, the other Colby.

A NICU team was called down to help with Colby, and Usha repeated her unanswered question, "What does she look like?"

"Purple," I answered. "But less purple now than when she came out."

Thankfully, she was still protesting fairly loudly, her cries of discomfort being comforting to us. The tension of the doctors was easing, but not gone, and aside from Colby's cries and medical lingo between teammates, the room was quiet.

Then, we heard the next comforting phrase, one that Colby would hear her whole life. "Look at that hair! Look at that pretty red hair!"

Pleased to hear she had red hair, and even more pleased that things had calmed to where that could be the focus, Usha and I were finally both able to smile at each other. Things were sounding much better.

By the time the doctor was done with Usha, the nursing staff had

Colby cleaned up and an orange bow in her hair. She was still being tended to by the NICU and others, but no one was sounding urgent, and there were no more signs of panic.

The doctor approached me to tell me things would be ok. We both saw the relief in each other's eyes. I hugged the doctor, and she hugged me in an embrace that could only be described as the bond between two people who had ventured right up to the line of disaster and managed not to fall over it: the skill and credit for which belonged to her and the unbridled appreciation to me.

That hug was a celebration. It was also downright scary because the doctor's display of emotion told the story of how close we were to a bad outcome for Colby.

Meanwhile, the other hero, Usha, still strapped to the table and only able to look up at the ceiling, was moving past her fear. "I want to see her!"

And for all the worries a child can give a parent, they are just as capable of melting those fears away just being themselves. Thus began the transition for all of us to the pure joy of bringing a child into the world.

Though second-born, all the joy was still there. But I wasn't new to the dad thing anymore. I smugly looked down on all those first-time dads from my lofty perch of experience and differentiated myself from them by waiting to be asked about my new baby instead of blurting out the details.

Of course, waiting to be asked doesn't mean playing it cool, necessarily. In the elevator, I'd position myself so others could see my joy-filled grin. I might have swung the empty baby carrier around just a bit too much or fiddled with an overnight bag a little too much, checking for bibs, etc. And, yes, I'll admit I have been known to wear my scrubs from the delivery room a lot longer than they were intended to be worn.

It started off working pretty well. Someone would release me from my suffering and ask if I had a new baby. That is, unless some *new dad* was already there blabbering on about his. Don't you hate those guys?

Sometime late in day one, my new plan's wheels came off in horrific fashion.

I stepped on the elevator on the fourth floor for a quick trip up one floor. The elevator had only one other occupant, a kindly looking lady with gray hair and a sweet, grandmotherly disposition. For this quick trip, I couldn't waste time, so I stepped in with a big smile on and asked, "Are you headed up to the nursery, too?"

"No," she said. "But you must be. Are you celebrating a new grandchild?"

Not child. She said GRAND child.

That stung. Heck, it still stings. It also made me a little gun-shy about what the next person would say. This is why, when Alex was born, six years after Colby, my guard was up. I considered it a victory that we made it through the entire hospital stay without anyone asking if I was a grandpa. I'd like to offer that as proof; as the older lady mentioned earlier, it was an aberration, but the truth is I probably stared at my feet a lot more as a self-defense strategy.

There were a few other marked differences between Alex's birth and those of his big sisters. Of course, there is the gender thing, which we are way too early into for me to have a handle on to write about.

The biggest difference was the delivery itself. With the girls, we didn't know when they would arrive. This time, we had to set up the cesarean procedure in advance. The morning Alex was born, we showed up in the hospital, went through all the normal tests and preparation, and then went off to the operating room, not in an emergency like with Colby but as scheduled.

Having been through the scary experience of Colby's birth, the haunting last few days of her life, and several tough memories in the hospital in between, we had been bracing ourselves for months leading up to that day. Years really.

If anybody were ever to debate if Usha and I are the optimistic sort—ok, nobody ever would but pretend with me—the fact that we attempted to have a third child should settle that question convincingly. You can talk about statistics all you want, and we certainly did, but when you walk back into the hospital world with the scars we carry, it's never going to be easy.

Our emotions ran the gamut from normal, excited parents to worries about Alex to the memories of Colby. Sometimes, tears of sadness. Sometimes of joy. Sometimes of fear. Sometimes of excitement. And on that day, there were all those tears combined.

There we were in the operating room. Usha, with her arms strapped down on either side of her, her eyes wide and darting about while the rest of her lay motionless. She has beautiful eyes anyway, but with her hair covered and the rest of her body below her neck blocked by the curtain, they are even more striking. Even more expressive.

And in that brief window of time between when they let me in the room and when things really got hopping, I sat there looking to comfort her. I was afraid to hold on to her hand because it had the IV in it. Her hair was all tucked into a cap, making it awkward to stroke. Patting her on the head seemed too condescending. So, I just stared at her face, trying to make sure that when she looked my way, she saw a confident smile looking back at her.

Then, it happened. The defining moment of our entire stay; it forever changed the way we think about something that always seemed so ordinary before. Something we knew would not just be a lasting memory but an iconic memory.

I'm talking about chicken pot pie.

Up to that point, I had tuned the doctors out, but in the midst of all that was going on, my ears were pricked by something I could not ignore. Usha's doctor had started talking about her dinner the night before. And if I have not been clear up to this point, this is while the procedure was going on. Her hands were on my wife's innards, and her lips were talking about chicken pot pie.

Now, in all fairness, this was by all accounts no ordinary chicken pot pie; this was from Wes Welker's new restaurant in Oklahoma City. Once the subject was raised, everyone had comments about it. The nurses were commenting on how fabulous it was; the other doctor was lamenting that sometimes he gets there too late, and they have run out. Everybody started chiming in with tips on calling ahead to reserve a chicken pot pie.

I mentioned Usha's expressive eyes above, and yes, that was, in part, a chance for me to compliment them, but they were full-on expressive now. Her lips silently mouthed, "Pot pie?" as her eyes said, "Are they really talking about that? Did I hear that right, or do they need to dial back the drugs?"

I nodded yes. We had braced ourselves for all sorts of things, but pot pie was not one of them.

Our eyes held a silent conversation that only old married couples are capable of having.

"Is chicken pot pie code for something?"

"I don't think so. I think they are really talking about it."

"Are they taking some kind of break?"

"They all seem too busy."

Then we smile at each other because we both realize that if they are talking about chicken pot pie, things must be going well.

Still, I couldn't let this conversation go without comment. "Did you say Wes Welker's restaurant? I've been meaning to try that place."

The head nurse looks over the curtain long enough to say, "You should," and then she looks back at her work.

Usha's doctor explained further, "That is Wes Welker's mom."

"Wow. Really? How cool is that? Wes Welker's mom is helping deliver my kid!"

I looked down at Usha, and she mouthed the word "Who?" I tried to explain but clearly discovered that it was not the time to be talking about football. Chicken pot pie talk from the doctors, yes. Talk from me about football great Wes Welker, no. (For all you new dads, that's a little tip from me to you.)

Of course, the chicken pot pie talk was exactly what we had surmised, an indication that all was going well. More than that, by the time we realized how long we had been distracted, the doctor caught our attention with another announcement, "Look at that hair!"

For a brief bit, I just knew Alex was born with red hair like his sisters before him. As it turns out, they were commenting about how much hair he had. And boy, did they comment. By the time I had seen him for the first time, I had heard so much about his hair, I half-suspected dreadlocks.

Then the talk turned to how big he was. Estimates were tossed around, bets were made, and nurses were chided to hurry up and clean him up so he could be weighed. When he hit the scales, he weighed in at a hefty 9 lbs.—3 oz.

This was something else we had not anticipated. In all the worries and concerns I had about what if he was born small or other issues, I had never considered the possibility he would be born such a healthy-sized chunk.

Indeed, looking over at Alex, he didn't seem like a newborn at all. You know, all those times you watch a movie and a baby is born, and everybody says, "That's no newborn! They never come out looking like that." Well, that's exactly what he looked like.

Later, when they showed Alex to Usha for her first good look, they joked, "Here is your toddler."

I don't want to give the impression that, at that point, all of our neurosis had dissolved. All parents have them, and we do even more so. But between the chicken pot pie and Alex's healthy size, our anxiety had dropped several levels; this began sinking in as they wheeled Usha back to her room, and the doctor and I trailed along behind. My thoughts turned. Even though everything had gone very well, I was still overcome with emotion and appreciation.

This story is almost three thousand words in, and all those thoughts and emotions above were whizzing through my head at the same time. I was so grateful to the doctor for shepherding us through this and the care she had given my wife and child. I tried to come up with the right words to express my appreciation to her, but the best I could muster was "Thank you" before my voice cracked and my eyes welled up with tears.

Usha's doctor is great. She is always outspoken, either with something witty or a strong opinion. But when I told her thanks, she responded with a sincere and quiet, "You're welcome." She knew this was no ordinary case and that there was more I wanted to say but couldn't without a complete breakdown. Hopefully, when she reads this, she will know just how much more was behind that thank-you and that I will always be thankful for her ... and for chicken pot pie.

CHAPTER 4

Diapers and Einstein's Theory of Relativity

In the opening chapter, I said this is not a parenting advice book, but allow me to sneak this one in. One of the things that frightened me the most as I prepared to be a dad turned out to be great bonding time and dare I say joyful. Such is the parenting life. What you expect often isn't what you get.

We had Alex a few years after this essay was written, and I was able to put these lessons back into practice.

I like to say that I only offer one piece of unsolicited parenting advice. That's not true, of course.

Like most other parents, I offer up lots of advice and comments to other parents. Sure, there is some part of me that is seeking to be helpful. The larger part is seeking validation over the parenting choices I have made by getting others to make the same choices.

It's a bad habit, I know. But at least I'm aware of my problem. Try being the only dad at a Girl Scout meeting, and you find out pretty quickly that the phenomenon is widespread and, in many cases, completely unfiltered. But I digress.

Back to my parenting advice, I should rephrase my opening statement to be more accurate. I only offer one *worthwhile* piece of unsolicited advice.

I should be upfront and confess this advice is not original from me. It's not even particularly earth-shattering, but pretty simple. However, it's not something I would have known had somebody not told me. Once you hear it, I think you'll appreciate it, and if you ignore it, you do so at your own peril.

But before I share it, I should provide a little backstory.

I remember the day very clearly; it was Christmastime 2002 and before we had children. We were sitting in a swimming pool in Tobago, overlooking an Atlantic beach. Caribbean breeze, warm sun, cool drinks—perfect conditions for relaxing. At that moment, I probably had the lowest level of stress I had enjoyed for the entire year. My biggest worry at that moment was wondering what would be on the buffet for dinner. Then it happened.

Usha leans over to me and whispers, *"I think I am ready for a baby."*

Stress meter to one hundred percent.

It's not like I didn't want kids. I figured we would have kids. Some day. In the future. Future meaning when we felt ready or, more precisely, when I felt like a real adult. I know that's an odd thing for a then thirty-one-year-old to be thinking, but becoming a dad seemed like such a grown-up thing, and I didn't feel that grown up yet.

It didn't take long to reason I would probably feel that way at any age. Truth be told, I'm years older now and still don't feel very grown up.

Putting that aside for a moment, a wave of more practical concerns began peppering my brain. How much do babies cost? How would we balance a baby with our work lives? How would we cope with the sleepless nights? What stuff do we need for a baby? What if we don't agree on a name? What if it's a girl, and someday she starts liking boys?

Then the daisycutter bomb hit. The one worry I had that hounded me until Ella was a few days old. A fear so great, it needs no explanation. Just the word itself strikes fear in soon-to-be dads: Diapers.

Having a baby meant dealing with diapers. Yes, it's a simple fact of life, but it did give me pause to consider if we could redefine "future" as that point in time where science and technology have developed a more refined and sophisticated method to deal with poopies and pee-pee.

Fast forward to mid-2004. Ella was on the way, and we were doing the types of things expecting parents do. I bought a camcorder, Usha bought books, we decorated the nursery, and we signed up for a birthing class. I had less apprehension about differential equations than I did about birthing class, but when in Rome.

Our instructor seemed like a nice and knowledgeable lady, and best I remember, the class started off okay. That I don't remember the details is testimony to how much effort I put into blocking out the details. Learning too much about the birthing process was antithetical to my strategy for the big day. My plan was to shut up and listen to Usha, the nurses, and the doctors. My dad often told me, "They don't pay you to think."; that was never more true than the day Ella was born.

Some of the other dads seemed to be aligned with my philosophy, some tried to debate points based off a book they had read, and one fellow was taking so many notes, I was sure his spiral would run out of pages before the class did.

Coming out of a class break, the instructor got a little off-topic and opened the floor to other questions about babies and parenting. Somebody brought up the subject of diapers. Whether it was out of fear or hope, I started paying attention.

The instructor talked about diapers with a beaming smile. She described one of the benefits of breastfeeding as—and I quote—"The dirty diapers smell like buttery popcorn." She went on to talk about how sad she was when her youngest child was fully potty-trained because she wasn't ready to give up changing diapers.

This raised a critical question in my head. "Who do we talk to about getting our money back from this class?" The only person who had to be more shaken by these words from our instructor was note-taker guy. He had been dutifully writing the words of this lady for two hours before she revealed herself to be full-bore crazy.

I think I tuned out everything from that point on. The only thing I really learned that day was that the Cheesecake Factory serves hard liquor.

So, a couple of months go by, and the big day arrived. Ella was born, and the day was filled with all of the wonderful emotions people try to prepare you for but can't. I had a full-on new dad buzz. If you've been in the OB section of a hospital, you have likely seen it, as I mentioned earlier in the book. I was that guy in the elevator who was smiling extra big at everyone, trying to mind-control them into making them ask about my new daughter.

There was only one thing killing my buzz: The anxiety over the dreaded first diaper change. All of the other recent new dads had been warning me for months with words of encouragement like "Just wait until that first one," "It's like tar," and "If I have another kid, I'm trying Goo-Gone."

A lovely Indian nurse changed Ella's first diaper at the hospital. If there was anything complicated about it, you couldn't tell by watching her; if you blinked hard, you would have missed it. My turn would come in the middle of the night. It wouldn't go quite as smoothly.

Usha was trying to get some sleep, a tricky thing between the new mom duties, a day of visitors, and the army of nurses parading through the room at all hours. I discovered Ella would sleep well if I pushed her around the halls, so we did lap after lap, her happy to be sleeping and me happy that she was safe and snug in her plexiglass crib.

Somewhere approximately between laps 250 and 275, it became apparent that her diaper might need to be checked. Once checked, it was apparent that it needed to be changed. I wheeled her back into the darkened room and set about changing it in hopes of keeping both Ella and Usha asleep.

The dirty part of the diaper turned out to be a lot less concerning than picking up her little legs. I know that not that long before, she had been through the whole ordeal of being born—not a delicate process. But those skinny, little legs looked so fragile, and I was doing my best not to hurt them or her.

I did a good job of not hurting her. What I didn't do such a good job of was cleanly extracting the dirty diaper. Ten minutes and 30 or 40 baby wipes later, she had a clean, albeit loose, diaper on. Usha never woke, a fact I attribute to her sheer exhaustion rather than my ability to be quiet. But I wasn't quite done yet.

I wheeled Ella and her crib down to the nurse's station and confessed, "I kind of made a mess of a few things when I changed her diaper. Can I get some new bedding?"

"Oh, sure. What do you need?"

"All of it. New blanket, new sheet, new cap, and some more wipes.

Probably better get a new pacifier, too," I said somewhat confidently, thinking they had seen it all. They laughed like it was the funniest thing they had heard and couldn't wait to share.

Later, in the light of a new day, Usha was holding Ella and asked me, "Why is she wearing pink socks? Where did her yellow ones go?"

"I threw them away last night. Don't ask."

More than a little intimidated by the first diaper change, it took me a few days to shake it. But by the time Ella was a few days old, I was starting to get the hang of it. Before long, rather than being something I dreaded, I was actually happy to do it. I couldn't feed Ella, but changing diapers was something I could do. It helped me feel like I was doing my part.

Before she was born, I suspected that we would have stand-offs or flip coins to see who was going to have to change the dirty diapers. But I soon found when she was dirty or wet, I wanted to change her. She is my daughter. Of course, I wanted her to be clean and comfortable.

Don't get me wrong; I have no desire to change other people's kids' diapers. That's just gross. And the buttery popcorn thing was a flat-out lie.

But despite my early anxieties, for Ella and later Colby, diaper changes actually were a positive part of fatherhood. You may not be convinced of that yet, but I have two more articles of evidence to back up my claim.

The first is the advice I promised you earlier. Somebody told me when you change a diaper, be sure to smile. Better yet, sing, laugh, and play while changing it. Don't make bad faces or complain; if you do, you are signaling to the kid that it's a bad experience or that they did something wrong, and soon thereafter, they begin trying to avoid or fight diaper changes. You're going to change thousands of diapers, so might as well make those times happy ones.

The second article of evidence is Einstein's Theory of Relativity. I know that probably seems a little odd and out of context, mainly because I've never really bought into that whole idea. But hang with me a bit, and I'll try to explain.

There is a classic layman's explanation of the Theory of Relativity. Put your hand on a hot stove for a minute, and it seems like an hour. Sit with a pretty girl for an hour, and it seems like a minute. Here is my twist on it.

Before I was thirty-one, I didn't give much thought to diapers.

At 31 and 32, the thought of diaper-changing freaked me out.

At 33, I discovered what a great bonding experience changing diapers can be.

At 38, my diaper-changing career got cut short when Colby passed away.

Now, at 40, I sometimes have dreams that I am changing her diaper, and we are being silly together. And when the alarm goes off, I hit snooze, pull the covers over my head, and try my best to dream about it all over again.

Back in that pool at the Tobago Hilton, I never would have imagined I would actually want to dream about changing diapers. But I do. Crazy birthing class instructor would be proud or would laugh. Or both.

So, if you are a soon-to-be dad, don't let the diapers psych you out. Remember, it's all relative. And most importantly, remember to smile while doing it.

CHAPTER 5

My Puzzle & the Time I Had Breakfast with the President

I've always had faith in God. That faith hasn't always looked the same. Colby's death required me to reexamine some things and though that may sound like wavering, the process resulted in a deeper, stronger faith.

This essay explores the idea of faith being like a jigsaw puzzle and then shares some appreciation for those who have helped me with my puzzle. It was written pre-Alex, but you can be sure that even though he isn't mentioned in it, he has added greatly to my puzzle as well.

In a recent period of introspection, the idea of faith being like a puzzle took root in my head. The simple thought has been tumbling around in my head like a grain of sand in an oyster for so long, I have finally decided it was time to try and spit it out into words and get a better look at it. And if you think that analogy is a little too self-serving, I'll point out that many ugly pearls get thrown back into the sea.

Somewhere along the way, I began picking up puzzle pieces of faith. I assume this is no different than anyone else, be it fostered in Sunday school classrooms or while pondering a full moon and the stars on a cloudless night. Though there may be a great deal of variation in answers, I feel sure that we have a great deal in common when it comes to the questions we naturally come to ask. Each question and answer becomes a piece of our faith puzzle.

Our earliest puzzle piece collections are like a child's first puzzle of a farmyard. Someone gives us the puzzle piece: we look at it, fumble it around with our fingers, and then apply our favorite method of learning—we put it in our mouths. This does not elicit a positive response and may even end that day's session. But sooner or later, we get the lamb-shaped piece placed in the right space cut out for it, and everyone claps and smiles at us at completing the puzzle. With our farmyard puzzle, we begin to learn our animals. With our faith puzzles, we take our first steps into figuring out the world is bigger than us.

The next puzzles up have a small number of big pieces. We begin to see how pieces fit together, and it takes a little more work to get them to fit. The first time it's complete, we enjoy not only the picture it makes, but also the pride in getting it there. We might build that same puzzle over and over again until it is so easy that all the challenge is gone, and with it, so goes our interest. Just as we move on to more complex play puzzles, the number and complexity of our faith puzzle grow with the more questions we have and answers we find.

My personal faith puzzle has been in various states over the years. At times, I felt like I had most of the pieces fit together. Then, someone would pose a question that would give me another piece, and I wouldn't have a place for it. Other times, I have used up all of my pieces, yet still had unfilled holes. I have been a poor caretaker of my puzzle pieces, having left them lying about, left some behind when moving, used some under the leg of a wobbly table, and paraded some around above me on a long stick, only to look up and see that they had fallen off.

Sometimes, when you lose a piece, it can be awfully hard to get back.

I have found that none of these problems compare to not knowing if a piece you have belongs in your puzzle.

Puzzle creators do all sorts of things to raise the complexity for their creations, such as designing with thousands of pieces, intricate shapes, confusing patterns, 3-D shapes, and two-sided pieces. If they really wanted to make a challenge, they would make a recreational puzzle like a faith puzzle. It would have 25,000 pieces inside a blank box with no picture and no instructions, save for one little note that says, "Includes your 500-piece puzzle and 24,500 leftover pieces from other people's puzzles."

It would be up to you to sort through all the noise and throw out the bad pieces. Some of the puzzle pieces would clearly stick out as foreign to your puzzle. Through color, pattern, or size, maybe even taste, you could swiftly cull it out.

But other pieces would be much more challenging. You may find there are two that are nearly identical. Perhaps they both belong; perhaps neither does.

Then you run across a piece that just almost fits, but not quite like it should. Maybe it doesn't belong; maybe it does; maybe it was manufactured with a defect. If you just nibbled a bit of the end off with your teeth, you could make it fit. But should you? Without nibbling, it may never fit; with some nibbling, it may fit but not as it was intended.

If any of this sounds cynical, it's not intended that way. It describes how I often feel and presume some others do, too. Yet, I know many whose faith puzzles are complete or nearly so. At least, it appears that way from the outside. Perhaps internally, they are still tinkering with pieces.

I have a great deal of respect for those who have mastered their puzzles. Their assuredness allows them to live their faith more deeply and more outwardly, which I generally find admirable. And if I am being honest, I have a bit of jealousy toward them, too. I bet they sleep better than those of us with messy puzzles.

Yet from that group with completed puzzles, another puzzle arises—a puzzle within a puzzle. Glance around at finished puzzles, and you'll see the pictures aren't always the same. Sometimes, they are just off by a few details here and there, and sometimes, they are nearly entirely different. Take a deeper look, and one might even wonder if they are like snowflakes, with no two exactly alike.

Are they supposed to look the same? Exactly the same? Or is "about the same" good enough? What do we make of the puzzles whose pictures contradict each other?

It also has to be said that within these completed faith puzzles, you can find every level of complexity. From the farm animal board cutout levels, which offer the simplest and non-cohesive platitudes, to the most intricately complex, begging the question, "Is the forest being missed because of the trees?"

Life has a way of challenging the easier puzzles and demanding you replace them with something more complex. When your child dies in the hospital, there comes a time when you have to walk out the doors without her. If there is a person who can do that with their faith puzzle intact, just as it was before, I'd like very much to meet them.

I'll give a few examples but know that these are things that are hard to say. It's hard enough to have doubts about how things work without having people add doubts about me. Yet I know that I am not alone. Others share these questions. Maybe someone will find comfort in knowing they're not alone in struggling with these puzzle pieces.

Let's start with the "God doesn't give us more than we can handle" puzzle piece. This platitude is given as positive encouragement, and I try to remember the intent as the actual words sear my ears. Did God give me the loss of a child because he assessed I could handle it? Looks like a bad puzzle piece to me, yet its use is very commonplace.

So, what role does God play in the loss of a child? If you think I pose that question to set up an answer, you are about to be disappointed.

Backing up a bit to when we got the first inklings that Colby's condition was serious, we began hearing lots of messages about God's plan and encouragement to take comfort in that. "Let go and let God" rolled off people's tongues with facial expressions like they just handed me a gift with a beautiful bow on it, just waiting for me to open it. Usually, I just smiled, but occasionally I would ask them to explain the mechanics of that for my particular situation.

I understand that if I had a falling out with a friend and had done everything I could to reconcile it, but was getting nowhere, then this might be very sound advice. Perhaps it would help me find some comfort in knowing that I had done all I could so then I could let go.

But this was not over hurt feelings or guilt. What exactly was I supposed to let go of? Quit pushing for answers? The daily struggle to get calories in her? Fighting to get appointments with specialists? The middle-of-the-night breathing treatments? The quest to fill her life with joy and hugs and laughs?

"Trust in God's plan" phrases and their variations were said to bring us comfort. It didn't. Or at least not in this case. Again, I can see its place in the puzzle, but when it gets invoked in every single aspect and detail of our lives, I think its usefulness devolves into a cliche and a useful crutch for people. Worse, when it gets invoked in the loss of a child, what you are really saying is, "God allowed your child to die. He planned it." It hurts to think that.

Yet, I don't believe that understanding. I believe that God's heart aches with ours in loss. I believe that he holds the wisdom of his plan—not a micromanaging of our life plan, but his Big Plan—and knows that one day our grief will fade away with immeasurable joy, but for now, he shares in our pain.

Is God the architect of every moment in our lives? Or is God the watchmaker who sets things in motion and sits back and watches it all unfold? Something in between, perhaps, or absent altogether? What does your puzzle say? Would it say something different if you went through incredible tragedy and loss?

I once heard a sermon that explained God's plan isn't for a specific path for you, but how you walk on that path. That helped me make sense of things. I'm holding on to that puzzle piece.

Don't even make me talk about the "God needed another curly redhead girl in Heaven" puzzle piece. And I'm glad for your blessing, but I hope you'll understand that I don't want to hear about how God answered your prayers for passing your chemistry exam.

Those are a few examples of what else has been given to me as comfort. There is more I could add, and maybe will one day, but to do so here would drive too far off track.

The idea isn't to give a full litany of puzzle pieces affected by our experience. The goal was to show that things happen in life to cause us to look at our puzzles differently. What shapes the way I look at mine may not hold true for you (hopefully). And you have experiences that I haven't, and those changed your puzzle. So, should we be surprised or offended or threatened when our puzzles look different? Probably not.

Of course, my puzzle began long before Colby was a part of my life, and it continues, at least for a little while longer. And it's not just the major events of our lives that shape our puzzles. Many people have helped me with my puzzle, and some will likely be surprised to know it. It would be an impossible task to list them here, but I want to share a handful of examples.

In high school, I was on the swim team, and after my freshman year, I sorta felt like I was in charge of the team. So, I had a fair bit of resentment when I was informed that at one particular meet in Midland, we would have a male chaperone joining us. This hadn't happened before (and I don't recall it happening afterward, either). I was not optimistic about how it would go; killjoy and boring were words that came to mind.

Then I found out the chaperone was going to be my teammate Logan's dad, Stan Hudson. Logan was cool, and I hadn't met his dad, but I had an impression of him. More adjectives were straight-laced, no-nonsense, and devoutly religious. No way was this going to be fun.

The bus ride down, I think he kept his distance riding up front and us hiding in back, trying to breathe in the last of our coolness bubble before it got popped. And when we got to the hotel, the bubble looked to pop in grand fashion. Room assignments were given out, and it turned out Mr. Hudson would be in my room. Groan.

We got into the room, and Mr. Hudson grabbed the remote control. As he clicked through the channels, I was expecting it to land on *The 700 Club* or the like. "All right! *Terminator!*" he said. The rest of the guys gathered around to watch, and though surprised, I skeptically stood back, feeling somewhat betrayed. The bubble of coolness hadn't popped; it had shifted.

The rest of the night went better than I had expected, but remember, I had low expectations. There weren't any lectures or nagging. There was more laughter than I predicted. I was warming up to this, but slowly.

Then, the next morning, our whole team headed off to Denny's for breakfast. As the others were seated and we waited our turn to order, a middle-aged Black man, who appeared homeless or close to it, approached us. "How y'all doing today? What's your name? I'm George Bush."

"Like the president?" I asked.

"Not like the president. I AM the president!" Well...we were in Midland.

I didn't need to hear anymore. I was happy to head toward my pancakes and let this loon go irritate someone else, but Mr. Hudson veered all of us off in an unexpected direction.

"Mr. George Bush, my name is Stan Hudson." He reached out to shake his hand and added, "Nice to meet you. Come join us."

Wait. What?

The man joined us, and never once did Stan let on that he didn't believe the man was not the president. The rest of us went from leery to prodding to trying to trick him and then to joking around. If I knew the things we said, I would be horribly embarrassed. But Stan's style wasn't to berate, and he was less concerned with us than Mr. Bush being fed.

Whether by muse or to avoid the check, George left rather abruptly and moved on. It wouldn't have mattered. Stan would not have let him pay anyway, and I have a dozen other stories to back that up.

As he left, Stan said, with a gentle smile, "Boys, I know we had some fun, but let's take a minute," and he reached for our hands. In a Denny's in Midland, Texas, we all held hands, and Stan prayed aloud for George Bush, his mental health, for help with any addictions or other challenges, and his well-being.

Where I had seen an outcast and an inconvenience, Stan saw a brother and an opportunity to put his faith into action, help his fellow man, and share love and kindness. I learned a lot from that day, including lessons about active faith, the power of teaching by example, and humanity. And the most surprising lesson of all—a faith-filled life can be cool. Those are some nice puzzle pieces, and I haven't always done right by them, but they have stuck with me ever since that day.

The rest of these examples won't come with as long of a story, but the pieces they yield are just as treasured.

Like the puzzle pieces from my brothers, who showed me that we introverts can play an important role in our church communities.

And the pieces from Ella and Colby, who have taught me the love a father has for his children, and a glimpse of what God's love for us must be.

And my wife, Usha, who is not usually well known for patience, yet has shown me endless patience in watching and supporting me in working on my faith puzzle.

And my Indian family, who has taught me that prayers said half a world away and in a language I don't understand can still move me to tears and wrap us in a warmth of love.

And Pastor Cheryl, with her numerous lessons and invaluable

encouragement with my puzzle but needing a special thanks for truly introducing me to God's grace.

And Dan Vaughan, our church music director, who lit up Colby's face with the organ and transformed my view on the role music plays in worship.

And the youth group at our church in Rockwall. The truth is it's not a hard step for a forty-year-old man worn down by life to come around to saying, "Lord, move my feet." It's a much bigger step for a young person and infinitely more beautiful.

And to Emily, the nurse in Colby's ICU room who gave up her day off to be with us and take care of Colby on the day we took her off life support. What extraordinary compassion to subject oneself to such heartache to bring comfort.

And Carl McCormack, a fellow grieving father who gave me a new perspective on communion that makes it my absolute favorite part of worship.

And to George Bush (our breakfast guest) who taught me not to be so quick to write someone off.

And for as frustrating as my puzzle can be, thanks to God for making my faith a puzzle that requires nurturing, tinkering, and continuous thought, lest I think it's done and put it away in a drawer. And for those pieces that I find too hard to figure out, thanks for giving us the ability to let go and let God. (See, even I think it has its place!)

Many of you reading this have helped me with my faith puzzle. And you are helping others with theirs, even though you may not realize it. I wish there were a way to thank you all, but this will have to do for now.

But someday, I look forward to catching up with all of you in Heaven, where we can all sit around and marvel at the unexpected ways each of our own faith puzzles was off the mark and how glorious they are in their heavenly versions. Maybe even uniquely glorious—wouldn't that be a hoot!

CHAPTER 6

Parenting Fail

Hopefully, the only tears this one will elicit are from laughter. Alex was six when this story occurred. The lesson here is that even when you think you have things well in hand, humility lurks.

I share some parenting wins in Facebook posts and conversations, but we all know the crowd favorites are the parenting missteps. If that's you, you are in for a treat. Today's missteps snowballed on me.

Alex is homeschooled, and I like to knock out Alex's computer assignments before we go on any adventures; this morning started off pretty well. He only protested a little, and we knocked out one lesson. We took a break, and when the next lesson started, things went downhill.

Sometimes, these balks last five minutes; sometimes they last an hour. The record is 15 hours, but that included 10 hours of sleep in the middle.

Somewhere around the forty-five-minute mark this morning, Alex told me, "You aren't my dad anymore."

He loves to start a distracting argument to get me talking about something else, so I just replied, "Ok, but you still have to do the lesson."

A few minutes later, Alex did his lesson, pausing between questions to remind me I wasn't his dad. To which I said, "You can pretend I am not your dad all day if you do your lesson."

With the lesson done, it felt like a win. But just put that little story in your pocket for a bit. You will want to refer to it later.

Our adventure today was pretty simple: Go to the park and play. Of course, our dog, Murphy, came along, too.

When we got to the park, I noticed it was fairly busy. The parking lot was full. It looked like a moms' group had a meet-up, and there were lots of kids playing in the sunshine. What there was absolutely zero of was other adult males. I cringed a little.

Now, I have nothing against mom groups. In fact, I believe them to be quite wonderful in almost all aspects. The exception is when you are the only dad around, you feel like a creeper of some sort. You may think that is just in my head. I used to try to believe that, too. But having been turned down for group outings because they were "moms only" means there must be some validity to it. Still, I mostly try to ignore signs of that and go about my business. And I should quickly add here that I have met many friendly playground moms, too ... so I definitely don't want to paint everyone with the same brush.

Anyway, back to the parenting fail...

I parked the truck down a ways from the playground, but I can see the walk all the way up to the entrance. Murphy needed some water before we left the truck, and Alex was anxious to get to playing. I made what at the time felt like a wise parenting move that allowed Alex some independence and showed him I trusted him. I told him he could go on to the playground, and we would be up there in a few minutes. It turned out to be misstep #2.

Murphy was thirstier than I expected, so it took a few minutes for him to drink up. Alex was already mixed in to a crowd of kids when Murphy and I came walking up the hill and sat on a bench away from everyone at the far edge of the playground. So far, so good.

But then, kids started noticing Murphy. One came over and asked to pet him, and I said ok. The kid sat down on the bench right next to me to pet the dog; that is when I realized there was a mom about to freak out.

In that moment, I was literally the guy they warned kids about when they talk about stranger danger. Beware the guy with no kids with a puppy. This was definitely a misstep, but I tried not to overreact.

The kid asked me, "What's his name?"

"Murphy," I answered, looking all around me, trying to assess the situation, and in doing so, probably making myself look even more suspicious.

"That's our dog's name!" the kid beamed. The kid hollered to a sibling, "His dog is named Murphy, too." Which, if you think about it, is exactly what the stranger danger guy would say, too.

I realized no one there knew I was with Alex, and I caught him looking my way, so I tried to wave to him. He was only thinking "playground" and blew me off. Meanwhile, I was catching the eye of other kids, and they saw our playful, happy, mixed-breed dog, Murphy. Soon, we had several kids surrounding us at the park bench at the far edge of the playground. Which, if you think about it, is the bench the stranger danger guy would have picked, too.

At this point, moms were starting to take notice. How could they not? I would have been on alert, too. Many were staring straight at me.

A couple of moms were moving toward their kids on the playground, and one brave mom started walking across the playground my way.

Now I really needed Alex to come over. He was standing between me and the mom marching my way. I was waving at him and hollered at him, but he was ignoring me. The mom reached him, pointed at me, and asked, "Is that your dad?"

To which Alex responded by looking my way, looking back up at her, remembering he was given permission to pretend I wasn't his dad, and said, "Nope."

And if you have ever wondered why I am awkward at the playground, now you know.

CHAPTER 7

Brownies Without Nuts

You'll be happy to hear that since this was written, I have mastered the practice of streaming television, though I am still prone to asking what channel something is on. And Mark, my long-time friend for whom this piece was written, has embraced using a Mac. The rest still holds.

A parenting journey is both richer and easier with friends. Cherish the ones who show up for you and endeavor to show up for them.

I like nuts in my brownies; he prefers plain.

He keeps his lawn pristine; mine, not so much.

I'm from the top of Texas; he is from South Texas.

His office is neatly organized; mine is organized according to chaos theory.

I can turn my TV on, change the channel, and adjust the volume. He knows every function on his remote, tweaks all the parameters on his setup menu, and has figured out all the cool tricks like streaming video.

He plays games like *42* with a strategic and calculated approach; I play more by the seat of my pants.

He would rather ride a motorcycle; I'd rather ride a horse.

I take the backroads; he takes the fast route.

I use a Mac; he uses a PC.

I order the grilled salmon; he orders the fried chicken strips.

So, what do you call two guys with those kinds of differences? Well, you can call him Mark, and twenty years ago, you would have called us new roommates. Not too long after that, you would have called us friends. Today, you would call us lifelong friends.

At this point, I should probably admit that I've embellished our differences a bit. It's not that any of the points above are false; it's just that I omitted examples of the many things we have in common. A full audit of our personalities, preferences, and philosophies would reveal our commonalities are more numerous than our differences. We certainly have a growing history of common experiences.

College, of course, covered a good bit of that history. Mark and I got each other into enough trouble to have fun and good stories, yet somehow kept each other out of serious trouble. We worked at the same grocery store. Both of us had cars that necessitated we buy motor oil in bulk. We were each other's counselors about girlfriend problems and played wingman for each other on occasion. Mark and I discovered and invented new ways to live on the cheap—some of which flopped tremendously. Our apartment always seemed to be the congregating point for our mix of friends. We had our disagreements, but on the whole, we had a lot more fun.

After college, Mark went south to Houston, and I went north to Lubbock. Somehow, we managed to stay in touch.

I was the best man at his wedding, having to fight through a hurricane to get there, missing rehearsal and barely making the rehearsal dinner. The next day, I pissed off his wedding photographer because I was being such a smart aleck, and he was having trouble getting the rest of the wedding party to cooperate.

He was the best man at my wedding as well. It was a small riverside gathering on a Texas Hill Country river. Mark had to help me clear off the dock, including moving the canoe, so we had room for the ceremony. He was a lot nicer to our wedding photographer, probably because he is married to her.

Our wives became quick friends, and we have all taken vacations together and regularly visit each other's homes. The wives both say that our personalities revert to our younger days when we are around each other. They like to make it sound like it's something they have to put up with, but I have a suspicion they find it adorable; at least, I like to think so.

Either way, I find it to be refreshing. If I put myself back twenty years ago, I don't think I could have imagined how things have worked out for each of us. A little age and responsibility have quite a transformative effect—mostly for the good, but still hard to comprehend at times. It's nice that some of the things from the old days linger on, even if it's only in the retelling of stories of things we either can't do any longer or know better than to try.

Perhaps the biggest transformation for both of us has been fatherhood, where we have quite a bit of shared history in that, too. The story I want to share is the most poignant one because it's a lesson I've recently learned about friendship.

I traveled to Houston to be there on the day Mark's oldest was born. Mark drove to Dallas to be with me on the day my youngest (at the time) died.

Explaining the first part of that is pretty straightforward. Mark and Tracy's daughter was born early on a Sunday morning, and on a spur-of-the-moment decision, Usha and I hopped on a plane to go see the new parents and their baby. We had the chance, and we took it. I know it meant a lot to them, and it meant a lot to us, but there was nothing hard in doing it. The flight down was full of excitement and anticipation, as we felt so blessed to get to share in their joy.

Explaining the second part is quite a bit tougher. The timeline is the easy part, so I'll start there.

On a Monday morning, we had taken Colby to the hospital for a routine surgical procedure. Early indications were good, but by that afternoon, things had gone horribly wrong. By that night, we were just praying she would live through the night. She did, and on Tuesday, the day started with some amount of hope. We were making plans for an extended hospital stay of many weeks. However, as the day progressed, the outlook grew worse. We were told to brace ourselves for the worst and that on Wednesday morning, some additional tests would be run, but that we shouldn't expect anything but the worst results.

So, it was Tuesday night, and we were doing our best to handle things one minute at a time. The next morning seemed forever away, and thinking beyond that was next to impossible. Our eyes studied the monitors, hoping to see something new. Our ears perked at every beep of the equipment, no matter how routine, and we eavesdropped on every conversation in the hall between doctors and nurses, desperate for something positive to cling to.

At that same time, many people were wanting to help, including Mark and Tracy. They wanted to know if they should come up to Dallas, and I didn't know what to tell them. I was still hoping that somehow, we were in for a long wait for Colby, and if so, maybe they should come later. On the other hand, part of me knew that there wouldn't be a later; I just hadn't accepted it yet. Not knowing what to say, I settled on telling them I'd let them know what the morning tests showed, and maybe we would know more.

The words texted back to me from Tracy still bring me to tears every time I think about them. "Mark says, 'I don't care what test results come in the morning. I'm going to Dallas to see my friend, no matter what.'"

And that's exactly what they did.

I can't imagine what their drive-up was like. It must have been a long four hours. They love Colby, too, and I know their hearts and minds were heavy with concern for her. Add on more layers of worry about Ella, Usha, and me. Mix in shock. Throw in some mystery from all the gaps in explanation in my rushed texts and e-mails. In the midst of all that, they were no doubt analyzing the situation over and over for signs of hope, too. And the entire time, asking themselves, "What can we do?"

At the hospital, the elevator ride-up had to be tense. They had to be wondering what they would see and what they would say. I think about the courage it took to walk into that situation, knowing how bad it would likely be and feeling like there was nothing they could do to help. I'd like to think I would have had that courage, but I know there have been times in my life when I didn't.

But they did come, and they did help. They helped in concrete ways, like driving us home that day and staying with us that night so that our house felt a little less empty. The next morning, they went with us to our pastor's office, where we were handed off to her care, then my brother's, then to more friends and more family, in a chain of care that continues on to this day.

But the biggest way they helped is by simply being there. It's reported that Woody Allen said, "80% of success is just showing up." Maybe that's true of friendship, too, where you don't always have to know what to say or what to do. Sometimes, just being there is enough, even when it's hard. Especially when it's hard.

They showed up for us in the same way countless others have. We are blessed to say that I could write many of the same things above about so many other people. There are countless numbers who have "just been there" for us in person or in spirit in difficult times, like with Colby. The list is lengthy: the others who visited us in the hospital, those who came to our home, the family members who shepherded us through things no parent should ever have to do, the hundreds who attended Colby's memorial service, the people who sent meals, the writers of cards that stuffed our mailbox for weeks, the callers, the friends of family, the family of friends, our church family, the coworkers, new friends, old friends, contributors to her memorial funds, the senders of flowers and teddy bears, Colby's team of doctors and therapists, the counselors and friends we've met with their own tragic losses. This list could go on. I can't imagine how we could cope without them.

Every one of these people shared in our grief, questioned what to do, and put themselves in an uncomfortable position to bring us some comfort.

To all of you, I say thank you. Thank you for your friendship. Thank you for the comfort you bring. And thank you for showing me the value in just being there.

And to my old roommate, Mark, maybe next time I'll make the brownies without nuts.

CHAPTER 8

Living and Sleeping in the Moment

Revisiting old memories can help us learn new lessons. This essay was written fifteen years after Colby's death. Some sleepless nights brought some cherished moments back to mind and reminded me to allow myself to linger in the present and soak it in.

Sleep and I aren't friends these days.

It's a shame, as sleeping has always been one of my favorite talents. Sleep on planes, no problem. Sleep in a tent, easy peasy. Once, I even slept on the concrete floor of a running cotton gin, using a pile of fan belts for a pillow. You'd think I would have used some fluffy cotton, but I didn't think of that until just now.

But lately it's not uncommon for me to still be awake at 3 or 4 in the morning. From my perspective, my mind is chasing thoughts about the past, about the future, and about the need to fall asleep. An outside observer would more likely describe it like a dog chasing his tail—lots of circling and no progress. That's the figurative language, but it is somewhat apropos of the literal action, too, as I roll over and over and over, trying to find that just right spot for sleep.

I've been trying several things to help. Reading books I find too dry, drinking milk, pretending I was on an airplane: none of these have helped. (Note to self: Pick up some fan belts at NAPA tomorrow.)

Last night, feeling the pressure of needing to sleep, I thought what I really needed was a good distraction. I contemplated moving to the couch and watching TV. This spurred an internal debate about whether the screen would be more detrimental than the benefits of the distraction. The not-watching-TV side won the argument, but that was mostly based on it being cold, and I was warm in bed under my blankets.

But the other thing to come out of that inner dialogue was something wonderful, a cherished memory that I hadn't thought about in a long while.

Colby, my second child, had breathing issues that at times required us to give her breathing treatments. If the words albuterol or nebulizer don't mean anything to you, count yourself lucky.

The albuterol was the medicine we used, and it came in these funny plastic vials that had tops that twisted off. They were like wax bottle candy, only not as fun and significantly more expensive.

Once the cap was twisted off, you squeezed the clear medicine into the nebulizer, which was a machine that atomized the medicine and pumped it through a tube into a mask that was held over Colby's nose and mouth. Imagine an air pump for an aquarium. Now imagine ten of them, and that is about the sound this thing made.

Some days, she didn't need any breathing treatments. Some days just one or two; bad days could be as often as every four hours.

There was one particular period when Colby was just shy of 2 years old that the nighttime breathing treatments began consistently hitting at 2:00 a.m. One of those nights, instead of giving her the breathing treatment in the rocking chair in her room, we did it in the living room, probably because that is where I had left the nebulizer.

For a reason I no longer remember, I turned the TV on. Back in those days, we had these things called channels. There was no Netflix home screen with thumbnails to scroll through. And the way these channels worked was that whatever channel you were watching when you turned the TV off would be the channel that came on the next time you turned the TV on. (I can't believe I'm trying to explain this, so if your birth year starts with a 2, just ask one of your old relatives for the rest of the details.)

So the TV came on, and being that our TV was tuned to kids' show programming ninety percent of the time, it happened to be on PBS. The show playing was *Gullah Gullah Island*, and not being familiar with it and knowing Colby had never seen it, I changed the channel to see what else was on.

Colby tapped my hand and pointed to the TV, and because she had me well-trained, I knew exactly what she wanted. I flipped it back to *Gullah Gullah Island*.

I don't know whether it was the bright colors, the singing, the dancing, or the characters that caught her attention, but she was an instant fan, which made me an instant fan. So, there we sat in a big comfy leather chair. She on one leg of my lap, me with one arm around her and one holding the mask close to her smiling face. She with her left hand grasping my pinky and the other patting her leg in rhythm with the music.

I can still picture her pajamas. My favorites were the onesie with elephants, the one with giraffes, or the light blue one with pink flowers.

The alligator pajamas were cute and a little sassy. Her curly red hair and bright blue eyes matched perfectly with everything.

The breathing treatments lasted about ten minutes. The show was on for thirty minutes, counting commercials. For you young people, commercials were—well, just ask your grandparents.

When the breathing treatment was over, I clicked the machine off, and the humming noise went silent. Colby looked at me. Being well-trained, I knew the look was asking if we could keep watching the show. The answer was yes, of course.

Done with the nebulizer, I have both arms wrapped around her. Her head would lean onto one side of my chest, and her little hand would pat the other side of my chest and rest there until the show ended.

This became our routine for a while, and afterward, we would go back to her room, change her to a fresh diaper, lay her in her crib, and I would lie on her floor, not trusting the baby monitor to convey the sounds of breathing. The sounds of her breathing as she fell back asleep were my lullaby, and soon I would be asleep, too. After sleeping on a cotton gin floor, sleeping on a carpeted bedroom floor was easy.

Back to my restless quest for sleep, these memories brought a huge smile to my face and a warm, peacefulness in my chest. Oh, what I would give to relive just one of those nights.

As I thought about it, I gained a new appreciation for those nights. Time has a funny way of teaching you new things about old memories.

The smiles and the snuggles were certainly great and key to those great memories. But what I didn't appreciate then, that I do now, is that for those thirty minutes or so, I was living in the moment.

It was too late at night to do anything about the chores I had left undone. It was too early in the day to stress over its to-do list and the accompanying logistics. In those thirty minutes, the past and the future weren't distractions. It was a perfect example of the old adage that the present is a gift.

I'm not good at living in the moment, and I admire those to whom that comes naturally (when they aren't annoying me).

I think it is a life skill that most of us have historically struggled with, and these days, that struggle has been exacerbated by hectic schedules, constant interconnectivity, and a flood of information and expectations.

I know I need more of living in the moment in my life, but I don't have any answers for achieving that. Maybe more inspiration will hit at 3:00 a.m. tonight. Maybe *Gullah Gullah Island* has an episode on that topic.

In the meantime, I'll just be thankful for those memories and the lessons they carry. And I hope by sharing them, it gives you a perspective to contemplate, too.

CHAPTER 9

Curls, Glasses, and Unsaid Thank-Yous

Some of the essays in this book came from the period soon after Colby's death. Well over ten thousand dollars was donated to a memorial fund for her, and we donated all of it to various organizations that we felt honored Colby. Along with the donation, I would include a story explaining their impact on us, some of which are included in this book.

At some point, I realized I had many, many more thank-yous to express, and this essay was an attempt at doing just that.

She didn't let the picture-taking interfere with her pancake-eating. I don't know her name.

I tried to talk to her a little bit to get her to smile, but she wasn't buying it. But despite her shyness or skepticism, she did let me take her picture. She was about five years old, with curly blonde hair, glasses, and cuteness to spare.

I was the volunteer photographer for a Kiwani's pancake breakfast, and she was just too much of a darling to pass up. That day, she did me the favor of letting me take her picture, and I made sure to thank her. Neither of us knew that she would touch my life again sometime later.

She likely never thought of that morning again; it probably would have fallen away from my memory, too, but life is spiked with unexpected twists and turns. One of those turns came in January when we took Colby to an ophthalmologist and discovered she needed glasses.

The news surprised us, as Colby hadn't shown any signs of vision problems. None of her previous checkups caught anything, and her behavior didn't indicate she wasn't seeing well. Apart from our surprise, our minds filled with other questions. *How do you get a twenty-one-month-old to wear glasses? How do you keep them on her head? How do you keep them from breaking? How will she look, and when she gets older, will they make her self-conscious? Will she get picked on because of them?*

I suppose these things are normal anxieties of anyone in that situation, and I had them all. Somewhere in that thought process, the memory of the cute, little, curly-headed blonde girl with glasses came to mind. As that memory soaked in, the concerns became more manageable. Oh, I was sure there would be issues, just as I am sure the girl from my memory faced some issues. It was just a reminder that plenty of kids meet those challenges every day and manage to look pretty cute doing it. Easing some of the anxiety was a welcome comfort because we certainly had plenty of other things to be anxious about with Colby.

Looking back, it's easy to think of many others who unknowingly inspired comfort or joy through simple gestures or comments. People who were never thanked, nor are they likely missing it because they don't know what a difference they made. The list contains more people than I could do justice to here but let me give a few examples.

There is the young lady who works the cash register at the Starbucks by Ella's old school. Colby was a fan of the oatmeal, pound cakes, cookies, and mango juice pouches. We were fans of her getting any extra calories, and particularly the potassium, so we made many visits there. Of course, with Colby's red curly hair, it didn't take long for all the workers to recognize her as a regular. And it didn't take too many visits for her personality to begin to shine through to the lady at the register.

It started with Colby wanting to pay her. She would take the debit card from me, hand it to the lady who would swipe it, and hand it back to Colby, whereupon Colby would put it back in my wallet and complete the transaction by transforming her look of concentration into a beaming smile. This became a routine, and the nice, young lady always smiled as she played her role and warmly nodded at the predictable comments from the others in the line. The women would sweetly say something like, "Would you look at that?" and the men almost always said, "Girls learn about those credit cards early" and "You are gonna regret teaching her that." (I don't, by the way.)

Then one day, the lady introduced a new step in the routine. She gave Colby a sticker. Colby was thrilled. She put the sticker on her shirt, on her hand, on her other hand, on the table, on me, and when the sticky part of the sticker wore off and it became just a piece of paper, she put it in my shirt pocket.

In subsequent visits, the sticker locations varied, but they usually started (and sometimes stayed) on her shirt. In fact, each time we approached the counter, she would begin patting her chest. At first, I was confused because it looked a lot like her sign for please, but it was most definitely a reminder that she wanted a sticker from the cashier.

So, to the lady at Starbucks, thank you. Thank you for the smiles and stickers you gave Colby. Thanks for playing her debit card game so well and for letting her rearrange all the merchandise on your shelves. Most of all, thanks for making her feel special and providing me with cherished memories to carry with me since she has been gone.

Another person who touched my life managed to do so in less than a minute. We were in the middle of a week-long hospital visit. Colby was slowly improving, but the pressure of mounting questions and bewildered doctors was taking its toll. Sleepless, I made a trip to the courtesy kitchen on our floor for something to drink.

Tired and worried, I stood in front of the microwave, waiting for it to boil water, when another dad walked in. He was a few years younger than me, and you could feel his upbeat outlook as he entered the room. We exchanged pleasantries, me groggily and him with an optimistic vibe. I don't even remember what was said after that. I just remember his positive outlook, being curious as to the story behind it, and him leaving me with a feeling of hope.

In under a minute, he was off down the hall, back to what I would later find out was his daughter's room. I would also find out that she had cystic fibrosis and spent her life in and out of the hospital. And in my mind, I knew that the smile he had in the kitchen would be ten times bigger for his daughter and that she drew strength from it, too.

Here was a man in the middle of a challenge few can imagine, but one which we all fear. A real-life nightmare. And with all of that, he not only found the energy to carry himself with joy, but he also found some words to encourage a total stranger.

To the loving father from the hospital, thank you. Thank you for showing me the value of carrying oneself with hope, even in the face of adversity—perhaps, even more importantly so, in times of adversity. Thank you for making it clear that the more uncertain tomorrow is, the more important it is to strive to fill today with joy.

Thanks to the ladies at the ear, nose, and throat doctor, who didn't see Colby as a sick child but saw the beautiful, sweet, and intelligent person she was. I already thought I was the luckiest dad in the world but thank you for making me feel not crazy for thinking so.

To the hundreds of ladies there who stopped and admired Colby as we walked around North Park Mall, thank you for making us both feel special. Thanks to the duck and turtle keepers there who care for the animals she took so much pleasure in watching. Thanks to the people who maintain the mall fountain, which always captured her attention. Thanks to the gardeners there who grew the lovely tulips that she couldn't get enough of. Thanks to the lady at the Starbucks there who scrambled to find a sticker, because Colby was expecting one!

Thanks to all the people who said prayers for Colby, many of whom did not even know her. They graciously found time to pray for her, and us, because we were friends of a friend of a friend. Knowing that prayers were being said around the world for our dear Colby was a comfort.

Thanks to the friends and family of our ICU nurse who sacrificed their time with their loved one so that she could be there for us on Colby's last day. It was a day she was supposed to be off, but she changed shifts and worked late just to help see us through what everyone knew would be a terrible day.

Thanks to thousands of other people for a million other things that touched our lives in ways, both small and large. I wish I knew how to express my appreciation to each of you, but I know it's an impossible task. This story won't make the slightest dent in my list of unsaid thank-yous. But that really isn't my point in writing it.

The point I hope to make is this: Every day, each of you impacts another's life. Most of these times, you don't get any feedback from these events, and it makes it easy to forget the power of a kind word or a helping hand.

Something we might dismiss as trivial or ordinary ourselves can leave a lasting impression on someone else. I hope that by sharing some of my unsaid thank-yous, each of you will reflect on the way your life touches others and that they help assure you that even the simplest acts of kindness matter.

And to the girl whom I opened this story with, thank you for just being you, because that leads me to my final point. The world is a better place with curly-headed little girls with glasses.

CHAPTER 10

Work, Worry, and Dogs Named Water

Somewhere along the way, stories from my own childhood began creeping into my essays. I placed it here because the last one left me teary-eyed, and I decided readers would appreciate the inherent comedy and struggles involved with a sixteen-year-old boy's reasoning ability. But many good things are borne out of struggles, and it's important that we parents stay mindful of that.

A friend was contemplating giving in to their kid's begging for a dog. Of course, the begging came with all the standard promises that the kid would take care of everything.

We've all been on the kid's side of the conversation. Begging for a pet and making promises that we don't know the size of. If you have kids, you've been on the other side of the conversation, too. And just as sure as we are all familiar with that conversation, we all know how it goes.

Thinking myself clever, my advice was to name the dog "Water." Maybe if the kid has to say Water every time he talks to the dog, he will occasionally remember to check the water bowl.

One memory of being on the promise-maker side of things was over a horse named Arizona. I was 15 or 16, and my parents knew I would handle the feeding and watering bit because I had already been doing that with the horses we had.

But Arizona was a three-year-old gelding that needed more than food and water. He needed to be worked. He was green broke in a very deep shade, but he had a great disposition. If he were a dog, he would have been a lap dog. He was 96% chill; the other 4% was rodeo bronco with mysterious triggers that came out of nowhere.

Of course, most of that we didn't know when we bought him at auction. All of it was potential and promises, neither of which any of us knew the size of.

Well, that's not entirely true. I did have one clue that Arizona had a bit of a wild streak.

At the horse auction, there was a bearded red-headed cowboy who people would pay to ride their horses into the sale ring. A ridden horse always fetched a better price. Many sale days, I spent part of my time behind the sale barn, watching that cowboy saddling and warming up horses of all types and dispositions. He made the gentle ones look peppy and the rank ones look rideable.

Needless to say, you don't take on a job like that unless you are a pretty good rider, and that cowboy certainly was. I enjoyed watching him, though I can't say I picked up any riding tips. I did observe a good marketing tip, though.

Hanging in the back window of his truck, the cowboy always kept a spare shirt. On the rare occasions he got thrown and his shirt got dirty, he would change to his clean shirt so no one would see the evidence that a horse had put him in the dirt.

Sure enough, when he rode Arizona into the sale ring that day, that cowboy had a different shirt on than when the day had started. But my heart was already set on that horse, and we all excel at dismissing evidence when we see fit.

I didn't tell my parents about the wardrobe change. And I must have made a great pitch or caught them on a really good day because they let me buy him.

The beginning–like most beginnings–started with a lot of enthusiasm. I strategically picked a freshly plowed field behind our house to start riding Arizona on, thinking if I got thrown off, I would have a spot place to land.

But as Dad often reminded me, "They don't pay you to think."

Arizona never threw me in a plowed field. None of the places he threw me were soft. He threw me on a caliche road, into a mesquite tree, and into a yucca plant. If you can't picture a yucca plant, you may be more familiar with its other name–Spanish Dagger. Once, I landed just shy of a cattle guard on a gravel road. I'm still not sure which would have been the better outcome.

As the spring rolled on, I worked Arizona less and less. It wasn't because I was scared of getting hurt. Ok, it wasn't just because I was scared of getting hurt; I was afraid of failing.

As long as Arizona was spending his days in the pen unridden, he was still a horse with potential that just needed attention. If I kept at it, my big fear wasn't that I would get thrown again. My big fear would be that he would turn into "that horse" that I ruined.

My mom nagged me about it pretty regularly. It was as effective as the nagging we all do as parents.

I ran cows on my uncle's land the summer I bought Arizona. One Saturday morning, we hauled Arizona and my first horse, Millie, out to check on cows. Dad rode with me, him on Millie and me on Arizona.

Things were going well, until out of nowhere, Arizona went crazy bucking. My dad just kept hollering, "Hold on! Hold on!" I did, even though it wasn't a little protest buck. It was full-on rodeo action. He finally stopped, and we both calmed down, and then he went right back to work like nothing had happened.

Later in the morning, we crossed paths with a rattlesnake. I told myself to be calm, but I know I tensed up, which horses sense. I was praying neither the snake or I would spook the horse and hoped to calmly walk right on past.

Arizona had other plans. He stopped right at the snake and bent his head down to smell it. In that moment, I knew how I was going to die. I was going to get bucked off and trampled or bucked off and bitten by a rattlesnake. Either way, I was eyeballing for a soft place to land.

But the snake slithered on over to the side, and I tried to figure out how hard I could prod Arizona into walking without pushing him to buck. He, on the other hand, was just trying to figure out what the fuss was about.

And that morning was the puzzle of Arizona in a nutshell. You never knew what triggered him, and the things you expected to bother him didn't.

He proved it again that afternoon.

We were missing a black heifer, but we spotted it in the neighbor's pasture. Dad didn't know the neighbors, so we went back to the house, and he swapped out with my Uncle Ivan, who lived there and did know the neighbors.

The two of us headed back on horseback to get the lost heifer. Along the way, when crossing some heavy brush, Arizona started bucking again. Uncle Ivan was worried Arizona was going to fall over backward and land on me, so he started yelling, "Jump Off! Jump Off!"

I was sorting out the irony of Dad yelling one thing and Ivan yelling another. I'm not sure if I jumped by choice or just got thrown off, but that was the day I landed in the Spanish Dagger.

Extracting myself was a delicate matter that took a minute to sort out. Arizona didn't run off in a panic. He was just a dozen yards from me, already calm and grazing by the time I was standing again.

When we got to the neighbor's pasture, the cattle were gathered up around an old, dilapidated homestead. My heifer was with them. So, we had to cut her out of the herd and push her up to a gate without her turning back.

Ivan knew the plan. I knew the plan. The heifer did not know the plan.

At first, it went well. We were calmly easing the lost heifer away from the group and toward a fence line that we could walk her down. But she decided she would rather stay with her new friends than go with us and took a hard U-turn between us and started running back to the herd.

Ivan told me to run around the backside of the old house and cut her off before she got mixed in again, so off I went.

Arizona was fast and smooth. I felt sure we would make it around the backside of the house in time. And we did, but not without some added adrenaline along the way.

Hidden in a weedy section was an old barbed wire fence. I didn't see it until we were right on top of it. I'm guessing Arizona hadn't seen it much before because he hadn't slowed. For the second time that day, I saw how I was going to die—this time in a high-speed moving ball of barbed wire, eleven hundred pounds of horse, and me.

But Arizona wasn't going to go out like that. He jumped and cleared that fence like it was nothing. My full panic switched to full joy. I couldn't believe it. Then, a few fast, long strides in, it happened again—another fence.

We—okay, he—didn't just jump a fence. We had jumped into an old garden that had been fenced off with barbed wire. Just as easily as he had jumped us in, he jumped us out, and he kept running like it was no big deal.

If he hadn't seen the fences or if he had decided to throw on the brakes and send me flying over his head, it would have been a real bad day. Instead, I felt on top of the world. Uncle Ivan was slack-jawed and didn't expect that out of the horse or out of me.

But that was Arizona: one minute putting you in the dirt and another making you look like the best stunt horse rider in the world.

I went home reinvigorated, but it waned. I may have ridden Arizona more often, but not as much as he needed.

Then one day, Mom came home from the feed store with a name and a phone number on a piece of paper. She met some man who trained horses on a ranch near Miami (Texas, not Florida).

I knew we didn't have the money to pay a horse trainer. Mom knew that, too, so she had made him a deal. She was going to send Arizona and me there for two weeks. The plan was that I would ride with him every day, and when we weren't riding, I would work off the lessons, room, and board by working.

One needed to be wary of Winnie Turner (my mother) when she had grown tired of nagging.

I showed up at the ranch on a Sunday afternoon. That evening, we went to the main house for dinner. I don't know if it was intentional or by happenstance, but the conversation throughout dinner and for a couple of hours afterward involved everyone around the table recounting every horse-related accident they could remember.

There were the broken legs and broken arms. There were the back surgeries. There were the getting hung up in the stirrups and drug to death. There were lots more.

Back at the small camp house with those stories running through my head, I didn't sleep very well, but I would have no trouble sleeping at night the rest of my time there. When you see the schedule we kept, you'll know why sleep came easy.

The day started at 5:00 a.m. with feeding the horses. While they ate, we ate breakfast. Then they were brushed and saddled before full dawn. Sunrises were seen from atop the horse. Everything was from atop the horse, including opening and closing gates and filling canteens.

Lunch was at 11, or 12, or 1. Maybe 2. It just depended on which pastures we rode and how the checking of cows went. The horses were cleaned and rested in the afternoons. We built fence, hauled hay, cleared trees in the creek, and some days worked with other horses.

Supper was at the main house at 7:00 p.m. or so after all the animals had been fed. After we ate, everybody talked until 10 or later. Afterward, we would go back to the small camp house and go to bed, just to repeat it all again the next day. I got Sunday morning off for church.

I liked the guy I was working for, and he never asked me to work harder than him, so I gave it my best. Arizona did too.

You might think it was the hours of riding time that were important and no doubt that helped make Arizona a better horse. But the hard, exhausting work mattered more.

See, I spent the first morning worrying about when the horse was going to spook or what mistake I was going to make next. I was thinking about all the things that could go wrong or hanging on too long to the things that did.

By day two, I was too tired to worry. I knew the day was going to be a long march, and the only way to get through it was working through the list one thing at a time. I was riding with a purpose, and once my mind was on the purpose, rather than the riding, things started falling into place.

Decades later, I can remember many details about those two weeks because they were meaningful. More importantly, I remember the confidence I left with. Not just confidence with Arizona, but the confidence that I could do hard things. A confidence that I have called on many times when a task is challenging, rising to that challenge—or at least attempting to—is worth it.

When this story came to mind, I thought it was because my son had started horse riding lessons.

Only when I started writing it down did I realize that what really brought it to mind is my daughter Ella, who will be leaving for college not long from now.

She is entering a world that is increasingly devaluing work. In a short amount of time, its virtue has been rebranded as exploitation, and that we should all somehow have the right to make it optional. I am afraid we don't have the slightest understanding of what the implications of that will be.

And I am not just talking about working at a job. I am talking about the work required to be put into our relationships, our families, our worship, and our communities. We seem to be on a trajectory where we expect everything to be easy, and when it's not, we quit or look for someone else to do it.

It seems to me that culturally we have fallen into a trap better coined by someone else; we put more effort into preparing the road for the child instead of preparing the child for the road.

I could be wrong about that. I'm not a sociologist, nor a parenting expert, child development specialist, or psychologist. I'm just an old guy with stories. And you should weigh any implied advice based on those credentials.

But that's okay. This story isn't about offering advice to others.

It's a reminder for me to let my kids try hard things. Let them fail. If they need it, help them get back up. Give them a push when needed. Do not deprive them of opportunities to create the confidence one only gets from hard work and conquering challenges.

Alex and Ella, pack an extra clean shirt because sometimes you will get thrown in the dirt. But don't shy away; that's where the best lessons and memories are made.

CHAPTER 11

The Bobs—Marley and Wills

There was a big love of music packed into that little girl. Colby soaked in music like a deep breath after a long run. It permeated throughout her and rejuvenated her cells. It prompted expressions of delight and contemplation. It sparked thousands of smiles.

The lesson in that? Lean into what moves your child's soul.

I s she fond of music?"

It seems like a straightforward question to ask. But as is often the case, context is everything.

Colby was fifteen months old at the time, and the question was being posed at her first geneticist appointment, where we were attempting to figure out why her growth had slowed. We had already given a full medical history, been through the weighing, measuring, and answered a couple of dozen behavior questions. We knew the doctor was looking for clues, but by this point in the exam, we had figured out that some answers led down darker paths than others. And while we were trying to provide the most accurate information, we couldn't help but try to read what was behind each question.

Fond of music—does not liking it enough raise questions about her intelligence? Does liking it too much raise concerns like autism or some other disorder?

We knew Colby to be an inquisitive, observant, intelligent, and happy girl. We put extra effort into making sure our answers made that clear. We explained that when she listened to music, what she did when it was on, and recounted as many music-related anecdotes as sprang to mind. The doctor was looking for a simpler answer, and she saw us struggling, so she attempted to clarify. "Is she *overly* fond of music?"

Usha and I looked at each other with one of those looks spouses can give each other to make sure they are on the same page. We both agreed Colby was not "overly fond," not quite sure exactly what being overly fond of music could mean, but fairly sure what the doctor meant didn't apply to Colby.

I've come to understand that she meant "overly fond" to mean to an unhealthy level. Still, it's a difficult idea to wrap my head around. Overly fond of chocolate, overly fond of television, overly fond of sleep—I can understand all those. Too well, perhaps. But how much does one have to love music to be overly fond of it?

Colby did love music.

Not long after that doctor visit, Colby became a fan of the song "Itsy Bitsy Spider." She would ask for it by moving her hands to show the spider crawling up the spout. Colby knew all the hand movements to the song, but she really could wash away that spider with style.

One time, Colby and I were in the waiting room of one of her granny's doctors. We played all over that room, and at one point, I was seated in a chair with my back to the door, and Colby was seated on the floor a bit in front of me. She was asking for "Itsy Bitsy Spider" over and over, and we were both really getting into it.

After a dozen or so times, out of the corner of my eye, I glimpsed someone, a woman, carefully inching closer to our side of the room and leaning in to try to angle herself so that she could see my face. I turned toward her, and about that time, she saw Colby, and immediately, a look of relief came across her face. I then realized from behind it looked like I was singing to myself, and I surely looked crazy. The poor lady had to have been contemplating calling security. Thankfully, she laughed as hard as I did after we realized what each other was up to.

After that incident, I began to theorize that the more people around for me to be embarrassed in front of, the more Colby would ask me to sing. Once she figured out she could ask me to sing whenever she wanted, she began to figure out how to ask me what songs to sing, too.

At night, I would rock her for a little while before I lay her down in the crib to fall asleep. We'd start rocking, and I would pick a song and start singing to her. If it wasn't what she wanted to hear, she'd pick her head up off my chest, look me in the eyes, and shake her head no, but would still be smiling until I stopped singing it. She'd then put her head back down and wait for me to pick another song to sing, and the process would repeat until I got to one she wanted.

She would tap her fingers on my chest as I sang. When the song ended, she would pick her head up again and show me her smile as her hands signed for more. Usually, I tried to limit the songs to three, but she was so sweet, and irresistible, so it wasn't unusual to sing four songs ... or five ... sometimes ten.

The songs were most anything. Old songs my dad used to sing

to me were in heavy rotation. The "How in the heck can I wash my neck?" line always delighted her as she put her hands in her hair, pretending to wash her curls. Other regular artists on the list included George Strait, Red Hot Chili Peppers, Guns 'N' Roses, Charlie Robison, and Robert Earl Keen. Tonight's favorite song might be the favorite for the next three or four nights, but never much longer than that. She liked mixing things up; her musical interests were truly wide and varied.

I remember taking Colby for strolls in the neighborhood with the iPod on shuffle the whole time. And when I say the whole time, it wasn't unusual for some of these strolls to last an hour and a half. Shuffle is a cool feature on an iPod, picking songs randomly from your playlist and letting you enjoy both the songs and the unexpected surprises in what order they get played.

In our house, the shuffle surprises can be pretty interesting. Our music library is a co-mingled mix of the musical tastes of both Usha and mine. Throw in a couple of sizeable handfuls of kids' songs, and we have a pretty wide spectrum of the musical world. I've often wondered after one of our strolls how many other toddlers listened to both Bob Wills and Bob Marley that day?

And not just listened but enjoyed. You could see it in the way Colby tapped her fingers. How I loved watching that little hand keep perfect rhythm. You could hear it in the questioning "ah?" she made, asking where the music went if the pauses between songs were too long. You could tell she enjoyed it because if you left the music at home, the strolls never seemed to last as long.

Sitting in the stroller listening to music was one thing. When not strapped into a stroller or car seat, she could let the music move her. Her dancing genes definitely came from her mom. Limited as my dancing is, I couldn't help but try because Colby loved it so much and wanted to dance with me. Sometimes we would dance around the kitchen, me holding her and moving in big, sweeping, waltz-like steps. The bigger the step or the dip, the bigger the laugh.

My absolute favorite memory of her dancing—maybe my favorite memory of all—was watching her dance all on her own the night Ella threw a belated Valentine's Day party for her. The two of them dancing with their mom, smiling and laughing, was a sight I will always treasure as the purest blessing of fatherhood.

One e-mail update I sent about Colby summed up her dancing with these two lines. Satchel Paige advised everyone to "Dance like nobody is watching." I believe Colby's advice was "Try and keep up."

No, she never hid her passion for music. She let you know how she felt about it quite clearly, as our pastor found out as she was getting to know us.

You see, Colby was a fan of the children's television program *Jack's Big Music Show*. I downloaded a few episodes onto my phone so that she could watch them during long waits at doctor visits. One morning, we were waiting for some blood to be drawn, and the wait turned into a rather long one. So, I pulled out the phone and let her watch Jack. As luck would have it, right in the middle of one of the songs, the phone rang. The show automatically paused, and I picked up the phone to answer it.

The caller was Pastor Cheryl, who I presume was calling to check on us. I say presume because, at the point when Cheryl introduced herself, Colby began howling with no intention of letting up until she got the phone back. I tried to fight through it, but it was no use. There would be no peace until the mobile phone went back to being a mobile television. Apologetically, I cut the call short, though I have my doubts she could hear me over Colby. Oh, how I would love to know the thoughts that were racing through Cheryl's head!

Once the song came back on, the cries of protest stopped, and her eyes locked in on the screen, except for a quick sideways look at me to make sure we had a new understanding. We did. If you were a regular visitor to my voicemail during that time frame, now you know why.

As much as she didn't like that phone call at the time, that call helped lead Colby to discover a whole other musical joy—the church organ. We began attending Pastor Cheryl's church regularly, and like with any toddler, time in the pew had its challenges. Colby liked getting dressed up for church, she liked all the attention before and after service, and she enjoyed exploring the ins and outs of the building. But she usually grew restless when sitting in the pew.

Restless, that is, except for when the organ was playing. When the organ played, she absolutely lit up. With a big smile and sparkling eyes, she scanned the room watching, as the music played. As adults, we often struggle to live in the moment, but Colby *lived* in those moments. In those moments, she didn't want to be doing anything else or anywhere else.

When the song ended, Colby's smile lingered on. She would clap, even if no one else clapped, and when she was done clapping, she would sign "more." If you get to Heaven before I do, find the organist and take him a cold drink with a straw. I'm sure he could use a little refreshment, because Colby is keeping him busy.

Stories about Colby and music seem endless. Her fascination with the song "Wombo Lombo," walking around the mall and stopping outside the doors of places like Abercrombie & Fitch just to hear the music playing inside and dance a bit, and my reluctantly developing an acquired taste for Yo Gabba Gabba through Colby—all of these are just a tiny scratch on the surface.

Out of all these many memories, one set of music stands out in my mind. We got a lot of mileage, figuratively and literally, out of the album *Undone: A Musicfest Tribute to Robert Earl Keen*. We played these songs a lot; it was the soundtrack on many car trips. These songs were our lullabies on nights we spent in the hospital, reassuringly calming us and drowning out the never-ending nighttime sounds you find there.

Maybe Colby liked it in the same way I liked the Yo Gabba Gabba songs, something that she gained an acquired taste for because her daddy liked it. Maybe she liked it because of the smooth soothing voices or the storytelling guitars. Maybe it was just part of her Texan DNA. Whatever it was, she undoubtedly liked it, and if you ask me, she loved it.

My appreciation of this album has simple roots. I have liked many of these songs for a long time, but what we were going through gave many of these songs a whole new meaning for me. It didn't take much imagination to give me a new perspective on the heart-resonating lyrics, even if it wasn't exactly what Mr. Keen intended by them.

I'd share the lyrics here but lack the permission to do so. Still, I encourage you to check out these songs and hear them through the ears of a dad with severe health issues: "Think it Over One Time," "No Kinda Dancer," "I'll Be Here For You," and "I Would Change My Life."

Colby's last car ride was early one Monday morning. We were headed to the hospital for a routine surgery to put tubes in her ears so that she could hear better. We were so excited about her hearing clearly. We knew it would help her speech development, but the thought had also crossed our minds that the music would sound even better to her. I joked that once she started hearing better, Colby would never want me to sing to her again because she'd know how bad I am at it.

We left the house a little after five, me hoping that she would go back to sleep and get some rest on the drive there. The *Undone* album was playing, and I listened for any sounds of her singing or tapping along. Hearing nothing, I was pretty certain she was back asleep.

A few miles up the road, one of the songs ended, and in the silence before the next one started, I heard the sound of her two little hands joyously clapping. Fluid in her ears be damned; it still sounded good to her.

Was Colby fond of music?

Very fond. She enjoyed it when it was played, and she asked for it when it wasn't. She soaked in every song and extracted full enjoyment from each one. Music wove its way into her play, her sleep, her learning, and every other aspect of her life. She strolled to it, danced to it, laughed, and clapped to it. Music enriched her life, and it enriched our lives by watching her. Colby was incredibly fond of music. Hugely fond. Massively fond.

Overly fond? Not even a smidge.

CHAPTER 12

Spoons

Some lessons take decades to sink in, at least for me. This piece reflects on the grace that spouses can afford each other. That is certainly a welcome blessing on a parenting journey.

B owl of oatmeal in hand, I stared inside the silverware drawer this morning and considered my options. There were 20 butter knives, even more forks, and 2 spoons: one was a large serving spoon, and the other a baby spoon. Not just small, but an actual tiny silver spoon designed for babies.

"Where the hell are all the spoons?" I asked myself silently. At least, I think it was silent.

Then I remembered I have kids and was immediately certain that was the answer. Oh sure, it lacked specific details. Was it a science experiment in the yard? Was it an ice cream party upstairs waiting to be cleaned up? We've been giving the dog meds with peanut butter and a spoon, so I suppose there is a chance Murphy has buried them under his pillow in hopes of a peanut butter fairy visit.

Who's to know? Or more precisely, how badly did I want to know? Turned out, not that badly. I grabbed the baby spoon, which I quickly determined was ridiculous, and went back for the serving spoon. Now there are no spoons in the drawer.

As I ate my breakfast, I couldn't help but think of a breakfast with my Uncle Ivan and Aunt Willie at their farmhouse in 1988. That story can stand on its own, but a full appreciation of it requires a little context.

Ivan and Willie did not have kids of their own, but our family is large, and kids visited often. Visits were special, and Uncle Ivan was a natural with kids. We all loved him. If others got crossways with Willie, I don't remember hearing about it. But I was more than a little much for Willie.

If she is standing next to St. Peter at the Pearly Gates, there are two certainties: My chances at getting in are shot, and the disapproving look she will have on her face will not have changed.

The seed of this fracture goes back to an overnight stay when I was about eight. Christina, my then twelve-year-old sister, and I were staying at Ivan and Willie's for the weekend because we were there for a swim meet. I was quite excited about it.

Staying at their house meant hearing Ivan's stories and sleeping on a fancy bed with crisp, clean sheets in the guest room. I am positive Willie actually ironed her bed sheets.

The bathroom had a fuzzy carpet seat cover on the lid, a matching one covering the tank lid, a pink tub, and it was plumbed with an actual showerhead that I didn't know how to work because we didn't have a shower at home. It also wasn't the only bathroom in the house, which meant no one was rushing you or barging in to use the toilet while you took a bath.

From my perspective, it might as well have been a five-star hotel. A five-star hotel with candy dishes!

We didn't have candy dishes at home. We seldom had candy around, primarily because I lived there and would eat it all.

All day long, I was picking through the candy bowl. Good candy, too. Lots of chocolate and other treats. Willie would sometimes chide me, "not to ruin my dinner," but I could tell she didn't mean it. By that, I mean she didn't take the candy away.

By bedtime, the candy in the bowls had dwindled significantly. And for some reason, even though I had been free-ranging on chocolate all day, I decided it would be best to hoard some of it.

I smuggled large handfuls of candy into my room and put them under my pillow for safekeeping.

Hmmm... I'm not much of a psychologist, but thinking about that sentence now, I'm guessing accusing Murphy earlier of stealing the spoons for peanut butter was what they call projection. Anyway, back to the story.

The next morning, I had long forgotten about the candy. As I brushed my teeth, Willie was about to discover it.

"What in tarnation?!?" reverberated down the hall. Christina and I dashed to Willie's voice to see what had happened.

She stood there with steam coming out of her ears, lightning bolts from her eyes, and holding a pillow with melted chocolate smeared all over the bottom side. The top sheet it had rested on looked no better.

For the briefest of moments, I was worried about the candy I had lost. But when Christina started belly laughing while looking at me, the sheer delight in her eyes was so profound, so pure, it could only mean one thing: I was in trouble. At that point, I knew that me losing the candy was not "the tarnation."

I don't remember the full unraveling of the rest of that day, but I do remember the car ride to the swimming pool was quiet. I remember good old Uncle Ivan, who always joked around, was not joking and had his eyes firmly affixed to the road in front of him. And I remember glancing at Christina, looking for clues about what to do and her just laughing at me.

Things never went back to normal with Willie and me. The rift persisting was probably not because she wasn't capable of forgiving and definitely not because I didn't try to make things right. I just wasn't very good at it.

On a subsequent overnight visit, Mom reminded me that Willie kept a very clean house, and she gave me tips. She told me to wipe the bathtub out with my towel after my bath.

I did that, and then stood, wondering what to do with the towel. It turns out that folding it neatly and hanging it back on the towel rack to make it look unused was not the answer.

Many years later, one of my nieces went to live with Ivan and Willie over the summer while doing an internship. I told her, "You'll like it, and they will like having you—just don't mention my name to Willie because she hates me."

My niece thought I was kidding or exaggerating. The next time I saw her, her first words were "Willie REALLY does not like you!"

Thankfully, in my sophomore and junior years of high school, Ivan and Willie did rent me about 400 acres of land to run heifers on. I had to go to the bank and get a loan, go to the sale barns and buy cattle, tend to them all summer, and sell them in the fall.

It was a great experience I look back at fondly, even if wistfully, and I owe them both a lot for giving me the chance. Willie could have easily used her lifetime chocolate candy incident card to veto the whole endeavor. At the time, I didn't appreciate that aspect as much as I should have. I was too busy being scared of her.

That takes us to that mid-summer breakfast in 1988. I had gotten up at 5:00 a.m. to be there for breakfast at 6:30, with plans to build a fence with Ivan for the day. I made sure to arrive early because Willie always thought I was lazy and wouldn't show up. She also took plenty of shots at me for not knowing how to do something the right way or being a greenhorn. She was right about that last part, but I was not going to concede "lazy."

At the breakfast table, Ivan was eating a bowl of cereal, and the two of us were idly chatting. Willie came around the corner, looked at Ivan, and disapprovingly said, "Why are you eating cereal with a serving spoon?"

He shrugged and kept eating.

That was not the correct response. I'm not sure there was a correct response, but that was definitely not it.

Willie turned back into the kitchen, but the spoon lecture continued. Just louder. And faster- paced.

Occasionally, there would be a brief pause, and I would wonder if it was over. Nope.

Ivan continued eating, at the same relaxed pace as before, just quiet now. He looked as calm as ever, but I was getting uncomfortable.

During one pause, I began to speak, "Why does it ...?" Ivan cut me off. Not with words, not even a head shake. Just a subtle nodding of no with his eyeballs.

The full question was going to be "Why does it matter what spoon he eats it with?" but I didn't need to finish it for Willie to know where I was headed with it.

She dismissed it very succulently. "Lord knows I wouldn't expect YOU to understand."

Ivan finished his bowl, got up, hand-washed the bowl and the spoon, and put them away. He put on his sweat-stained straw hat, and we headed out to build the fence. Willie was still talking about spoons as we walked out.

Ivan wasn't going to talk about it. Actually, he didn't seem bothered at all. Mentally, I logged two lessons.

The first was never to get married. Thankfully, that didn't stick.

The second was to know when to hush. I'll never win any prizes for that one either. Whether it's from simply being a smart aleck or not being able to resist a principled stand, my hush button malfunctions regularly.

But back to the first lesson.

Watching someone get so upset over a spoon really did spur lots of contemplation about relationships within me. And I have thought about it often over the years.

The "never get married" evolved into "Be careful who you marry," then to marry someone optimistic and always capable of the benefit of the doubt. Older now, I think there is some truth to that, but I also recognize it's an impossible standard.

The best of us have bad days. The best of us get upset about little things and don't know why. The best of us get upset about bigger things we don't recognize or don't deal with, and it gets expressed in small, unrelated things. Irrational things.

Those things can and do happen.

Maybe the real lesson is to find someone to love like Ivan loved Willie. To him, the spoon size was a tiny, little thing, but so was a few minutes of fussing. It was a pebble in his boot to shake out and keep going. He could have festered on it and carried it with him or fought back.

Up until this morning, I had always focused on the lack of grace

Willie had shown Ivan. This morning, I realized the other side of the coin was the amount of grace Ivan was showing Willie.

I don't mean to imply it was a one-sided thing, as I'm sure the shoe was on the other foot at times.

And that's what couples do—or should try to do. Take turns being the strong one, the rational one, the calm one, the optimistic one, the quick-to-forgive one, the not-keeping-score one, or the don't-kill-the-nephew one.

Or maybe serving spoons really do matter that much, and I just haven't caught on yet.

Now, if you'll excuse me, I'm going to search for spoons before it's ice cream time.

CHAPTER 13

Watching Mom

This book wouldn't be possible without my wife, Usha. Not only because she made me a daddy, but she has helped me be a better one than I could have ever been without her. This was a Mother's Day essay written about her in 2011; that was pre-Alex, but the sentiments hold for him as well.

On occasion, I've watched her doubt herself as a mom. In those moments, I want to fill her thoughts with the other things I have seen her do.

I've seen our daughters imitate her, even though they might not even know what it is they are copying, because just being like Mom is reason enough.

I've watched them playing with a toy with great interest and suddenly toss it aside at the sounds of her footsteps entering the room and rush to her as she returned home.

I've seen her beam with pride at their accomplishments and watched them soak it in like flowers in the sunshine, helping them grow a little stronger and stand a little straighter.

I've watched her fight for them, cry alongside them, and sacrifice her comfort for theirs.

I've witnessed Usha take the time to teach them how to do it on their own, give them the space to let them try, and provide a well-timed push when they doubt themselves, sometimes with the biggest obstacle being me.

I've seen her be silly and watched the resulting belly laughs they all shared, making some of life's most perfect moments appear out of thin air.

I've watched her dance with them and fill the room with smiles and squeals, flooding my heart with tremendous warmth and filling my mind with what will be my most cherished memory.

I've watched her give me room to be a better dad, step in when my patience was wearing thin, and help me sort it out when I veered off track.

I've seen her take pure joy in the wonderful highs of motherhood and watched her endure the immense pain that no mother should have to face.

Yes, I have seen Usha doubt herself as a mom, and I think that's what great moms do. They pause from time to time to question themselves as part of their endless endeavor to do the best they can for their families. And I'm sure she won't be stopping that anytime soon.

My hope is that whenever she doubts herself, Usha never doubts the deep love her daughters have for her and the indescribable appreciation I have for her in being both a wonderful mommy and wife.

Happy Mother's Day, Usha.

We love you,
Ella, Colby, & Neil

CHAPTER 14

887 Pairs of Goggles

The previous chapter told of our kids watching and learning from their mom. This story will let you know the apples didn't fall far from the tree.

Ella has since retired from swimming, but not before she worked hard enough and swam fast enough to compete at national-level meets. There was a lot of hard work from Ella supported by a great deal of family sacrifice involved. This explores the rewards.

It started with Ella's first week of swim lessons.

At the end of the week, her instructor pulled me aside after the session and told me, "Swimming is Ella's sport. When she is old enough for volleyball and basketball, those coaches are going to want her because she is tall. Don't do it. If she does anything but swim, it will be an injustice. She is made to swim."

Now, when someone tells you something like that about your child, you take notice. It makes you think about your responsibility to make good choices for your kid, and, in our case, that we should seriously consider swimming. It makes you feel special.

That is special until you overhear her giving the same spiel to another parent at the next swim lesson session, and you realize it wasn't advice but a sales pitch. Parents are suckers, and sports parents are the biggest suckers of the lot.

Sales pitch or not, Ella did take to swimming pretty well, and when some of her friends decided to try out, she decided to relent to her teacher's encouragement to try out, too. Nervously, we watched her make her way down the pool doing freestyle and come back doing backstroke. A backstroke so painfully slow as she tried to make sure her arms moved perfectly that her not sinking surely defied the laws of physics. The coaches made notes on their clipboards, and soon we were told the good news—she had made the team.

We celebrated! Then we thought about what was next.

That was a process that has been repeated many times and will continue for as long as she swims.

There was Ella's first swim meet. We celebrated and then looked forward to when she would win a ribbon. The first ribbon was followed by wondering when she would win her first medal. Her first time to swim breaststroke was followed by wondering when the first time would be when she would swim it without being disqualified.

USA Swimming sets time standards that range from B to AAAA to categorize athlete performance. Her first B time was followed by looking up BB times, which was followed by looking up A times. She was on track to get her first A time later in the spring, and when she did, I was sure we would look to see how much she needed to cut to get to an AA time.

At some point, you realize that after every celebration, there will always be another level. Another, what's next?

Look around a swim meet and you will see a few hundred kids dreaming of the Olympics. Who knows, maybe one or two will make it. If they did, they would dream of the medal podium. The bronze winner will dream of gold. The gold medal winner will dream of eight, and after she gets them, she will dream of returning to the next Olympics.

If the top swimmer in the world is dreaming of "what's next," it really makes you wonder what is the end game here? What are we trying to accomplish? What is the ultimate goal?

A lot of sports parents answer that question with hopes of a college scholarship. No doubt that is quite an accomplishment and, in many ways, an admirable goal. Financially, it may not be quite as practical as it sounds. Factor in twelve years of swim club fees, all the miles back and forth to practice, out-of-town travel for meets, entry fees, swimsuits that you don't want to know the prices of, swim camps, and an estimated 887 pairs of goggles, and that amount of money put into a 529 would fund college quite comfortably.

Now, don't get me wrong; I don't foresee Ella reaching the level of swimming that would merit a scholarship—but if she did, I would not turn it down! But that's not the reason we've worn ruts in the road between here and the YMCA pool.

I think about these things, usually at swim meets. I enjoy celebrating her improvement and accomplishments, but not long into it, I find myself wondering what is next.

Last weekend, Ella swam at the Phillips 66 Meet of Champions. Last year, she didn't have qualifying times for the meet. This year, we were thrilled she qualified. It didn't take long before just being there wasn't quite enough, and Ella began dreaming of making the meet finals. When she began dreaming of that, our hopes for her followed right along.

On Saturday morning, she swam in the prelims for three events. In the first two, she had good swims and dropped time, but did not finish in the top six, which was what was required to make the evening finals. But the third event was one of her favorites, and she swam great. When the results were announced, she was in sixth place and squealed with delight. She would be in the finals.

Ella was excited, and her teammates, coaches, and other parents were excited for her. And she spent the next couple of hours repeating, "I can't believe I made the finals." The girl was floating on air.

Later, back in the hotel and letting Ella rest up for finals, I began wondering what was next. I was curious how close she was to an A time, so I opened the Meet Mobile app to double-check her time from the morning prelims. When I did, her place had changed. She was now listed as seventh, one spot out of the finals.

I decided it would be best to break the news sooner rather than later and that maybe there was a mix-up earlier. Maybe Meet Mobile had it wrong, but if it was right, maybe something happened to cause the update, and if so, she might not be swimming in the finals.

Ella was smiling as I was explaining, leftovers from a smile that had been on her face all afternoon. As my words began sinking in, the smile turned quickly, and her eyes welled up. She flopped face down on the bed and kicked and punched and sobbed uncontrollably. One place separated by a tenth of a second—the difference between being on top of the world and feeling the entire weight of it in the pit of her stomach.

I tried to calm her. Tried telling her not to worry until we found out for sure. Tried explaining possible explanations. Of course, none of it mattered. She was crushed. The rest of the afternoon was periods of sobbing, interrupted by rage about what was fair.

We showed up at the pool well before finals warm-up to see what we could find out. Turns out that a girl in that event had been disqualified for a false start. Unfortunately, the person entering that into the computer tagged the wrong swimmer—the swimmer who happened to have the fastest time. After prelims, the wrongly disqualified swimmer's coach and the officials sorted it all out, restoring her to first place and bumping everyone else down a spot.

Ella got knocked down to first alternate. The uncertainty removed, the tears returned.

I stepped away to check on something, and when I returned, Ella's face was in her hands, and she was still sobbing. The difference was that one of her teammates had shown up and was sitting next to her with her arm around Ella. Such a sweet thing to see.

I took a spot on the opposite side of Ella and put my hand on her knee. The three of us sat there for a bit, not saying anything and just letting Ella cry.

Soon, one of her coaches showed up, and I knew I was superfluous. I stepped away to let them talk and took a seat on the opposite side of the pool. A minute or two later, a smile reappeared on Ella's face. Tears still flowed, but there were definite signs of improvement.

Add in more supportive teammates and another coach, and before too long, Ella was in her suit and warming up on the off chance that, as an alternate, she would get to swim. Throughout warmups, I'd see her teammates continuing to console and support her.

As the finals started, all the girls put lots of effort into cheering each other on. They would space themselves out up and down the pool so that their teammate would hear shouts of encouragement the whole time.

Then, Ella's event approached. She moved herself over to a chair by the starter, where hopeful alternates would sometimes sit, hoping to get their shot. She had her swim cap on and goggles over her forehead, ready to go if called. She looked at me in the stands and flashed a smile and a thumbs-up. A couple of hours before, I never would have predicted that reaction possible.

As the top six took their spots behind the blocks, harsh reality set in again. Her face was angered as she stood to walk back to her team. She ripped the cap off her head, and her red hair sprang out like flames, matching her anger.

I left the stands to go wait for her in the lobby. Some time passed as Ella changed into street clothes, and when she entered the lobby, she didn't pause for hellos or hugs. She marched right past me to the door. Outside the door, tears flowed again, but they weren't sad. They were angry.

"I watched the race. I watched the girl who took my spot."

I clarified what I thought was an important point, telling her that the girl earned the spot and shouldn't be penalized for a clerical mix-up.

"Dad, this was my first time to make finals. It wouldn't hurt so bad, but this was my first time! They should not have gotten my hopes up!"

No, more clarifications weren't needed. Just an acknowledgement that the situation sucked.

From there, we went to a local pizza place to meet up with the team. We took a few extra minutes for Ella to compose herself before going inside.

Once inside, parents gathered around one big table and swimmers around another. Ella was surrounded by other swimmers of all ages, each with their own experiences of triumph and disappointment. They had a track record of sharing, including hours upon hours of practice, aspirations, inside jokes, common challenges, and each other's support. That night, they shared about two hours of laughter and food.

When we left to return to the hotel, Ella wasn't talking about missing the finals anymore. She was talking about how much fun she had at dinner, how much she appreciated her teammates, and how glad she was that she would have one more chance to make the finals the following day.

I stood in admiration of her. Ella had been kicked in the teeth, battled through it (with lots of help from her team), dusted herself off, and got herself ready to try again. She went to bed that night with more optimism than disappointment. Truly remarkable.

By morning, fueled by optimism and determination to avoid the alternate chair, she was mentally prepared for prelims and another shot to make finals. How prepared?

First thing she said was "Dad, can you iron my team jacket? I want to look good when I make it onto the podium tonight at finals."

What's the goal here? I think we found it. Working through disappointment and finding another path forward. The immense value of teammates and friends to support you, and the importance and fun of supporting them. The role hard work and confidence play in meeting your goals. These things are the point. This is what makes the hours and the goggle budget worthwhile.

I left the swim meet with an incredible new appreciation for her teammates, her coaches, and the other team parents.

Ella left with a wealth of new experiences and life lessons.

She also left with a fifth-place finish in the finals, a plaque, and a picture of herself on the podium.

And, yes, Ella looked great in her jacket.

CHAPTER 15

Kolaches

Some of my best lessons from college didn't happen in the classroom. One of the greatest lessons was in finding gratitude in the everyday people and things around us. That's a lesson we all need, and we should look for opportunities to ingrain that gratitude in our children to counteract the modern narratives of divisiveness.

For those who are unfamiliar with kolaches—more accurately just kolache without the s—they are a Czech pastry made with a yeasty dough depressed in the middle and filled with sweet fillings such as fruit, cream cheese, or poppy seed.

I've been craving kolaches for a while now. I finally got around to making a batch. While fumbling my way through the recipe in a manner that would have driven a Czech grandma to dark liquor, I realized I wasn't really craving kolaches.

Well, that's not true. I always crave kolaches. But I was really hungry for something more.

In what seems like a lifetime ago, but also seems like yesterday, I lived out in the countryside past the town of Snook, Texas. It was while I was in college, and while the distance between home, campus, and work seems odd now, I loved it at the time.

The setup had lots of things to appreciate, including high up on the list Thursday, Friday, and Saturday mornings. On those mornings, a group of grandmotherly types of local women opened their kolache shop. There was nothing fancy about the place. I don't even recall a sign out front. It was just a simple, small house that had been converted into a bakery in the back and sales counter up front.

At first, I wondered why they would only be open three days a week. Slowly, I discovered the marketing genius. Wednesday nights always held the excitement of fresh kolaches in the morning. If they were open every day, Thursdays would have been nothing special.

On Saturday mornings, excitement changed to mild panic with the knowledge that this would be the last chance for kolaches for several days. I soon came to appreciate that these savvy ladies had concentrated a full week's worth of sales—possibly more—into three days.

Needless to say, I was a regular. The ladies came to recognize me and over much time warmed from skeptical of me to slightly less skeptical of me. Very slightly. They were never rude or unkind. They just had a practical approach to the dispatch of business.

This was our relationship for almost two years. Me needing (okay, wanting) kolaches and them selling them. Transaction done. Moving on.

That relationship changed in an unexpected way.

After an early work shift, I was driving back home and just barely out of College Station, I saw a Monte Carlo broken down on the side of the road with a priest looking over it and scratching his head. I had been up since 4:30 a.m., so I was tired and ready to be home. I was having trouble reconciling a Monte Carlo-driving priest. Despite all that, I pulled over and backed up to his car.

Once outside of my truck, I asked him what I could do to get his car going, and he said what he really needed was a ride to his church in Somerville, which was another fifteen miles past my house. Another thirty minutes or so between me and my nap seemed a small price to pay to help out, so we got in my truck and off we went.

After the perfunctory expressions of appreciation and "glad to help," we settled in for a pleasant talk. College was great fun, but being a broke college student working two jobs had a number of stresses. I can't tell you the specifics of all we talked about, but I remember feeling uplifted and more empowered by the end of the ride—a ride I admit I wasn't ready to be over.

As he got out, the priest invited me to church. I said I would, and I meant it. I am not Catholic, but I had been to a fair number of Masses at that point in my life and found them intriguing.

The next Sunday came and went. I didn't go to Mass. I was probably working or maybe just too lazy that day.

But the next Sunday, I did attend his church in Somerville. It was a perfectly fine service, and I got to say hi to my new friend and shake his hand. I even saw a few familiar faces—the ladies from the kolache shop. We didn't speak.

Thursday rolled around, and when I swung by the kolache shop, it started out completely normal, but as I paid, something different happened. The lady taking my money asked me a question.

"Are you going to start attending church in Somerville?"

"No, ma'am. Father Richard invited me, so I was just visiting."

Not understanding, she asked, "Where do you know Father Richard from?"

"Oh, his car broke down a week or so ago, and I gave him a ride."

"That was you?"

"You heard about it?" Now I was the one not understanding.

"He told us about you helping him and your ride together in his Sunday sermon the week it happened."

She handed me my change but took away my kolache bag. She turned back to the kolache pans and added a couple more to my bag. She gave it back, and I said thanks for the extras. I stood there for a bit, trying to figure out if there was more to this exchange. There was not. She was well back to work, and I slowly figured out I had been dismissed.

But from that day forward, I always got one or two more kolaches in my bag than I had paid for. And sometimes, if the shop wasn't too busy, I'd even get a little smile or pat on my hand.

A couple of years after graduation, I was visiting Usha in College Station, and I took her to the kolache shop. To my surprise, the ladies still remembered me. We even got a couple of free kolaches in the bag. I dare say we even had thirty seconds of small talk.

But that's the thing: We didn't need to talk a lot for it to feel comfortable. To feel community. To know we all knew what was important.

As I finished making my kolaches this morning, I was pondering all of that. It's been many years since I set foot in that shop. I don't even know if it is still there. But the feeling lingers—the feeling of being part of a community.

The old man in me wants to say things have changed and long for the good old days. But rationally, I know that is not true. It is a hundred percent absolutely not true. I see people every day helping their neighbors, kids, or someone in need.

People haven't changed. What has changed is the narrative. The narrative that "We are more divided than ever" and that people should be judged and classified first and foremost by their politics. It's the idea that says it's not important what you do, but what you say. That somehow being compassionate only requires looking and sounding compassionate.

My dear kolache ladies were antithetical to today's narrative. Their actions spoke volumes. They didn't need to.

As I eat my poor excuse for a kolache, I have but two wishes. One—that I could make them half as good as that Snook kolache shop. Two—that we listen less to those motivated to minimize us and instead celebrate the many good acts that happen all around us every day. Only then can we truly appreciate them, and only then will they reach their potential to inspire us to do more.

CHAPTER 16

Tripping Over the Line of Irrationality and Into the Land of Cracker Kisses

This one is a lesson in grieving. More accurately, it's a lesson in supporting others who are grieving or struggling with a challenge. Not everything makes sense. Providing comfort means you don't have to try and make sense out of it.

A few days ago, I felt like I had been too harsh with Ella, so after things calmed down, I apologized to her. Her response was delivered in classic Ella-style: sincerely sweet, yet devastatingly to the point. "It's okay, Dad. I've kinda gotten used to you yelling at me."

Clearly, in addition to whatever behavior I wanted Ella to improve upon, I have my own things to work on. I tell that story so you will better understand the following one.

I yelled at Colby once.

As explained above, the reason I didn't do it more isn't because of any special parenting skills. But it is a great testimony to how good a child Colby was.

It happened when she was about eighteen months old and happily playing and exploring in the house. Her play was punctuated with giggles of delight, and she was largely taking care of herself. At some point, I looked up and found her poking at a light socket.

"No!" I blurted. Emphatically. Sharply. Loudly.

Colby took a startled step back. She looked up at me, her eyes welling up with tears, and her bottom lip stuck out and quivered. As she further processed my yell, she broke into a heavy cry. My heart crumbled.

Now, I have traditionally considered myself a rational person. I'm not particularly driven to analyze things to the nth degree or gather every single fact, but whatever facts I have, I'd like to think I usually do an okay job of treating them fairly.

Rational thinking would say in that moment I was protecting Colby from getting hurt and, beyond that, teaching her to stay away from electrical plugs. After all, she never did go near another plug. Maybe you could say the short-term tears were worth it. I wish I could.

I'm sure in those moments between the yell and the full tears, Colby was wondering why I scared her and not making sense of why I looked so angry. A simple "no" would probably have sufficed. Although she was sometimes unhappy with being told no, she always complied. Those tears and, even more so, the fear on her face still haunt me. Is that irrational? Maybe. But the lines of rationality that look so clear at a distance can get blurry when you get a closer look.

For instance, let's suppose you have something in your refrigerator that is out of date. You throw it out. It doesn't take a lot of thought, and perhaps the most you dwell on it is factoring it into future buying patterns. That is the rational thing, right?

A while back, I threw away a packet of fruit puree snack. For the previous seven months, it had been staring at me every time I opened the refrigerator door. It gave off an odd vibe, mixed between comfort and taunting. As the days went by, it dared me to do something with it. The cringes it induced morphed into moments of despising it. Sounds pretty irrational, doesn't it?

Maybe it is.

But there is a little more to the story that has to be told. The snack was something called a Peter Rabbit squeeze packet. We discovered these at Starbucks and had always been on the lookout for things Colby might eat well, so we bought one and let her try it. She loved it. I remember one trip to Starbucks when she finished one. She walked back to the case and picked out another one and insisted on having it, too. She didn't have to ask twice.

Even better than her just liking them was that they contained things like mango, bananas, and strawberries. All of these things are high in potassium, which was something we had to keep a close eye on as part of Colby's regular care in managing side effects of her medicines. Once we saw how much she liked them, we quickly started buying them by the case on Amazon.

When Colby died, we probably had most of a case left over in the pantry. Sometime over the summer, Usha packaged it up with some other items for the local food pantry. But one of these fruit snack packets remained behind in the door of the refrigerator, right where we had put it, anticipating having it ready for Colby the next time she asked for it by giving the sign for "drink" and "bunny." As it turned out, it was waiting for an occasion that would never come.

For someone else to drink it seemed wrong. It was for Colby. I must not have been the only one to think that way, because although we have never talked about it, nobody else in our house had touched it either.

To throw it out didn't seem right either. It's not that we haven't dealt with many of Colby's things. As you can imagine, it's a painful process, and Usha has taken the brunt of handling it.

Items that may otherwise seem ordinary or trivial hold dear meaning and invaluable memories. Sorting through them and deciding what should stay and what should go is a task where the hubris of rationality dare not tread.

So, there it sat. One packet of fruit puree with a cute, little bunny making me smile, making me sad. Until one day, as part of a full refrigerator clean-up to mask the singling out of a lone expired Peter Rabbit fruit squeeze packet, I threw it away. And I cried.

If that story gives you even the slightest twinge of sadness, I should point out to you that a few minutes ago, you probably didn't think a discarded packet of food could have that effect.

Welcome to the blurred lines of rationality.

If you are a parent, this is not completely unfamiliar territory. If your child is like Colby, you've been on the receiving end of some sloppy kisses. One of Colby's specialties was the cracker kiss. Oh, how I miss Colby's cracker kisses and the closely related banana smooches.

You know the cracker kiss. A mouthful of Ritz crackers seems to trigger a desire for a toddler to kiss her parents, leaving behind a residue of mushy and dry bits of cracker that grosses out observers. But if you are the lucky parent of that sweet child, it's not gross at all. Those sticky crumbs are the mark of being blest. Clearly, the lines of rationality can be in the eye of the beholder.

The euphoria of parenthood leads to quite a few irrational behaviors. It's what moves us to retell the stories about our kids that only we find interesting. It's what explains why we sing when changing the dirtiest diapers. It's why we splurge on that cute outfit they will only get to wear twice before it's too small, or on that special tee ball bat made of a special carbon alloy and promising greater swing speeds.

It's why, after so many nights devoid of sleep and so many days filled with worries, many of us choose to try and have more kids. It's the only explanation I have for why my mom didn't change the locks at least one of the many times she was on the receiving end of a phone call from one of my unhappy teachers. Lest you think I am exaggerating, you should know the attendance ladies' nickname for me was "Speed dial #6."

But those aren't the things I am talking about here. I've been putting the lines of rationality to far greater tests lately.

Last Thanksgiving, we were in Florida, celebrating with several family members. Enough family members, in fact, that we rented an eleven-passenger van. Most of that weekend, we were never all headed the same way at the same time, but for Friday night dinner, we all climbed into the van to head into town. Just before we pulled out of the driveway, someone did a quick headcount to make sure everyone was accounted for and noting no empty seats, they remarked, "Perfect number of seats."

But it wasn't. There was no seat for Colby, and my mind could not escape thinking about it. The number of seats and Colby's absence occupied my mind from that point until I fitfully fell asleep. The thoughts were primarily of anger and sadness but sprinkled in was some confusion. I suspected my feelings were irrational, but the hurt was so real I couldn't be sure.

I held no grudges against whoever had announced the seat count. In that moment, they were right after all, and I have long since forgotten who even said it. My anger and sadness weren't at a person. It was the unfairness of it all and the cruel reminders that slap me in the face even when I least expect it. It was not the perfect number of seats. We should have needed one more. Somebody should have had to follow along in a different car, or at the very least sit on the floorboard.

I knew I had plenty of reasons to be sad about Colby's passing. But to be angry at the number of seats in a van? Surely that's not rational. *Is it?*

Not long after the van incident, Ella and I were riding to school. Too cold to walk, my favorite conversation time of the day was abbreviated to the length of the drive. The topics that get discussed sometimes repeat and sometimes are unexpected. This one started off the former but took a hard turn into the latter.

Ella asked, "Colby is all better in Heaven, right? Her heart is good, and she is growing, right?"

This was not a new question, and my answer wasn't new either. I reassured her that Colby wasn't sick anymore and that God had made sure she had everything she needed. But this time the answer did not satisfy Ella's curiosity.

As we neared the drop-off point, Ella asked a follow-up question. "Well, if her heart is all better, why can't He just send her back down here?"

I empathized and answered, "What a wonderful thought, and I wish it could happen, but it just doesn't work that way."

Both of us sat sad with that thought throbbing in our heads, and I was even sadder for sending Ella off to school in that state. We said our I love yous. She headed into the warmth of the school building, and I headed back to the coldness of a house without any giggling of girls.

As I drove back home, I reexamined the question. Why can't He just send her back? Maybe if He knew how bad we hurt? Maybe if He knew how much we missed her? Maybe if my faith were stronger? Maybe He would let me trade places? Maybe my answer was wrong. I thought about what I had said and replayed it, over and over. It certainly sounded like a sucky answer.

Not too deep down, I knew "it just doesn't work that way." But I was willing to suspend that and daydream in the realm of irrationality for as long as I could linger there.

As you read these, maybe the lines of rationality stay clear for you. Maybe even you've noticed that I'm usually aware when I am tripping over it, even if my feelings make me confused about it. But there are some that are much more difficult for me to discern and more difficult for me to talk about.

There is one that haunts me so much that this story has sat unfinished on my hard drive for more than six months. I've opened this file dozens of times only to stare at the blank space, afraid to fill it with the words that once shared can't be unwritten. Yet leaving it blank nags at me because these words are a part of Colby's story and mine, as well.

So here it goes.

Doctors will probably deny this, but your appearance matters in how they treat you; it's human nature after all. Well-dressed people get better service, do better at interviews, are more likely to be listened to, stand a better chance of getting seat upgrades, and seem more trustworthy in general. You think that way, I think that way, and a doctor who claims not to is being, well, irrational.

As the number of Colby's doctor appointments increased, I began to take notice of this. If I showed up in stay-at-home dad shorts and a T-shirt with remnants of cracker kisses, the doctors asked fewer questions and were less likely to give credence to my answers. However, if I wore a pressed shirt, slacks, and some nice loafers, suddenly I was taken more seriously.

Now I should note that this mainly applied to doctors we were seeing for the first time or irregularly. Colby's regular doctors were quick to fall under her charm and gave her top-notch care. Those doctors did not give one wit about what I wore as they kept their focus on the curls, the smile, and solving the puzzle of her condition.

But for the new doctor visits, hospital doctors, and new nurses, I needed every edge I could get to make sure they would slow down to hear all the details and nuances of Colby's case. I noticed a big difference, and I became pretty obsessive about it. The pattern became so clear that whenever I had on nice clothes on during a weekday, Ella would ask, "Does Colby have an appointment today?"

All the appointments leading up to her ear tubes procedure, I kept this policy. That morning, we had to leave the house at 5:30 a.m. to get to the hospital on time. Because of the early start and the stresses of getting shuffled around the hospital, I opted out of my normal policy and dressed in shorts and an old sweatshirt.

The shorts were the cargo type, with several oversized pockets, perfect for keeping up with the mix of toys to keep Colby occupied as we waited for our turn. The sweatshirt was worn because hospitals can be chilly, but also because it was a soft surface for Colby to lay her head as she snuggled. A starched shirt wouldn't stop either of us from snuggling, but who wouldn't prefer the comfort of thick, soft-knit cotton?

Off we went, with hopes of returning home around lunchtime if things went well. Because of some risk factors that had required us to have the procedure performed at a major hospital, we had been advised that there was a small chance that they might want to keep her for a night for observations. We had packed a full overnight bag for Colby, and I threw in a change of underwear for me just in case.

Maybe someday I'll write about the specific events of that day in greater detail, but this is the part relevant to this story. We would later find out that Colby's full case history and the events leading up to the procedure had not been given to the anesthesiologist assigned to her surgery that morning. In the time given to visit with him prior to the procedure, I conveyed the most critical of those details to him, thinking I was mostly confirming to him what was in the chart.

If I put myself in those doctors' shoes, I realize every day they are dealing with nervous parents and spend a lot of time trying to dismiss unfounded worries. That probably explains why many of them put so much faith in the chart and so little in the actual words coming from the parents' mouths. I'm sure that is even more true when the parent is wearing an old sweatshirt and shorts.

Had I gotten up a little earlier and dressed a little nicer, would he have listened more? If I wore khakis and a pressed shirt, would he have stopped to look me in the eye as I spoke rather than nodding along with his back to me, pretending to hear me as he flipped through pages of old information? If I had worn a tie that day, would he have paused things long enough to make a call to find out why the procedure had been rescheduled to take place at this better-equipped facility? If I were wearing two-hundred-dollar shoes and a fancy brand watch, would he have ordered Colby's post-op care to take place in the more intensive cardiac observation unit rather than the standard recovery room?

We soon learned that Colby's condition was causing her heart to deteriorate quickly. Had she not gone into cardiac arrest on that day, the chances of her seeing her third birthday were very slim. And no one knows what those days would be like. For a girl who loved the outside, loved exploring and playing, weeks or months in the hospital would have been torture. For all the unknowns, I accept that we were on a quick course with an unhappy conclusion.

Yet, I wonder. If I had dressed up that day, would we have had another good month? Maybe make it to one more Christmas? What memories would we have made? What other treasured stories would I be left with today? How many cracker kisses did I miss?

Irrational? Maybe. Maybe not. I'm probably not the best person to ask. I'm also not the best person to try to convince one way or the other, because I'm not sure it matters.

Rational analysis would be an inherent part of this discussion if it were about guilt or blame. But that isn't what this is about. It's about being sad. It's about dealing with questions to which there are no answers. It's about the human instinct to want understanding and adjusting to a life where you will never know why. It's about me missing my daughter. You can't reason your way out of those things.

It's not that I no longer value rational thinking. I do. In fact, I think our world could use a lot more of it. And I readily agree that it even has an important place in the grieving process. But I have come to realize that rationality is not an antidote for grief, and not every grieving action needs a rational explanation.

My prayer is that God will help me to remember that lesson when I seek to provide comfort to others who are grieving.

CHAPTER 17

Scratched Glasses

Parents, the lessons you impart to your kids will go on long after you think they have stopped. I'm still learning from my parents long after they have gone.

I need to start with two confessions.

The first one is that I wear glasses mostly out of vanity. Much of my vision issue could be solved if I simply increased the font size on my phone and computer. That and a pair of readers that I could keep track of would smooth things up pretty well for me. But a bigger font seems ... well ... seems more appropriate for a more seasoned person, let's say.

So, I have opted to wear glasses all the time instead, which may seem like an odd trade-off. But I have found that I am less likely to lose them if I wear them all the time. And it's not like I can change hairstyles, so at least I can change my glasses every once in a while.

The second confession is that most of these thoughts came to me in last Sunday's sermon. One minute, we were at Jacob's Well, and then things went off track mentally. For me, anyway, I assume the pastor delivered the sermon as he intended.

It's not his fault I tuned out, and I can explain. But I need to back-up several weeks to the root of the problem.

Alex and I were on a camping trip earlier this spring, and the weather was still on the chilly side. In the mornings, my glasses would always be fogged over with condensation. One morning, whatever I grabbed to wipe them clean must have had something gritty-embed-ded. Right in the center of each lens, I managed to leave some scratches.

Now the scratches weren't terrible, but they were very annoy-ing. I could read and see well enough, but I never could not see the scratches. Thankfully, I have a pair of prescription sunglasses, and I made use of them as often as I could.

When we returned to Oklahoma, I took my glasses back to the place I bought them. The good news was that they had a six-month warranty that even covered scratches. The bad news was that I had them for seven months. They kindly looked past the date and replaced them for me anyway. Had they not, I gladly would have paid to be rid of the annoyance.

Which brings us to church. There I was, with my new glasses, and they must be ever so slightly different than my previous pair, and I had not fully adjusted to them, yet. As I would glance back and forth between the projector screen and the pastor, I couldn't quite hold my head just right for sharp focus. The edges were always slightly fuzzy.

So, I took them off.

Soon, Alex looked my way, and then I saw him do a double take. He isn't used to seeing me without glasses. I remembered feeling the same way about my dad. Rarely did I see him without glasses, and when I did, it always took me back a little bit.

Dad truly needed glasses in every sense. He liked to tell people he was "blind in one eye and couldn't see out of the other."

My mind drifted back to looking at my dad's face. His glasses were thick bifocals, magnifying his eyes and his eyelashes. I was thinking about how his Texas Panhandle-sky blue eyes looked huge. And when I said something that made him raise his eyebrows—which was often—the lenses made his big eyes and eyelashes look Snuffleupagus-sized.

And as I sat there contemplating that, I could remember something else about those glasses.

Scratches.

Dad's glasses put in an honest day's work every day and took the abuse that comes with that. In addition, he kept the same glasses for many years at a time. That meant every annoying scratch was going to be there a long while.

Now I'm sure Dad would have liked to replace his glasses more often than he did. But we never had much money. And what extra money my parents did have, they spent on us kids, especially me, the youngest.

Dad didn't have the luxury of prescription sunglasses. And he certainly didn't have the luxury of just doing without. Instead, he put up with worn-out frames and scratched lenses for as long as he could. Sacrificing. Doing without. While at the same time helping me keep my go-kart going, or helping me take care of my horse, or running me up and down the road to the hundred places I thought I needed to be.

I've known for a long time that my parents made sacrifices. But there I was in church in my fifties, just now realizing how deep those sacrifices were sometimes.

But this story really isn't about those sacrifices. It's about how thirty-three years after I left home and many years after their deaths, I am still learning from my dad and my mom.

I'm sure that would give them both a good chuckle, considering how averse I was to listening to their guidance when I did live at home.

And for me now, it gives me hope. With a daughter about to leave for college and a son already showing early signs of being a teenager, I often feel like the things I say are just wasted breath. But maybe one day they will find meaning or useful guidance in something I said or did. Let's hope they are faster learners than I am.

In the meantime, I'll try to keep reminding myself that I wasn't the best listener at their ages, either. And as my pastor will tell you, sometimes I still struggle with it.

CHAPTER 18

Things Kids Say

Capturing my emotions of losing Colby is challenging. Not just the sadness and tears, of which there are many, but the desire to get it right. Trying to capture those stories for young Ella is beyond challenging. It's impossible. Yet, this essay tries to do it in some small way, and it produces my biggest tears.

From the spring to the fall of 2008, we had a number of visitors pass through our house. For Ella, this was just one of the many upsides of having a new baby sister. Lots of visitors wanting to meet Colby meant lots of visitors for Ella to be entertained by—and for her to entertain in return, too.

One day, when Ella was just a little bit past her fourth birthday, we were on the way to school, and she was mentally going over the list of visitors. "Dad, I've met Abuela, Nana, and Granny. Where's your dad?"

There is a lot to explain in those few words, so let me catch you up a bit before I carry on with my response. Abuela is the Spanish word for "grandmother," and what Ella calls my mom. We have no

Spanish heritage, and I actually worked to get Ella to call my mom Me-maw, which I consider to be a good, solid term of affection for rural Texas. My suggestion wilted under the more powerful influence of *Dora the Explorer*, the cartoon character. Ella called my mom Abuela once: we laughed, it stuck, and forevermore it has remained in our house despite the confusion it causes from others.

But the confusion doesn't stop there. Around here, and elsewhere, I presume, another popular term for grandma is Nana. Ella has a Nana, but her Nana is her *grandfather*. Ella's mom's dad is from the state of Gujarat in India. The Gujarati word for mother's father is Nana. If this use of Nana sounds odd to you, consider that from Ella's perspective and a billion or so people in India, it is all completely normal.

Then we have Granny, who is Ella's maternal grandmother. The name Granny may seem pretty run of the mill, but when you realize the person carrying it was born in the U.K. of Dutch and Irish heritage, grew up in Kenya, and lived most of her adult life in the Caribbean, the phrase "run of the mill" pretty much goes out the window. Phrases like "Jambo, Granny" are commonplace in our home.

If you are keeping track, that covers all the grandparents, except my dad. He passed away in 2001, and that brings you up to speed on Ella's question, "Where is your dad?"

I'd anticipated getting that question someday, but that doesn't mean I was necessarily ready for it. Not knowing exactly where to start or how deep to go, I started with, "Well, it's kinda hard to explain."

This was our first time talking about death, so my explanation was all over the place, in very vague terms, and trying to mix in concepts of Heaven without opening another can of worms. After muddling along for a while, I tried to bring it to a close by asking Ella, "Does that make any sense?"

"Uh-huh," she said in a tone that meant "nuh-uh."

"Well," I sighed, "like I said, it's hard to explain."

About a week later and out of the blue, Ella tells me, "I know what you were trying to say about your dad. I know where he is."

"Oh yeah?" I responded, surprised in both that she had been thinking about it and in that she had it figured out.

"Yep. He is in Spain," she said confidently.

In fairness, that does sound remarkably like "hard to explain" and probably made as much sense as anything else I actually did say.

I love that story. It's not the funniest example of the humorous things Ella says, but it still makes me laugh. But beyond the giggles, it was a little window into what was going on in her head. She knew a lot more than I gave her credit for. Not only was she able to reason that someone was missing; she was able to articulate it very clearly and concisely. Heck! She even knew there was a place called Spain. Where she got that from, I still have no idea, but Dora probably gets credit for that, too.

The other thing I like about that story is that it reminds me that the words we tell kids aren't necessarily the words they hear.

I realize I'm far from the first in appreciating the things kids say. The list of aficionados includes parents, teachers, pastors, uncles, neighbors, *Reader's Digest*, and on and on. Art Linkletter and Bill Cosby were masters of the art of it. Expressions like "out of the mouths of babes" testify to it. If you want to be entertained, to hear the unvarnished truth, or hear a new perspective on things, find a kid and just listen.

And while I'm not a pioneer in the field, I have accumulated enough hours of listening to Ella that I have earned my "Observer of Things Kids Say" merit badge. That's actually a bad analogy because it carries the connotation that I earned it. This badge wasn't earned; it has been a blessed gift and one far greater than I deserve.

Friends of mine on Facebook see regular postings where I recount something Ella said that I find particularly interesting. The stories about her getting the best of me at something are usually the crowd favorites. The examples I am about to share aren't those kinds of stories.

The stories I am about to share are some of the things Ella has said about losing Colby. I've shared my thoughts and feelings on that topic, at least some of them. I don't claim to be able to speak for Ella, but these stories offer a little insight into her mind. My hope in putting them down is that it helps me to learn from them and one day gives her a look back that she will appreciate.

Maybe you'll find something worthwhile in reading them, too.

Sometimes it's hard to know where to start. In this case, that point seems pretty clear.

In the final hours of Colby's life, we had family bring Ella up to the hospital for her chance to say goodbye. Colby had previous hospitalizations, and we had always shielded Ella from seeing that. And of course, Colby had always come home before. This time was different, and as much in shock as we all were at that point, Ella for sure didn't know what she was walking into.

I met them in the lobby, where Ella was smiling and happy. A lot of people comment that Ella smiles a lot, and that is generally true. Plus, she hadn't seen her parents in a few days, so I'm sure she was happy to see us. The hospital was a new adventure, and those usually excite Ella, too. For all the pain and crying of the last few days, and for as much as I had been dreading what I was about to do, I have to admit that smile made me feel like I was breathing for the first time in a long while.

I told you earlier that I knew one day I'd have to tell her about my dad being dead. Up until about twelve hours prior to this moment, I had never anticipated the conversation we were about to have. In those twelve hours, I had lots of worries but no ideas about what to say.

When things like the death of a child happen, it triggers a lot of questions about where God is in all of this. I have had a lot of those questions, and I confess to very few answers for them. Don't ask me to explain which prayers get answered and why. But what happened next, I don't have a better explanation for than God's help. Lord knows I wasn't up to the task on my own.

I took Ella in my lap and hugged her tightly. When I began to speak, she matched her attention to my tone. The words came easily and evenly. They were heavy words, laden with seriousness and sadness, but they came with a calmness I didn't expect. I told her how much Colby loved her, how much Colby knew Ella loved her, about how things don't always go as planned, about the machines she would see when we got up to Colby's room and not be frightened by them. I told her how much we didn't like what was happening, but the doctors had done all that they could. I told her Colby wasn't in pain. Then I explained Colby wouldn't be coming home with us and would soon be in Heaven. I told her that today, we would be saying goodbye to Colby.

As I spoke, Ella's expression changed to match mine, her wide eyes locked on my face. When I had first started talking, she would interject a comment or two, but by the end, she was quietly listening to my every word.

When I finished, I had a surreal feeling of unbelief that I was able to deliver the words without falling apart, under-explaining, or over-explaining, as I am more apt to do. Still, as pleased as I was with my words in delivering this unwelcome message, I didn't know if it made sense to Ella. But when I stopped talking, Ella spoke.

"Dad, is Colby dying?"

"Yes, Ella. Colby is dying," I answered, knowing that Ella understood even if she didn't fully comprehend. How could she comprehend what all that would mean when we didn't either?

The details of our goodbyes that day are for another day. Maybe. But that four-word question was just the beginning of many thoughts more profound than we give credit for to five-year-olds.

Here are a few of those thoughts and stories.

LOOKING PAST THE STARING

Kids stare at others in public, and we teach them it's rude. They don't mean to be rude; they are just observing and learning. In fact, there is a good argument to be made that it should be okay for kids under ten to stare. Aside from social graces, it's really a wonderful thing. In that moment, they are captivated, quiet, calm, and soaking in information. Normally, we would be thrilled!

But in our house, we have befallen to the conventional stance on staring, too, and admonish Ella not to do it.

The exception came not long after we lost Colby. As my dad had done with me, I took Ella with me to the barbershop. In this age of iPads and endless cartoons, free lollipops are still a powerful draw.

There I sat in the barber chair with Ella sitting across from me on the bench with some book or toy in hand, waiting for me to be done. Those of you who have seen my hairline are likely thinking that exercise should take no more than a couple of minutes, but you'd be wrong.

First, barber school must do an excellent job of covering bald etiquette, because nobody cuts my hair as fast as they could. I think they must feel obliged to dawdle a little bit, so as to make sure I feel as though I am getting my money's worth. Next, there is always that one hair that wants to stick up higher than the rest. It's like that one corn stalk that grows a foot higher than the rest. In a full, lush field, it's not that big of a deal. But if all the other stalks get mowed down to a tenth of their height, that one stalk really sticks out.

Ella was sitting patiently, and I was trying to make out what the barber was talking about as the clippers buzzed too close to my ears for me to hear clearly. Somewhere in there, a customer walked in with two daughters, one about 5 and one about 2, the same spread as Ella and Colby. As quick as they walked in the door, Ella lost interest in whatever was in her lap and her eyes locked onto the girls.

As I saw what was happening, my initial instinct was to discreetly signal to her not to stare, but I paused. I contemplated what she might have been thinking. Did she notice the similarity in ages to hers and Colby's? Was she jealous? Did it give her heart pangs? Did she just want to tell them how lucky they were to have each other? Or was all that just me?

For the rest of the haircut, she sat there, expressionless, barely blinking, and had even lost interest in her lollipop. After getting settled in their spot, the dad surveyed the room and noticed Ella staring. He glanced my way for clues as to what it was about and, not knowing what was up, went about his business, ignoring her as best he could.

When the haircut was over, I got up, patted Ella on the leg, and we made our way out. In the car, I asked if she had seen the two other girls.

"Yes."

"What did you think about them?"

"I'm not sure," she said quietly.

It's never hard to get Ella to elaborate, especially when she was five, but that didn't seem like the thing to do at the time. She was still thinking, and Ella having the opportunity to do that uninterrupted seemed more valuable than me knowing what she was thinking.

We rode onward in silence.

Now, Ella is nine, and on occasion, I still have to remind her not to stare. Unless she is staring at two sisters, in which case I just let her stare and think. It still happens, the last time as recently as two weeks ago. There isn't much we don't talk about, but I don't ask her about what she thinks while staring anymore. Sometimes it's nice just to be able to think and feel without having to put it into words.

CONVERSATIONS WITH TORNADO SIRENS

The spring following Colby's death, Ella was in kindergarten. Up to that point in her life, we had taken shelter in the closet under the stairs a few times during tornadoes, but she never really understood why we were doing what we were doing.

That particular year, our area had quite a few tornadoes, and Ella was gaining a better understanding of what they were and what they were capable of doing. She had seen a few news reports, and of course, being in school increased her awareness, too.

One particularly active weather day had an afternoon with multiple warnings in the area. She was at school when this started, so they had already taken shelter there a couple of times, including one that was delaying release. The weather looked like it was breaking up with the bad bits past us, so I went up to school and gathered her up to take her home.

I wasn't sure what to expect, whether she would be scared or hyper from all the excitement. Turns out neither. She was just glad to be going home. Apparently, the novelty of taking cover wears off after ten minutes or so, and more than an hour of it felt more like punishment. She was glad to be headed home.

But once we got home, another tornado cell was spawned in the area, the tornado sirens kicked back on, and off we went to the closet under the stairs, grabbing an afternoon snack on our way.

There we sat, listening to the weather radio surrounded by emergency kits and flashlights. On a shelf behind us even sat a backpack left over from the year before with special supplies for Colby. The sirens lasted for a long time. Or at least it felt that way. Un-airconditioned spaces in Texas houses in mid-May don't take long to get uncomfortable.

I was making a conscious effort to show Ella that we needed to take this seriously, but at the same time to not make her panic. I wanted her to learn to respect the power of a tornado but didn't want to create any phobias in her. She must have sensed I was searching for the right tone and trying to gauge her mindset.

"Dad. Don't worry. I'm not afraid."

"No?" I asked.

"Nope. If I die, it will all be okay. I'll get to see Colby!"

I'd be lying if I said I hadn't thought the same thought every day since Colby died. But I never said it aloud. I feel confident that Ella is in no rush to die, but I also get where she is coming from. Heaven with Colby sounds much sweeter than it ever did before.

WONDERING WHO IS TAKING CARE OF WHO

As Colby was dying, we got some valuable advice on grieving with Ella. They told us to make sure we didn't hide our grieving from Ella, told that it was important that she see us cry and that we didn't try to shield her from experiencing those emotions. "She needs to know that it's okay to cry," the counselors said.

The balancing act is that she deserves her childhood, too. It would be completely unfair to ask her to witness all our lows and struggles. So, there were (are) times when we share our sadness and times we chose not to. Or at least so we think.

One evening, Usha was away for work. At Ella's bedtime, I took her upstairs to tuck her in. I had been struggling with Colby's loss throughout the day but thought I had masked it pretty well. As we said our evening prayers, my thoughts turned to how we used to pray for Colby's health.

Maybe my voice cracked, or maybe I lingered too long between words. Maybe Ella glimpsed a tear or could just read the pain on my face. Maybe she knew I had been struggling extra that day and just hadn't said anything up to that point.

Whatever it was that tipped her off, Ella didn't want to part without saying something.

Ella took my hand in one of hers and patted it with her other hand. Then she said, "Daddy, if you need me in the middle of the night, I'll be right upstairs."

Well, the tears certainly flowed from there. And the hugs. And the smiles.

As I walked down the stairs, I pondered who was taking care of who, and I was grateful for the answer.

Ella still sees us cry from time to time, and she is quick with the hand pats, the hugs, or just that knowing nod. She doesn't press or try to rush the moment. She just lets us know that it's okay to cry. I'm still not sure if we taught her that or if she taught us that.

CONVERSATIONS ON
THE WALKS TO SCHOOL

When we lived in Rockwall, our house was a ten-minute walk to school. These days, we live several miles from school with a major interstate between home and there, so walking is not an option. I miss those walks. Free of interruptions, they were prime conversational opportunities. Topics could be about almost anything. Once, we gave great consideration and speculation as to where roly-polies would take summer vacations.

Of course, sometimes the conversation was more serious.

"Dad, does Heaven have a gift shop?" Ella once asked out of the blue on a walk to school.

"I don't know. I haven't ever thought about it."

"Hmmm. I wonder how we can find out."

I suspected it was about Colby, and that was good enough for me in that moment. That she was thinking of her little sister and wanting to send her a present was plenty to fill my mind with happy, sweet thoughts.

That night, during bedtime prayers, my suspicions were confirmed. I said the prayer aloud as we normally did. Before the amen, Ella added an extra bit. "And if Heaven has a gift shop, please give Colby a stuffed animal from me. A REALLY big one!"

Amen.

Recounting this story now, the silliness of the roly-polies pales in comparison to the silliness of my answer of uncertainty about Heaven's gift shop. Of course it has one. It's Heaven!

CONVERSATIONS ABOUT ANOTHER SIBLING

Soon after Colby passed, Usha and I quickly decided we would not try for a third child. But as firm as we thought we were in that decision, time would soften our stance. At some point, we began discussing options between just the two of us, and we eventually began getting serious about the adoption route.

It became so serious that we eventually included Ella in the discussion. We made it clear to her that there were no guarantees and that the process was difficult. We did not want to falsely raise her hopes, but we also did not want her to overhear something and misinterpret it. We did our very best to be clear that it was just a possibility we were trying to find out more about.

That turned out to be quite a task. Ella's understanding of the adoption process was along the lines of you went to the baby store, you picked one out, and you took it home. She had no idea how much more complicated reality is, and it turns out neither did we.

When progress wasn't happening as quickly as she liked, Ella would prod things along with questions or talk about adoption. I am sure the process never made much sense to her, as it makes very little sense to me, either.

On one walk to school, Ella decided to push things along again.

"Is adopting a baby expensive?"

"Yes. It can be very expensive."

"Well, I want you and Mom to know that you can have all the money in my piggy bank, and you don't even have to pay me back."

Turns out her patience was rewarded, though it took a couple more years and did not involve adoption after all. I'm hoping she remembers those generous loan terms when it comes time to send her baby brother to college.

IT'S OKAY TO BE ANGRY, TOO

Most days, Ella comes home from school with something to be upbeat and happy about. But not always.

The topic of siblings comes up at school much more often than you realize. It's a very normal thing to discuss, and unless you have some reason to be sensitive to it, you'd likely never notice how often siblings get referred to.

We have been very blessed by how supportive and understanding teachers, staff, and usually the other kids are about our loss and how they handle that, particularly in regard to Ella. Ella also deserves a lot of credit for being able to graciously handle awkward moments or comments, especially when no harm is intended.

But she is still a redhead. And a protective big sister. Which means that not everything gets a free pass.

Teachers are wizards at keeping kids engaged and getting them to be cooperative. If I was a gym teacher and it was time to put up jump ropes, I'd say, "Everyone put up your jump ropes," at which point half the class would be crowded around the jump rope-holder, shoving each other out of the way and the other half would be ignoring me. By the time I got it all sorted out, either the kids or me would end up in tantrums. Probably both.

But Ella's gym teacher was great, and she would even make putting up jump ropes fun by playing games like "Everyone who has a birthday in October, put up your jump ropes," and off they would go until month by month, all of the jump ropes were put away.

The put-away game changes from day to day, and one day, Ella announced, "Everybody who has a little sister, put away your jump rope." Ella did not hesitate; she popped right up and headed for the jump rope rack, at which point a few of her classmates cried foul.

"Ella, you don't have a little sister. Your sister died. She doesn't count."

Ella is feisty with her parents. With her friends, she can be quite the pushover. But if they thought they were going to back her down by saying her little sister didn't count, they miscalculated. They poked the bear.

With a red face and ferocity, she made it clear that Colby most certainly did count. Fifteen minutes later, when she came out of the school doors to go home, she still had a red face and a clenched jaw. My own fight-or-flight response was alert, so I can imagine how her classmates felt.

When we got to the car, she explained what had happened. As soon as she had told the last of it, she caught her breath. Then she cried.

I had a mix of emotions. I was proud of her for standing up for herself, I ached for her for being upset, and I was more than just a little pissed off at those kids myself. Later, Usha was the voice of reason that got both Ella and me to admit that they probably didn't mean to be hurtful but just let the competitiveness of being first to put away their jump ropes get the best of them.

Still, I felt better knowing that Ella had stood up for herself and for Colby.

THE ONE THAT HAUNTS ME

Hearing Ella's perspective on losing Colby has helped me make better sense of things, too. Her observations are sometimes sweet, sometimes sad, and sometimes uplifting. I think the select few that I have shared here show that and, hopefully by sharing them, it will help ensure that I don't forget them.

There is one that is in no danger of me ever forgetting. It puts a pit in my stomach each time I think of it, and I think of it often. It haunts me. I have tried to deny it, but it is true, and I'll always carry the guilt.

Ella only said it once, and it was painful enough to hear that I can't even remember the context, but I certainly remember the words. They were said with anger and resentment. The words were justified, and they were directed exclusively at me.

"Dad, you didn't let me hold Colby enough."

I protested at first, but I quickly knew she was right. Ella was always wanting to hold Colby. And I do mean always. But many times, I said no because saying no was easier. It was easier to let Colby play on the floor or for me to hold her than to have to stand watch, looking out to make sure that nothing happened to Colby...like Ella would have ever let that happen.

Sometimes I look through old pictures, and I come across pics of Ella holding Colby, and I think, *I did let her hold her some.*

Some.

And then I try to reason with myself and say, "None of us got to hold her enough" and "No amount would be *enough.*" Both true. But not enough to invalidate Ella's sentiment.

Now she has a little brother to hold. I still sometimes say no to her requests to hold Alex, but you can bet when I do that, I have a better reason than it just being easier for me. And you can bet that when she holds Alex, she cherishes every moment.

MAKING SENSE OF IT ALL

A little while back, Ella was reflecting on the day that Colby died.

"Dad, I wish I had understood more about what was happening at the time."

I asked her what she would have done differently, and she admits she doesn't know.

I don't know what I would do differently either, but I understand the desire for a do-over. There was so much trauma involved that it's difficult to remember all that you want to about such a day. That there is no right way to handle such a tragedy still doesn't stop the feeling that somehow, that day could have been handled better. And the days that followed. And certainly the days before.

Just a couple of days ago, someone asked me if Ella remembered losing her sister. It was sort of an odd question, phrased such that losing Colby was confined to one day. The reality is that each day without her is a loss. And as the days go by, our understanding evolves and our coping skills adapt, but the loss continues.

And as desperately as we try to cling to every memory, sadly, that is an unwinnable endeavor.

So, Ella, these stories are for you. I want to preserve some of these memories and stories for just a little longer. As the years go by and your understanding deepens, I want you to be able to look back at how you handled it at the time. While I know that you wish you had better understood what was happening at the time, I want you to know how remarkable you have been throughout it all.

You surrounded Colby with love, which she felt then, and I have no doubt that she feels today and forever more. You've carried on her memory with all the passion and strength of a big sister. You've made us better parents, helped us with our grief, and been our strength in ways you may never understand.

You are a great daughter and an even better big sister.

CHAPTER 19

Some of You May Know

We found out about Alex's autism diagnosis when he was three. While we had some suspicions, we were not ready for it. He had actually started some therapies when he was two, and it stepped up greatly once he got the official diagnosis. In the early days, we were scared about lots of things, including the labels that would be put on him.

It wasn't until he was five that we made the announcement to all our friends and family. This was that announcement and the beginnings of Alex becoming an autism advocate and of Okie School of Adventure and Charm.

Some of you know about this. Many of you don't.

I'm an over-sharer on Facebook, but that isn't the "this" I am referring to. All of you know that I over-share on here. But there is something we have been careful not to say here up until now. We haven't been keeping it quiet because we are ashamed or disappointed. We have been careful about who we tell because it's a label that causes people to treat kids (and their parents) differently.

Alex has autism.

To be clear, Alex has lots of other labels. He is courageous, creative, fierce, smart, funny, hard-headed, demanding, charming, adventurous, loud, thoughtful, hard-working, inquisitive, handsome, quick, talkative, stubborn, deep-thinking, energetic, problem-solving, and loving.

He just also happens to be autistic.

Over the past year, we have shared a lot of his homeschool adventures. From the outside, it may just look like loads of fun, and every day is a party. Well, it is loads of fun. But I can assure you it's not always a party. I say that not for sympathy for us, but because it shortchanges Alex.

Make no mistake, Alex absolutely works his butt off.

From the time of his diagnosis until now, he has made tremendous strides. We owe so much to many wonderful therapists and teachers who have helped unlock his potential and have started us down this path of growth. This includes teachers at our local traditional schools who did absolutely fabulous work with him.

Despite some great professionals and lots of effort on everyone's part, last year showed us that, for now, a traditional classroom wasn't a good fit for Alex. It wasn't good for him, it wasn't good for his teachers, and it wasn't good for his classmates.

That is why we decided to try homeschooling. We knew as part of that decision, we needed to put an emphasis on educational opportunities beyond traditional schoolwork, though Alex does plenty of that, too. That is the core reason behind the trips and adventures you see us post about.

Alex learns best by doing, so we look for ways to expose him to a combination of his interests and learning opportunities.

So why are we sharing this news publicly now?

Good question. And it has a few answers.

One of the reasons is that there are a lot of misconceptions about autism. We know because we had (and maybe still have) them, too. The truth is there is as much variety amongst autistic kids as there is amongst neurotypical kids. There can be some barriers and adjustments in getting to know these kids, but it's our belief that it's absolutely worth doing.

Sharing that Alex has autism is asking for your patience. It is also–hopefully–knocking down some of the fear and misunderstanding surrounding autism. We hope that Alex reshapes people's ideas of autism the way he has reshaped ours.

Another reason is that we realize how lucky we are to be able to provide Alex with those learning and adventure experiences. Several times over the last year, we have been encouraged to share what we are doing with others. Autistic or not, all kids can benefit from adventure learning. We hope that by sharing what we do, it inspires others to go on their own adventures, and/or they can learn by following along with ours.

Toward that goal, we are going to start sharing Alex's adventures in our "Okie School of Adventure and Charm" on its own Facebook page and YouTube channel. We are hoping that friends and family who enjoy following along will continue to do so there. But it will also be open to the public as a resource for other kids–autistic or not, homeschooled or not, Okie or not.

If you are one of the ones tired of me oversharing, good news! I'll be reducing how much I post about our adventures on my personal page. It won't be down to zero, but it will be less–so enjoy that.

Finally, on behalf of Usha, Ella, Alex, and me, let me say thanks to all of you who have known about the autism diagnosis and supported and encouraged us along the way. Thanks to all of you who have suspected it, but it never stopped you from accepting us all. And thanks to all of you who had no idea for understanding why we haven't shared it earlier, and the encouragement I am sure you will have going forward.

CHAPTER 20

Chasing Redemption

Like so many of my essays, this one was rooted in my trying to make sense of my world. A thought gnaws at my brain, and eventually I am driven to a keyboard to process it. Sometimes those stories never get finished. This story did, and The Oklahoman, our state newspaper, published it. I hope you find value in it, too.

I saw it coming from a mile away.

Ok, it was eighteen feet away. But I knew it was coming.

Alex and I were seated at a cafe in Wyoming for breakfast. A kindly grandmotherly type sat four tables away, catty corner from ours, with a disapproving look aimed at me. I knew exactly why.

Alex had his iPad out, and I had my iPhone. Neither of us was paying much attention to each other. She clearly did not approve.

Occasionally, I would glance her way. She maintained her watchful eye on us through her coffee sips, while waiting for her food, and while eating it. Each time, I mulled over what words she would say to us. There were lots of possibilities, all of which centered on our use of screen time.

The truth is I didn't know exactly which words she would choose, but I was certain that she would be saying something. Absolutely certain.

Inside my head, I chuckled that she herself had been sitting opposite her husband for the entire time without talking to each other. But maybe she had her reasons, too. Reasons like I had but that she couldn't possibly know.

She couldn't possibly know that Alex and I were in the midst of a 31-day trip together, during which we would seldom be more than 5 feet apart. She couldn't have known that the day before, we had to drive almost 100 miles to find a place to sleep for the night. She couldn't know that I was on my phone looking for camping options for that night while I still had Internet access—and that doing so meant we could spend our day in Yellowstone without having to rush.

And of course, she could not have known that I wasn't just his dad, but also his teacher. And that Alex accompanies me to cotton gins and works alongside me in the shop. Or that Alex teaches me about trains, or that I teach him to drive a boat, or that we learn about fishing together. Nor could she know the challenges and backstory behind all those things–those tremendously blessed things and so many more.

If she knew those things, or at least some of those things, perhaps she would have given me a pass. But the lady couldn't have known, so all that remained to be seen was what words she would choose.

By the time she and her husband had finished and paid, we were well into our own meal. The mountain air and hikes did wonders for Alex's appetite, and he was plowing through pancakes, eggs, and bacon without much prompting from me. I took a pause in my eating so as not to have a mouthful when she came by our table on her way out.

As she approached, I didn't want to act like eye contact was warranted, but as I casually glanced up, she spoke, "Time goes by before you know it. You should enjoy time with him while you can."

My mind said, "If she only knew."

But my voice said, "Yes, ma'am. Sounds like good advice." I meant it respectfully, but if she was satisfied, it didn't show on her face.

My thoughts quickly turned to finishing up our meal and getting on the road. Once we did, the lady's words came back to mind. They were almost exactly the words said to me by another stranger more than ten years before at a Panera Bread.

On that occasion, I was with my daughter Colby just a few months before she passed away. We were just getting barely a grasp on her condition, and although we had no idea what was coming, we knew it to be well within the realm of possibility. In that interaction, there were no screens involved, and the stranger wasn't offering a rebuke. She was just another grandmotherly type who was watching an adoring dad playing with his beautiful daughter and wanting to make sure I was soaking it all in.

But my reaction was the same: "If she only knew."

I can give you two dozen good reasons why we have decided to homeschool Alex. And I can give you just as many good reasons why we did such a big fall trip. On top of those, I always knew there were some selfish reasons, too.

The most obvious of which is that I got to see some new places and revisit some favorite ones.

Stronger, but perhaps less obvious, is that I need to feel like a good dad.

Neither of those reasons were unknown to me. I was very conscious of them both. But on the road to Yellowstone, it hit me. Every laugh, wonder, breathtaking scene, hike holding hands, unrushed moment, praise from a stranger, nighttime snuggle, deep thought, or spark from his mind—none of those were getting me closer to feeling like a good dad.

No. Just the opposite. The harder I run toward it, the faster it slips away.

Because every one of those moments was a moment I didn't have with Colby.

I want to sleep in a tent with her. Let her throw snowballs at me. Stand quietly twenty yards from an elk and just stare. Build a campfire and watch the stars. Throw 100 rocks into a lake and then throw 100 more. Mostly, I want to watch her eyes light up at new experiences and see the joy and wonder.

You see, I knew I had been chasing redemption. But it wasn't until then that I figured out I would never catch it.

I've still been trying to process that morning at the café with Alex and that story. I'm still not sure what the takeaway is for the rest of you or what it should be.

I'd like to say be careful when doling out parenting advice because there are sure to be some "if you only knews." But armchair parenting is deceptively simple when you are watching your friends, family, or fellow cafe patrons. The advice springs forth awfully easily.

So instead, I'll close this story with a humble benediction. Be kind to yourselves and to others as you examine parenting successes and failures. It's a very hard test, and you should grade others on the curve in hopes you will be, too.

CHAPTER 21

Marriage is a Roller Coaster

This essay came from our twentieth wedding anniversary.

Yes, it is a metaphor.

No, it's probably not the one you are thinking of right now. Sure, marriage has ups and downs, unexpected curves, some slow parts, and some fast parts. But that is life in general, whether you are married or not.

This metaphor needs a story to explain it.

In 2001, which also happens to be the year I married Usha, Six Flags Over Texas introduced a new roller coaster named the Titan. Just short of a mile long, lasting just over 3 minutes, 245 feet high, and with speeds up to 85 mph, this roller coaster invented a whole new category—the hyper twisted coaster. It was an impressive design and debuted with much hype.

Less impressive was its tendency to get stuck at the apex.

Sometimes they could restart it. Other times, after an hour or two of being strapped in cars on their backs, firemen or park employees would assist passengers out of the cars and walk them down the steps back to the ground.

Now you should know two things about me for the full context of this story. I don't like heights, and I never ride roller coasters without peer pressure.

Of course, the most effective peer pressure is from my beautiful wife, whom I still try to impress when given the chance. And of course, Usha wanted to ride the Titan.

I tried to dissuade her with the long line. She was willing to wait.

I pointed out alternative attractions. No interest.

So, I stiffened my resolve and got in the Titan line. Now I want to be clear here. I was okay with riding a coaster. Not thrilled with the idea, but I have learned over the years that I can bear them, given I have something to hold on to tight enough with both hands. I am especially fine during the fast parts, which, if nothing else, is progress toward the end. And even sometimes, at the end, be glad I rode it.

No, riding it wasn't the fear.

The fear was getting stuck at the top. The slow clack-clack on the way to the top, lying almost entirely on one's back, is bad enough. But if it stopped at the top, I knew I would not handle it well. Just thinking about the waiting and not knowing how long we would be stuck makes me stressed, even thinking about it now.

The second worst part in my mind would be them trying to coax me out of the car and me not wanting to let go with either hand, much less both.

The worst part I feared was all of that happening in front of Usha. So, for ninety minutes in line, all my thoughts were pretty much trying to figure out how to look somewhat manly while a fireman was rescuing me like a scared cat stuck in a tree.

At the ninety-first minute, we stepped up to the platform gates to be on the next run. While the group in front of us took off, I did what I had been doing every other departure. I watched them climb the starting hill and race down the track. Only this time, it didn't race down. It stopped. It was stuck.

For a moment, I was stuck, too. Then, I said to our group, "Well, we tried. Let's go."

Usha didn't flinch. "Give them a minute."

Which at the time seemed about the most ridiculous thing you could say. In retrospect, it definitely was the most ridiculous thing to say.

A few minutes went by. A man showed up to look at the control console. I watched him closely.

First of all, and I don't mean this unkindly, but he looked incompetent. I mean, there is a decent chance he wasn't an electrician at all but just on break from selling cotton candy.

Then he opened the control console and stared at it like a man looking for ketchup in the refrigerator, as if he just stared long enough, the answer would magically appear. He reached in and pushed a reset button, and nothing happened, and then he just stood there dumbfounded like that was the only thing they had covered in roller coaster controls school.

"Doesn't look good," I said, attempting to sway the others.

And maybe it would have worked, but at that exact moment, the twelve-year-old girl running the ride nonchalantly announced, "We apologize for the delay. It could be a few minutes. It could be down the rest of the day. If you leave, you lose your place in line."

"Welp. Let's go," I said, taking a few steps away for emphasis. No one followed.

"Let's wait a little while," Usha pleaded.

And there I was. Torn between trying to make my new wife happy and trying not to embarrass myself in front of my wife. My brain said "go" and my heart said "stay."

I stayed.

A few minutes later, a motor started whirring, a clutch kicked in, and the stuck ride started moving again. Passengers on it cheered and screamed. Those waiting in line applauded.

I looked back at the electrician. He was still staring blankly at the panel. Then, he gave a little shrug, closed the door, and walked away. My confidence was not lifted.

The attendants called for us to load into the waiting cars while the other set completed its journey. I gave Usha one last "Are you sure?" look; she was sure. Sure not only about the ride, but she was sure enjoying me squirm.

We loaded into the car. I checked my restraint a couple of dozen times and tested different grip positions. I braced myself and began a repetitive silent prayer. "Please don't get stuck. Please don't get stuck. Please don't get stuck."

The ensuing clack-clack-clack kept perfect rhythm with my prayer.

My eyes were staring dead ahead, looking for any signs of losing momentum. Steadily, we climbed to the peak, to the point where it would sometimes stall, but we kept moving.

As everyone else let out a scream as we dropped over the top, I took a big sigh of relief.

As we raced downhill, something unexpected did happen. The ride went underground. As much as I had studied the runs before ours, I hadn't noticed that. I guess the viewing angles hide that feature unless you are on the ride.

So, we raced and curved and zoomed, and the rest of the ride was pretty fun. Of course, I was still full of euphoria that we hadn't gotten stuck.

As we got off the ride, I could feel myself relax for the first time in about two hours. Usha looked up at me and said, "Well, what did you think?"

I answered, "I had no idea we were going to go underground!"

To which she replied, "We went underground?"

Her eyes had been closed the whole time.

She talked me into going on a roller coaster that I didn't want to ride, and she closed her eyes during it.

You know those souvenir photos they snap of you at the scariest point of the ride? When we looked at ours, yep, there she was smiling, screaming, and her eyes squeezed shut.

I was thinking about that story the other day, and that's when it hit me. Marriage is like a roller coaster.

You get out of your comfort zone, and you aren't ever sure what will happen. But if you are with the love of your life, whatever happens, you will always have that—and almost always that's enough to ensure that it is all going to work out just fine.

We had a great time on the Titan. There were laughs in line before and lots more laughs afterward.

If we had gotten stuck for five minutes, it would have been a different story to tell, but we still would have had a great time.

If we were stuck for hours, it would still be a different story and one I couldn't guess the details, but in the end, it would have been a good one because we would have been together.

And if we had left the line, even that story would have been better than anything that would have happened if I were there without Usha.

Everything in my life is better with Usha than it would have been without her.

In married life, the twists, turns, ups, and downs aren't as trivial as a roller coaster. You don't get to pick your path like an amusement park ride. Our ride has been amazing, but it hasn't always been smooth or fun. We've flown off the rails and picked up the pieces together, only to get blindsided again. Good times and bad times, they are always better with her.

Wife, what lies ahead for us, we can't be sure. But I am absolutely sure there is no one but you I would want by my side as we find out.

Happy Twentieth Anniversary, Usha.

I love you.

CHAPTER 22

Mending Hearts and Sails

On the surface, this is the story of kindergarten Ella starting on the path to become a heart ambassador for the American Heart Association. But it's really the story about the power of sisterly love. It can change the world... and it can certainly conquer a doubtful dad.

We've all heard the expression about taking the wind out of someone's sails. Tuesday afternoon, I saw the most vivid illustration of this saying I have ever witnessed. Unfortunately, I was the guilty party, and worse, it was my own daughter's sails.

School was letting out, and Ella bounded out the doors with a huge smile and arms spread wide. Her jacket flapped behind her like sails as she ran to me.

"Daddy, we are going to raise money for people with bad hearts, and I want to raise a thousand dollars—at least. Probably more! They are going to send home information on Thursday, and we watched a video and it helps people with bad hearts. They showed some kids who were six years old like me that it helps. And there are jump ropes and the gym teacher…"

What her words lacked in detail and organization, she was making up with speed and enthusiasm. The words I fixated on were the "more than $1,000" portion, and that is what I chose to interrupt her with.

"Darling, a thousand dollars is a lot of money. Trying to raise more than a thousand will be very hard."

"Well. At least a thousand dollars then," she replied.

"I don't think you understand how much money that is." At this point, we had stopped on the sidewalk, no longer making progress to the car.

"No. You don't understand." She said it firmly, but not disrespectfully. Her voice had a tone of one part frustration and two parts determination. "They help kids with bad hearts. They help kids like Colby."

It all became very clear, very quickly. For Ella, this wasn't just another school activity to be excited about. This was personal. This was about her sister. This was a chance for her to be actively involved in making a difference in another child's life—a child who was facing some difficult challenges, like her little sister did.

Now, I need to clarify something here. Colby's condition went far beyond heart problems. It's hard enough to explain Geleophysic Dysplasia to medical professionals and even harder to other adults. Explaining it to a six-year-old seemed riskier than the potential benefits, so for now, we've kept the explanation simplified for Ella. So, her basic understanding is that Colby's heart was very sick. That is true, but obviously, there is much more to it all, but we are saving those conversations for another day, and this was not the day.

Understanding her better, I tried to explain the situation better to Ella. I told her how good it was that she wanted to help other kids and let her know that we would help raise some money. But I again tried to point out how much money a thousand dollars is and that we shouldn't set such a high goal.

Part of it was out of protecting her from disappointment, and part of it was protecting myself from getting wrapped up in asking people for donations. I told her we would look at the information on Thursday and talk about it more then.

She didn't protest anymore, but you could see her mind at work, not only trying to make sense of what I was saying and why I was saying it but also trying to figure out just what it was that she could do. Our walk to the car resumed, but her smile was gone, as was the bounce in her step and the flap of her jacket.

Gone was the wind in her sails.

That night, I thought a lot about that exchange. The more I thought about it, the worse I felt about what I had done. I had robbed her of the joy she was feeling about trying to help people and robbed her of the chance to dream big. The idea of protecting her from failure lost merit the more I thought about it, and even if it hadn't, if it was at the expense of her ambition and joy, the price was too high.

How many times had I told Ella she could accomplish big things if she worked hard? I realized I didn't want to make those words hollow.

The next morning, on the way to school, I apologized to Ella. I told her I had made a mistake and that I was sorry. We spent some more time talking about what a big goal raising a thousand dollars is but that if she wanted to try, I would support her however I could. We also talked about what it means to do our best and that if she fell short of her goal, she had nothing to be ashamed of if she had done her best. Whatever amount she raised, she would be helping kids with sick hearts.

Her smiles and nods let me know that she understood. Ella wasn't worried about falling short. "Dad, that's all I want. I want a chance to try."

I posted that story on Facebook, and within 24 hours, she passed her $1,000 goal. By the end of that year's campaign, she had raised approximately $6,000. The following year, Ella raised over $12,000. The full tally of her Jump Rope for Heart career and Sweetheart program participation exceeded $70,000.

But that only tells part of her impact. The American Heart Association took note of her success early on and made her a heart ambassador. She did TV interviews, spoke to schools, spoke at coordinator meetings, was featured at two Heart Balls, appeared in national fundraising videos, and so much more. Harder to quantify, but no doubt real, her indirect impact has easily been several hundreds of thousands more.

My favorite memory of these events was when Ella was asked to speak at the Heart Association headquarters in Dallas. Seven-year-old Ella walked up to the front of a room full of adults. As she struggled to look over the adult-sized podium, and the room struggled to see her face, a quick-thinking volunteer snagged a box for her to stand on.

Ella leaned toward the microphone and opened with the line, "I knew I should have worn my heels today."

With that line, the crowd was eating out of her hands. And I was yet again reminded that if you give her space, if you give her a chance, Ella will find a way to succeed.

CHAPTER 23

Unsung Siblings

Here we jump from Ella in kindergarten to her senior year.
I think it is a fitting follow-up to the last chapter.

Ella, my oldest, will be a college freshman this fall. Being on the parent side of this experience, I've noted a lot of absurdities in this whole process. The cost, the extravagant facilities, the cost, how much of it relates so little to actual education, the cost, the parking, the cost, the out-of-control dorm décor, and the cost, to name a few.

If you think I repeated the cost too many times for comedic effect, I can assure you of two things. One, the costs keep coming. And, two, there is nothing funny about them.

There are a lot of scholarships out there to try and ease that burden of college expenses. But even in looking at those, absurdities abound.

Extracting some levity out of the college admissions process, Ella read aloud from an Internet list of crazy and unusual scholarships to me one afternoon. She would read me the criteria; I would scoff and make a snarky comment; she'd feign laughter, pleased that my crankiness was aimed elsewhere; and we'd repeat.

A scholarship for people wearing duct tape attire to prom—Ha!

With the price of duct tape these days, it might cost more than the scholarship.

A scholarship for people with a dedicated commitment to the art of puppetry—Snort! That one doesn't sound super competitive.

The nude recreation enthusiast scholarship–Ewww! That sounds like a committee of creepy, old men.

The vegetarian scholarship–Ugh! Beef cattle management majors need not apply.

The scholarship for students with special needs siblings–Hmm. Not going to laugh at that.

Hmm. I wonder what motivated someone to create that one?

No one has ever accused me of being a quick study, but thinking it over, it didn't take long to recognize that particular scholarship targeted a deserving demographic, and Ella is a great example of why.

Ella is a big sister to two special needs kids. For those who don't know, her little sister Colby had a genetic condition that affected her heart. She required a lot of interventions before she passed away at the age of two. Ella's little brother has a very different special need: he is autistic.

Having experienced the special needs family life from a couple of circumstances, I see a common theme. The parents receive a lot of support and sympathy. The affected child gets lots of attention and encouragement. And the siblings–well, the impact on the siblings is often overlooked.

There is an important distinction to make here. Anybody who has watched Ella grow up knows that she hasn't been overlooked as a kid. She is well-loved by many and has been blessed with many opportunities and experiences.

But it's also true that her childhood has been interrupted, accelerated, and altered by having special needs siblings. And in most cases, that does get overlooked.

An exhaustive list of these impacts would take longer than I am prepared to write and longer than you are prepared to read. Even then, it would certainly be incomplete because I am not the one living through it; she is. But for the purposes of context, let me share a few examples.

Imagine expecting your mom or dad to pick you up from daycare, but instead it's your uncle, aunt, or neighbor. On the one hand, you are excited to hang out with people you love and have an impromptu sleepover. On the other hand, you know it means your sister is in the hospital again, and you don't know if it will be for a day or a week. And you are four, so nobody knows how to talk to you about it or what you will understand.

Then there are the holidays you spend apart from your immediate family because of more hospital stays. There is watching your parents worry and their schedule fill up with doctor visits and hearing the cracks in their voices as they soak in what seems like sweet, innocent moments.

There are your nightly bedtime prayers for your little sister and wondering if they will be answered. Then one day, you go through the whole sudden hospital routine again and find out the answer is no, they will not.

Imagine you have to make sense of all of this—and you are five.

Things only get weirder from here. Your parents are hugging you tighter than ever but crying more. People clearly want to comfort you, but they don't know how to talk to you about it. So, the world flips upside down, and you end up being the one to comfort them. You end up being the one working to establish normalcy in your home.

You are five and shepherding adults through a world that you, nor anyone else, understands.

That may seem vague, so let me give you one tiny example. When a commercial for the Children's Hospital would come on, Ella would change the channel or provide some other distraction. No one taught her to do this. She could just see my eyes welling up, and she took action to make it better.

It's not an exaggeration to say she is the reason I got out of bed each day.

She had ambush-type situations to deal with, too. At school, what do you do with the assignment to "draw a picture of your family"?

At the donut shop, how do you answer the lady who asks, "Where is your little sister? I haven't seen her in a while"?

And then there are the kids who are mean about it. In grade school, I told myself they just didn't know any better. That high road is a little harder to take when the mean verbal attacks on her come from eighteen-year-old boys from high school. To the rest of us, the idea that a kid would tease another kid about having a deceased sibling seems unfathomable. For Ella, it's reality.

In some ways, her experiences with Alex have been similar, and in some ways not. She has certainly been an observer of her parents' worries and watching us try to work through things.

We managed to accommodate her intense swim schedule and Alex's intense therapy schedule, the key part of those phrases being "tense." Late pick-ups, early drop-offs, lots of waiting around in between things, with not enough time to go home. We got through it, but the crankiness it imparted took a toll on all of us.

As Ella got older and could drive herself, it was a huge logistics relief, but it also meant our only time together was at the very end of the day, when we were exhausted with no tolerance for frivolity or energy for casual chitchat.

Rare was the time we could all be at her school or swim events. We did parent tag-team, and Ella became accustomed to one or neither of us at her events.

Maybe the worst was a stretch of time when Alex was physically hurtful to Ella, kicking her or pulling her hair. Thankfully, as his communication and coping skills have improved, we have worked past that, but there is no denying she took the brunt of many of his frustrations.

Autism requires a lot of adaptation on the part of a household. Those changes can be hard on anyone. Imagine being asked to adapt your life around another as a teenager–not a time of life we normally associate with self-sacrifice and thinking beyond yourself!

Being the youngest of 7 myself, I can assure you that in my decades of experience, 6 out of 6 older siblings agree that the youngest kid gets all the attention and generally ruins the lives of the older kids. I'll never agree with them.

But the siblings of special needs kids have a pretty strong case that their childhood is significantly changed.

Make no mistake, through all of this and more, Ella loves her brother and sister wholeheartedly. Through the struggles and the heartaches, I feel confident she would go through it all again because Colby and Alex mean that much to her.

And every day, it's my hope that Ella recognizes how much we love her through all of it. I also hope she knows that we see the challenges, frustrations, fears, and yes, the unfairness, that she has been through as a special sister.

I hope Ella sees that we are better parents because of her. I hope she knows her siblings' lives are richer because of her. And I hope she understands she is stronger and better because of what she has been through.

And to the scholarship programs that honor other special siblings like Ella, I get it. I don't know if you could have zeroed in on a more deserving group. A group that seldom, if ever, gets recognized for what they have been through and who they are.

Now, excuse me, I need to go buy Ella a puppet and print out that form for the puppetry scholarship.

CHAPTER 24

Dear Mooches

When Ella was an infant, I began calling her Mucha-cha, mistakenly thinking it meant "little girl." Quickly, it became Muchachita, which I reasoned meant "itty bitty girl." Later, someone pointed out the flaws in my Spanish, but it was too late. My nickname for her had stuck.

It's one of many nicknames, but it remains my go-to. The one that makes me smile just to think about.

As Ella grew, the itty bitty part seemed unfitting, and the shortened versions of Mooches or Mooch generally took over. Funnily enough, just like when your own parents call you by your full name when you are in trouble, in serious times, the full Muchachita still makes an appearance.

This was a letter I packed in her bag as she headed off to her first big swim meet trip without either of her parents. It was penned as encouragement, but it also serves as a reminder of the importance in letting kids have opportunities to grow strength in their independence.

Dear Mooches,

I remember waiting and waiting for you to put your face underwater at the swim pool. It took countless trips and seemingly endless persuasion. When you finally did it, we all celebrated the achievement.

The first time you swam a full lap, we celebrated with hot dogs. Your first swim practice, your first meet, your first ribbon, and on and on ... every one of them was a hard-fought achievement, and every one of them so much fun to watch.

This week, you leave for the Central Zones Long Course Championships as a member of Team Oklahoma. Never, ever, when I was trying to coax you to put your face in the water, would I have dreamed of what you have accomplished already. What you have achieved has brought us great joy and, yes, pride.

But as happy and proud of you as we are for your achievements—and we are!—what we are most impressed and thankful for is your attitude, team spirit, and perseverance.

Recently, you were describing swim practice to me, and you said, "Practice is simple. It's just hard work and having fun." What an amazing attitude. You carry that attitude with you in life, and you will go as far as your dreams will carry you.

I've seen you dive into the pool next to great friends, and from start to finish, you both battle to come out on top. Sometimes you are faster, sometimes not, but as soon as the race is over, you become each other's biggest fan. You are a good teammate, and you appreciate the good teammates around you. Keep up that team spirit, and you will not only achieve more personally, but you will have much more fun along the way.

More than once, I've seen you grasp for the golden ring and just when it was in your fingers, it is yanked away. The following tears and anger were expected and normal. The picking yourself up and dusting yourself off was commendable. The classy way in which you raised your head back up high with renewed resolve is remarkable and inspiring. You will encounter obstacles throughout your life, but if you continue to encounter them with that kind of perseverance and determination, those obstacles will shrink away.

Someday, your last meet will be swum. Your collection of ribbons and medals will be complete. The achievements along the way are wonderful. But what will endure are the memories, friendships, and the lessons learned–those are priceless. And in those areas, we are thrilled to see you making the most of the opportunities you have been given.

On this trip, I hope you achieve all your goals. But more importantly, I want you to remember who you are, take care of the things you are supposed to, don't worry about the things you can't control, and have an absolute blast. If you do these things, you will return victorious no matter what else happens.

We will celebrate that, too. Maybe this time we will skip the hot dogs.

Love,
Dad

CHAPTER 25

Memories of My Own Big(gest) Sister

When my oldest sister, Jennifer, passed away, I spoke it at her memorial service along with my two brothers.

It may seem odd that this qualifies as a Daddy Essay, but many of my lessons about being a parent came from siblings. Of course, I didn't recognize them as lessons at the time; I suppose that is part of what makes them so special.

This is a tough task.

Tough day.

Tough to watch Jennifer's daughters, Whitney and Jessica, with grieving hearts.

Tough on all of you.

But thinking of memories to share about Jennifer, that's not hard at all. Like the rest of you, I have a lot of them.

For those of you who don't know me, I'm Jennifer's littlest brother ... well ... all her brothers are little brothers to her, but I'm the littlest at twenty-five years younger. So, by the time I came around, Jennifer was married and not too far off from having her own kids.

For most everybody else, a twenty-five-year gap between sister and brother is quite unusual. It was probably a bit weird for Jennifer, too, but for me, it is all I have ever known.

There aren't many other siblings with twenty-five-year gaps to model a relationship off of. So, we made it up as we went along. In doing so, there are a lot of memories to share. Narrowing it down to one or two … that's a tough task, too.

I could tell you about being five and her fighting with me to take a nap. I won that battle.

I could tell you about being six and her locking me out of the house because I wouldn't nap. Jennifer won that war.

I could tell you about all the times she took us to the zoo … or the Rangers game … or Six Flags … or the pool … or the Japanese Gardens. There were lots of adventures in the Texas summer, even though she was no fan of the heat.

But on the ride home, there was always an ice cream shop to be found. I could tell you about those. Jennifer always found the best places and new places to try for sandwiches, or Italian food, or whatever … but especially for desserts.

I could tell you about betting on racehorses together. Some days we were lucky. Most days not. But we always—always—had fun.

I could tell you about being sixteen and her letting me know I was too big for my britches. There are at least a few of you in here who want to shout an "Amen" to that one. Thank you for not doing so.

I could tell you about the day that we buried our dad. When they asked if anyone had anything to say, I stood there thinking there was no way I would have the courage to do so. But Jennifer stepped up.

Voice cracking and tears in her eyes, she talked about "Her daddy and pecan pies."

She probably didn't realize that she was teaching me a lesson in courage, but she did.

I could tell you about all those times she questioned what decision I was making by silently raising that one eyebrow. And sometimes her critiques weren't so silent and made me wish I had just gotten only the eyebrow.

But I am not going to tell you any of those stories. Instead, I've picked two that really stand out to me, because I think they say a little about us and a lot about her.

That twenty-five-year gap meant that our relationship was always in flux. Sometimes a sister, sometimes more like an aunt, and sometimes more like a mom. And it could change in a moment.

Jennifer, Mom, and I were on some trail ride in God knows where and with what group. We'd stopped for lunch. Mom and Jennifer sat on the ground and ate picnic-style. I thought it was "more cowboy" to not get out of the saddle unless I had to. So, we had lunch, I watered all the horses, brought them back, and they mounted back up.

We started heading down the trail, and a hundred yards in, Mom started squirming and shouting, and the next thing you know, she stepped down from her horse and began pulling her pants down. She was hollering in pain. I was hollering from embarrassment, and in all the chaos, we figured out what was going on. Fire ants.

Mom was tough, and it didn't take long for her to get the giggles despite the stings. She was thoroughly enjoying how embarrassed I was that my sixty-two-year-old mom had stripped her pants off.

Jennifer chided her. "Mom, don't embarrass him! That's enough.

Get your pants back on." I was happy to have my sister take my side. Who knows. Maybe she was embarrassed a little, too.

Fire ants dead, pants back on Mom, she got back in the saddle and off we went again. This time, I rode back a little further, trailing behind the two of them.

Then I saw it. Jennifer twitched in the saddle sharply. Then she twitched again. A few seconds later, her feet were on the ground, and her pants weren't far behind. Fire ants had gotten her, too.

Mom's giggling went into full-on laughter. My face was so red from embarrassment that the ants might as well have been stinging me, too.

"What happened to not embarrassing me?" I hollered out.

"These damn things hurt, so get over it!" she hollered back.

Jennifer fought off the invaders, and we all got going again. This time, I trailed back even farther. But I could still hear the giggling ... this time from both of them as they soothed their stings with the salve of enjoying my embarrassment.

Years later, they still laughed whenever that story was told.

But my story that best explains Jennifer comes from when I was in college. Our family had met at her house for Christmas, and she noticed I didn't have a coat, for which I received an eyebrow.

I told her I was a broke college student and had better things to spend my money on. Besides, I explained, College Station never gets too cold. We didn't talk about it anymore that night. I had won the battle.

The next day, we went to the Hulen Mall, and she won the war. She bought me a coat.

I appreciated the coat, I really did. But to put it on would have been ... well ... it wouldn't have been hard-headed, and if we have a family tradition, being hard-headed is it. So, I didn't put it on.

The next day, I headed back to College Station, and the coat sat in the seat next to me. Stopping at the gas station, it was a bit chilly, and with no one around to see me capitulate, I slipped the jacket on.

I had just put on the coat, and I was waiting for my tank to fill, so my hands did what hands naturally do. I put them in my coat pockets. When I did, I felt something unexpected.

No, not fire ants.

Jennifer had folded up three $20 bills and slipped them into the coat pocket.

Observant. Caring. Insistent. Generous. And a little bit sneaky. That's Jennifer.

I'm sure we all have stories like that, and none of us more than her kids and grandkids.

She wasn't just creating memories with you. She was teaching you a lesson. A lesson on how much she loves you. A lesson I know you all learned well.

CHAPTER 26

100 Years

Like most, I struggle with gratitude. I need regular remind-
ers of the blessings all around me, so easily taken for granted.
This occasion caused me to stop, reflect, and renew my
gratefulness.

A hundred years ago today, my dad was born. He only lived to eighty-two, but the day still seems worthy of note. In some ways, a hundred years is a long time. In others, not so much.

Alex is 4 and some change, so technically, he and my dad are 95 and some odd years apart. I don't think I am bending the laws of mathematics too much when I round that up to say grandfather and grandson are separated by a whole century. I think about those one hundred years a lot.

My dad was born in a farmhouse in the Texas Panhandle. No doctors or nurses. No epidurals. Heck, I don't even know who would have cut the umbilical cord. I can't fully wrap my head around all of that, but I can understand it enough to know what a dangerous time childbirth was for both woman and child back then.

The first thing to consider when contrasting Dad's birth to Alex's birth is the location.

One of Dad's favorite songs to sing in the truck was a Woody Guthrie tune called "Oklahoma Hills" that included the lines:

> *Way down yonder in the Indian nation*
> *I rode my pony on the reservation*
> *In the Oklahoma Hills where I was born*
> *Way down yonder in the Indian nation*
> *A cowboy's life is my occupation*
> *In the Oklahoma Hills where I was born*

Little did he know that one day he would have a grandson born in Oklahoma.

Alex was born in a hospital facility that no one could have ever even dreamed about back in 1918. We had a room full of doctors and nurses. A fantastic neonatal ward and all sorts of modern monitors, tests, and screenings were there for our benefit.

Even with these facilities, I can't wrap my head around how tough modern-day moms are either. Though I would never dare call it easy, thank God we have the means to drastically reduce the deaths of women bearing children by almost ninety-nine percent.

It wasn't just childbirth that was dangerous. Dad had a sister who passed away as a teenager. Dad told me once that she had a bad headache and laid down and never got back up. When I was older, I was told it was an ear infection. These days, you hear some folks judgmentally say, "Parents run their kids to the doctor for every little ear infection. What did they think happened in the old days?"

Well, I can answer that. Some kids died because of a simple ear infection.

Now the worst part about the ear infection (aside from the bill) is the diapers that follow an antibiotic. I don't think there is a big line of people wanting to go back to the old days of ear infections.

I do know of one time that the doctor made it out to my dad's house. When he was a young boy, he had to have his appendix taken out. Once again, no anesthesia. They gave him a belt to bite on. It left him with what us kids thought was a second belly button.

I asked him once, "Did it hurt?" When someone tells you there is no such thing as a dumb question, you all now know there has been at least one.

Aside from the medical world, think of all the ways the world has changed.

When my dad finally got a telephone, it was a party line, which means you shared it with several other houses. You counted the rings to know if they were calling your house. Other houses could listen in to your calls, and if you had a call to make, you had to wait for their call to finish. I can't imagine the latter happening too often, though, because phone calls were expensive. One source says a transcontinental call costs the equivalent of $135/minute today.

I don't have to tell you that most of us can call anywhere in this country for free—or at least free on a per-minute basis. Heck, it's only pennies a minute to call anywhere in the world, and we can have video calls with most anywhere in the world for free. Not to mention that our phones do so much more than voice communications. We carry the world in our pockets, and in the span of just ten years, we have gone from being amazed at this ability to considering it a fundamental right.

I also think about how much cars have changed. I'd love to take a teenage driver today and put him behind the wheel of the first car my dad drove and, at the same time, put my dad behind the wheel of a modern-day car loaded up with the latest gizmos and let them have a race. I'm pretty sure once my dad got past the keyless start aspect, he'd be on his way, albeit frustratingly so, with all the gadgets beeping at him. The teenager wouldn't get out of the parking lot.

I could cite a laundry list of things my dad's car didn't have that we would consider absolute necessities, but I'll just name one. He didn't have a defroster. He would drive with a candle on the dashboard and rub an onion on the outside of the windshield to try to control the frost.

When it came to school, my dad went to school for a while in the fall until the cotton was ready to pick. Then he had to drop out for the year to help on the farm. I think he made it to about the third grade before he dropped out for good.

He was really good at math and read well, but as I got farther into school and too big for my britches, I used to look down on his lack of education. I can remember coming home from school and telling him I learned how FDR got us out of the Great Depression by priming the pump with government spending.

He just laughed and said, "You think so?" Of course, I did. That's what my teacher taught me. He went on to tell me that those policies extended the Depression, and despite him having actually lived through it, I dismissed it.

Now, being older and having much more exposure to Keynesian and Austrian economics, I often think back to how smart my dad was on matters like that, despite being given so little opportunity to indulge in those studies.

I also often think what fun it would be to be able to take my dad to see modern cotton farming. I bet his back would start aching at just the sight of fields with yields that have increased sixteen times from what he grew up with. I think about the hours he spent sitting on a wagon full of cotton pulled by mules, waiting his turn at the gin as it pressed out a bale or two an hour. Oh, how he would marvel at the gins running 70 bales per hour or more, and some ginning 200,000 bales in a single season.

I could go on and on. I'm sure you could, too, with your own examples. And the best ones are not even related to technology.

When my dad was born, his mom didn't have the right to vote. Meanwhile, Alex's mom works alongside senators, congressmen, governors, and other state and federal officials, and they contact her to seek out her expertise.

We are safer. We are more food secure. We have made more progress on civil rights for everyone in the last fifty years than in all of human history before that. Literacy has skyrocketed. Life expectancy has increased.

Let's all pause a moment to appreciate indoor plumbing!

We are not without problems, but so much has changed, and we have so much to be thankful for ... in just a hundred years ... in just the time between a granddad and a grandson.

But that isn't the modern narrative. The gratefulness of how far we have come and what made those advances possible is a tiny drop in a pool full of discourse about the ails and flaws of our society. To be sure, we have both ails and flaws, but we spend so much time lost in them and validating our modern struggles, we have lost sight of how bad struggles can be.

We need the context of the past and the acceptance that life will always have imperfections to realize that we are living in a golden age. If we want to preserve that golden age, improve it, and expand it to more people on this earth, we need to start by appreciating it.

So, on this hundredth anniversary of Bill Turner's birth, I'm going to spend some time appreciating all of the ways the world has changed for the better. And I'll spend some time appreciating all of the work my dad did for me in helping me to enjoy it.

And, lastly, I am going to spend some time thinking about the many ways his grandson is so very much like him, even though the world is so different. How they both point with their middle finger. How their eyes are the same shade of blue. How they share a sense of humor. How they both get down to business when there is work to be done. How much both of them like singing in the car.

And how, no matter how hard he tries, Alex will never be able to fathom the world his grandson will be born into. Nor can I imagine the world Alex's children will inherit. Let's all do our part to make sure it's a good one by appreciating the one we have now.

CHAPTER 27

A Mother's Day Story

Mother's Day takes a different tone after your own mom passes away. It becomes a time of reflection, and those times often offer new appreciation.

When I was a senior in high school, a buddy of mine named Wade was having a rough patch at his home. My mom and dad let him move in with us for a while, which helped him out of a jam, and it was great fun for me.

My parents put an extra bed in my room, and Wade and I began figuring out being roommates, as well as friends. Somewhere in all of this, a great prank war broke out. Truth be told, we had been playing jokes on each other for a long time. Having more access and proximity, the roommate situation created lots more opportunities.

For instance, I put a bowl full of marbles in the freezer. Said marbles then ended up in Wade's bed as he slept, or at least he was sleeping when the prank started. Of course, as he tried to roll away from the marbles, they just followed him.

A few nights later, Wade retaliated by sticking straight pins along the edge of my mattress so that when I slid into bed, they would poke me. I guess the first time I got into my bed, I sort of hopped in and missed them. So, Wade would get up, turn the light on, and get back into his bed. I would then have to get out of bed to turn out the light and slide back into bed. It took about three tries before I got stuck with the pins.

I howled with expletives, and he howled with laughter.

And on it went, with the escalating cleverness and sometimes viciousness.

So, one day, we came home from school together. I sat down in the living room, and Wade disappeared back to our room, which had its own bathroom. A few minutes later, Wade barrels into the living room, pounces on me, and starts pummeling me with his fists.

I was trying to figure out what the hell was going on, and my mom was yelling from the kitchen, "You boys settle down!" I was all in favor of things settling down, but Wade was plenty mad.

I was yelling, "What?" and he kept telling me I knew what. Mom came into the living room, and she was yelling now, too. So, Wade told her what the problem was.

"Neil put something on the toilet seat, and it's burning my ass!"

I protested, "I don't know what he is talking about!!!"

My mom's face shifted from mad to thoughtful, then she began laughing. "Oh no! I was cleaning you boys' toilet, and I had just put liquid Comet on the seat, and the phone rang. I went to answer it and must have forgot all about the toilet seat and never wiped it off."

By the time she reached the end of the explanation, she was laughing so hard, she had tears in her eyes. I was still trying to figure out what was going on but felt better knowing that I was vindicated.

Meanwhile, Wade was getting madder because the pain was only intensifying. He dropped his pants back down to get a look at the damage and see how he could soothe it, and sure enough—there was a red blistered ring around his posterior right where the seat had been.

My mom was laughing so hard at that point, she had to sit. I was laughing because—well, because it was funny. And Wade was in too much pain to see the humor. Even though he knew who did it, he couldn't hit my mom, so he punched me again, which made my mom laugh even more.

Nobody has ever described my mom as jovial, but when she got on a roll of laughter, it was something to witness. She had once laughed so much, they threatened to throw her out of the hospital—and she was the patient! That day with Wade was probably the hardest I had ever seen her laugh.

Though that story might seem to be mostly about Wade and me, it really captures a lot of my mom. Sometimes a little scattered, which sometimes led to funny things. No nonsense—at first, she didn't care what was going on; she just wanted us to "cut it out." A bit twisted, which allowed her to find joy in Wade's misfortune, then mine. A bit paradoxical in being a tough woman who had lived a hard life and could still laugh with such abandon.

But most of all, what that story tells about Winnie Turner—after raising 7 kids whose ages span over 25 years*—is she found room in her home, her time, and her heart to care for one more. She clearly loved mothering.

---

* That's more than 43 years of having kids under 18 at home.

CHAPTER 28

St. Patrick's Day

This was written over ten years ago, and, yes, dress socks still make me itch.

It's another wedding anniversary note and a reflection on marriage and having someone to lean on. Parenting provides ample opportunity to put that blessing to work.

My parents were not practitioners of openly showing affection. Years may have faded some memories, but I can only remember a few distinct such occasions.

One was before Mom was leaving on a trip, and they exchanged "I love yous." Once, seemingly out of the blue, I recall a peck on the lips between them. I distinctly remember where we were because such a thing was so unusual.

And there was the unfortunate time when I was in the eighth grade, when I was out of athletic socks and went to borrow a pair from my dad. I walked into my parents' room without knocking and left even quicker—without socks. I'll leave it to your imagination what I witnessed, and I suspect you won't be wrong.

I wore a pair of black dress socks with my sneakers to school that day.

"Hey, look at Neil's socks!" someone tried to tease.

Normally, I would deflect such things with humor, but I was not to be messed with that day. "Say another word, and I'll make you eat them."

Black dress socks still make me itch.

It's not that my parents hid all their emotions and thoughts. They shared the stresses and strains of marriage much more freely. By the time all my siblings had left home, I was the only one left to talk to and was regularly on the listening end of one venting about the other. When that didn't relieve the pressure, I'd often find myself stuck in the middle as they vented toward each other.

I don't say all of this to criticize my parents; after all, their marriage lasted until death did they part. Almost fifty-six years. I share all of that to set the stage for the biggest lesson they taught me about marriage. It involves the one other moment of affection between the two that I remember.

It was St. Patrick's Day 1980, and we were at a church at my grandma's funeral service. I was eight and a veteran of funeral services at the Methodist Church in McLean, but this one was different. The other services were for distant relatives. This one was for my grandma. I was too young to comprehend the implications and struggled to find the balance between the grief of the loss and the natural joy of having all my siblings home. In this weird mix of emotions, I could barely figure out how I was feeling, much less what anyone else was feeling.

As the service ended and we stood to leave, my dad began crying. Only then did it really dawn on me that he wasn't mourning the loss of my grandma. He had just lost *his* mom. Not only that, it was the first time I had seen my dad cry.

My mom took notice, too, of course. She hooked her arm into his. He leaned into her. Together, they made it to the door and down the steps to the car. My mom helped Dad into the passenger seat of our station wagon, and she got in behind the wheel to drive to the graveside. At that time, Dad always drove. It was never even a question. But that day, Mom drove. And it was never a question then either.

My mom's tenderness in helping my dad left a deep impression on me. But so, too, did my dad's vulnerability and entrusting my mom with it.

I suppose I never suffered any illusions that happily ever after equated to always happy. The youngest of 7 spread out over 25 years, I was a kid amongst a bunch of adults. Between my parents and other conversations, I overheard and witnessed a lot of the work and struggles that go along with marriage.

In our house now, we often say "I love you." We kiss and hug more than Ella is comfortable being around. We hold hands less than Usha would like, but we do still hold hands. We get fussy and frustrated with each other, but we also enjoy a good laugh or the occasional moment of pure silliness.

The moments of friction are normal. The happy times are wonderful.

But on this St. Patrick's Day 2014, the most beautiful and cherished moments of our marriage to me are when we lock arms, lean into each other, and help each other put one foot in front of the other.

And for that—on this night of takeout dinner, a kid recovering from oral surgery, coping with the curves of newborn schedule, the eternal ache of missing our sweet angel, no presents, and not even a card—my heart is full of gratitude for you, our marriage, and our life together.

Happy anniversary, wife.

CHAPTER 29

Ella in Chat Mode

Much of fatherhood is simply listening. If there is ever an audio version of this book, you might want to play it at double-speed to get the full effect.

E lla attended a Lone Star Adventure Nature Camp this week. They spent all day yesterday and today together, including a sleepover at the Trinity River Audubon Center. The center is located in a 6,000-acre forest in South Dallas. She was a little excited about it when I picked her up—I wish I had had a camera.

Below is my attempt at capturing her words.

> Dad! Look, I lost my tooth! Not yesterday, but on the hike this morning. I wiggled it and wiggled it, and then I couldn't feel it with my tongue, and I looked at my fingers and there it was. So, I put it in my pocket so I could keep it safe, but I kept taking it out to look at it and one time, it wasn't there, so I can't show it to you. But it's all okay, because I'm going to write a note to the Tooth Fairy and explain what happened. That's okay because she accepts

notes if you have a good excuse. We all talked about it and agreed that is the way it works. Even the counselors said so.

And today we worked with owl puke. When owls eat, they can digest the meat, but not the fur and the bones. So, they puke that up. We had to pick through the balls of fur and find the bones and try and identify them. Owls kill their prey with their talons. And if that doesn't work, they use their beaks.

I've been so hungry! They didn't feed us much for breakfast. Only a granola bar and some fruit. They said we couldn't have more because they didn't have anything else. They said sometimes that's the way it is when you camp. I like camping, but I like breakfast, too. I was so hungry, I ate all my lunch. It was so good. I was hungry.

I missed you! I'm so glad to see you. But now I miss my camp friends and the counselors.

We stayed up until four in the morning. We had to be in our tents at eleven, but we were so excited for the morning that we couldn't sleep, so we just kept talking. We all decided, and I don't mean all of us, just the girls in my tent, the four of us. Well, we all decided, the four of us, which boy we thought was the nicest. We picked the funniest boy. He says stuff like, "Wanna pineapple?" He is so funny.

We went swimming today. Not in a pool. In a real pond with mud on the bottom and everything! Well, mud and fish poop. And we found clams with our feet. Not the ones with pearls in it, but the ones with meat in them. And we swam all the way across the pond. And my feet turned brown, and it won't wash off.

I thought this was just going to be camp, but they kept teaching us stuff. I didn't know we'd have to learn things. But it's okay. The learning was fun.

I am tired. Not because we stayed up until four. I was the second to last person to fall asleep. I'm tired because we did so much. We hiked. We canoed. We bird-watched. We saw the biggest bird over by the entrance. It was big. Not big like an ostrich, but still the biggest one we saw. We played games. We ate Cool Ranch Doritos. We hiked a bunch. We even went on one at night.

One hike we had to crawl through a fence, and I got chiggers all over me. I thought I shook them off, but I got a bunch of bites. I'm okay though. We saw bobcat tracks, and then we started wondering if there were mountain lions. We were scared that we might see a bobcat or a mountain lion, but the counselors told us not to worry. Then we saw hobo tracks, and then our counselors got scared, too! What? Why are you laughing? Trust me, if you were there, you'd have been looking out for hobos.

What did you do yesterday?

"Well, I worked all day and then last night for dinner, I had -."

You can tell me more later. I learned how to paddle. Do you want me to tell you about the single paddle or the double paddle? Well, I'm going to tell you about the single paddle because I already knew how to use the double paddle. It shaped like a shovel. Except the handle end doesn't have a hole in it. You put one hand on the handle end and the other hand on the other end. And when you paddle, you act like you wave your hand, but you don't really have to wave your hand. Only if you want to.

Did I tell you about breakfast? They only had these little bars. The pizza the night before was pretty good, except I didn't like the crust. They only let us have two pieces. Well three, but it seemed like two. I wish we had more for breakfast.

Oh! The owl puke had been sanitized. Our teacher said to be sure to tell our parents that part. He didn't want you to freak out. I'm still freaked out about it a little though. I can't believe I had to work with owl puke. It was sanitized though. We saw coyote poop, too.

Ah! Good memories.

Can I put on my pajamas when we get home?

CHAPTER 30

Little One-Room Schoolhouse

With the title referencing a one-room schoolhouse, you might think this is another story about my dad. It's not.

Early in Alex's homeschooling journey, we spent much of it on the road. This essay tries to capture what that time did for us.

I t snowballed on us pretty quickly. I mean that in a good way. A great way, actually.

A little over a year ago, we made the decision to homeschool Alex; that was a popular choice at the time for COVID reasons. Our reason was that a traditional classroom can be a hard place for a young autistic boy, and a young autistic boy can be hard on a traditional classroom, too.

Alex is smart, creative, and a natural learner, and we needed to provide him with a space to flourish. Little did we know what that space would turn out to be.

Mid-summer, I started looking ahead and trying to plan activities. I found a nature group that had meet-ups once or twice a month at area state parks, and that sounded perfect. Alex loves the outdoors, and nature topics would provide lots of learning opportunities. Exercise, fresh air, exploration, social interaction—it all sounded perfect.

But as I was signing up, I ran into one problem: No dads were allowed. This particular group was strictly for moms and their kids.

I contacted them just to make sure that was correct. It was. I wanted to argue. I didn't. I realized their group wasn't as much about the kids as they claimed.

Instead, I had a very petty reaction. I decided I would out-nature adventure their misguided club.

It didn't take long to realize my guide rails were off, too. This was about Alex, not me. I refocused and started giving thought to camping for a week in Colorado.

I started looking at tents, and I was lukewarm. Then I saw one of those tents that sets up in the bed of a pickup, and I was intrigued. Then I saw a rooftop tent, and I was in love. I showed the idea to my wife, Usha, and she enthusiastically encouraged us to try it.

I ended up with a stack of research at a local retailer. They listened to what I wanted to do, persuaded me to throw out some bad ideas, and helped me source parts during a nationwide shortage.

The plan started out as a week of camping in Colorado. It turned into an extended trip into Montana, and ultimately, it turned into a year with over 80 nights camping in our Roam Tent, covering 29 states. We camped in the San Juan Islands off the coast of Washington, on the beaches of South Carolina, on Lakes Superior, Michigan, and Huron, and lots of places in between.

Now I don't know if there is such a thing as a "typical" rooftop tent user. But I am certain what we do isn't common. I know a lot of their market is overlanders exploring very remote places. That's some cool stuff, but that is not us.

We typically stay at state parks or national forests instead of dispersed camps, though we have done that, too. We have seen lots of the great outdoors, including canyons, mesas, prairies, mountains, islands, forests, glaciers, deserts, and oceans. But we have also explored state capitals, civil rights sites, historic forts, farms, factories, the Soo Locks on the Great Lakes, and tons of other places with paved parking lots accessible by any vehicle.

It may not be typical, but I assure you it is an adventure, and our rooftop tent base camp makes it all possible.

The education taking place is broad and deep. We take what we learn during the day and integrate it into the core subjects. Math, science, social studies, reading, writing, geography, history, economics, and art lesson opportunities are everywhere. It's been a wonderful treasure trove of experiences.

Alex hasn't just studied dinosaurs; he has walked in their tracks!

But there is also something beyond those things—something almost magical.

When we are adventuring and learning, Alex's autism isn't an obstacle. He isn't struggling to be still or quiet. He has the freedom to intensely focus on the topics that interest him for prolonged periods and explore more deeply than I ever expected. At other times, his brain is ping-pong hopping between a dozen different things, and that's okay, too. It may seem chaotic to me, but he can be processing multiple channels of information at the same time.

Of course, there are triggers or meltdowns. They can be frustrating, for him and me, but they don't disrupt others' learning or cause him to miss his learning window. We can take our time and often use the environment around us to reset. I mean, if you needed a mental break, wouldn't you rather take it skipping rocks at a lake?

When we saw how much Alex was benefiting from adventure learning, we decided to share those experiences with other kids with autism so they could learn from some of the things that Alex does and be inspired to take their own adventures. So, along the way, we set up a Facebook page and even a YouTube page.

The videos have turned out to be valuable tools for Alex, too. It helps reinforce what he learned and also gives him the chance to practice his communication skills. Not only does he narrate, he helps create the outline and has input on what we include, in what order, and how best to explain the subject.

Once we began sharing the videos, we quickly found out that the audience extended beyond autistic kids. Some teachers have begun using his videos in their classes, including some high school and college classes. We have also been touched to hear that some children in other countries who have had their schools closed due to violence have been using the videos as a resource.

Not long ago, Alex spent most of his school day hiding under a desk. That same little boy's videos are now a window to a world for some children in a South African home who can't leave their home due to unsafe conditions.

And that brings me to what really makes my heart swell and eyes water.

Alex isn't just teaching the world about beekeeping, waterfalls, mushrooms, cows, and artesian springs.

Alex is teaching them—he is teaching all of us—that autistics have a place in this world and that when we make room for them, they can be world-changers.

And it started in a little one-room (rooftop tent) schoolhouse.

CHAPTER 31

Ella Goes to College

Long before we dropped Ella off at college, I had begun a mental list of all the advice I would dole out to her. It seemed impossible to tell her all the things I thought she would need to know.

It turned out to be a much simpler task.

Ella,

Over the last few months, and especially over the last few days, I've thought of a hundred pieces of advice to give you.

I've settled on just one … be you.

Be you because you are already incredible and awesome and have everything you need inside you to soar high and soar happy.

Forever my moochachita.

Love,
Dad

CHAPTER 32

Tree Dedication

When we lived in Rockwall, Texas, our church outpoured huge amounts of love and support to us as Colby battled her illness and as we coped with her loss. Colby loved flowers, and the church planted a crepe myrtle to honor her. This was my speech to the congregation on the day of the tree dedication.

Before we go any further, I need to share something with you. Some of you may already know this and have just been too kind to comment on it. But here it is. Most weeks during worship, at some point, we end up crying a little. Sometimes a bit more than a little. And that is just for a regular Sunday.

This Sunday—this special Sunday—has been on our minds for some time. I can tell you what you already know. There is a better chance of me dancing on top of the piano than of us getting through the day without crying. In fact, that may be the only way I won't cry, but the rest of you surely would.

In anticipation of this day, I came up with a plan. It was a good plan and one I was quite proud of—until Usha told me I couldn't bring tequila to church.

So, we are moving on to Plan B, and it's important that you pay attention because all of you play a role in Plan B. Plan B is *did anybody else bring any tequila*?

Ok. Not really. That isn't Plan B. Plan B is that if at some point my blubbering gets out of control or the snot bubbles become too distracting, all of you start applauding and laughing, and we'll just pretend I did a good job.

Deep breath.

Our family remains constantly surprised and in awe at the number of people Colby touched and who supported her and continue to support us. It is truly phenomenal, and we appreciate the comfort it has brought us.

But when it comes to this church, surprised isn't really the right word. Surprised means unexpected or unusual. Anybody who has spent any time here knows that the kind of love you have shown us is not unusual or unexpected. We've seen you do it time after time, for all sorts of people, in all sorts of situations. Without hesitation. Without reservation.

When I realized my words started to rhyme, I wanted to read this in my Al Sharpton voice, but Usha nixed that, too.

Feel the love. Be the love. It's not just the motto here. It's the truth. And just because we aren't surprised by it anymore doesn't mean we aren't in awe. And most definitely, we are and will always be in appreciation of it.

We are so honored to have a tree here in Colby's memory. We hope it does inspire wonderful memories of our sweet, little girl.

But we also hope you see Colby's tree as a tribute to you. A constant reminder of the very real difference that "Feel the love. Be the love." makes. A beautiful growing reminder of the difference each one of you makes.

Thank you for helping us honor Colby's memory and thank you for providing us with such a wonderful church home.

Let the snot bubbles flow.

CHAPTER 33

Slug Bugs and Pastors' Cars

During the time we lived in Rockwall, the church in the previous chapter was pastored by Cheryl Taylor. To say she has had a tremendous impact on our family is the largest understatement in this book.

She was at our side when Colby died, and she led her memorial service. It's really unthinkable to ask so much of anybody. Yet we did. And she obliged with all the beauty and grace that only people of her talents and her heart can do.

Growing up, we called it Slug Bug. Apparently, competing for the right to hit somebody else unabatedly and without retribution, based entirely on an arbitrary event, is pretty widespread. My wife, who grew up three thousand miles away from here, played it, too; they called it Punch Bug. Slightly different name, but the same simple concept. The first one to spot a Volkswagen Beetle "Bug" gets to punch/slug their opponent.

Somewhere in the past year, Ella has picked up on this game. For her, it's all about a chance to beat her mom or dad, much more than the act of punching—though she can land a pretty solid right-hander. Not to mention, we normally play it while in the car, and it's tough for her to get a good angle on my arm from the backseat. So sometimes we just keep score.

One day while playing, I got on a lucky streak and was several points ahead of Ella. As Ella is prone to do, she decided to expand the rules to her advantage. She spotted a Toyota Prius and shouted, "Pastor Cheryl car!" and slyly added it to her total, waiting to see if I would challenge her.

Normally, I am a purist and don't like expanding the rules. Jazzing it up with punch-backs or other complexities always seemed a distraction. But there was such a sweetness and excitement in Ella's voice when she said, "Pastor Cheryl car," it gave me pause.

"Ella, do you think we should count cars like Pastor Cheryl's?"

"Yes," she replied with a slight hint of disbelief that she was pulling this off.

So, I gave in, but not without a little more tweaking. "Do you think we would honor Pastor Cheryl in a good way if we punched each other every time we saw a car like hers?"

"No," she replied very thoughtfully.

"So, what should we do?"

"Hmmmm." Pause. "I know! Every time we see a Pastor Cheryl car, we can say something we are thankful for."

Now that is a good way to honor Pastor Cheryl. I think that inspiration says a lot about Cheryl and her impact on Ella.

And with that, the Pastor Cheryl Car game was born, and I've grown to be quite a fan. Naturally, it encourages her (and us) to be more reflective and appreciative of the blessings in our lives. But the best part has been that whenever Ella spots a Prius, we get a snapshot of what is going through her mind. The answers are sometimes routine, sometimes surprising, and always bring a smile.

And my shoulder likes it better, too.

CHAPTER 34

Learning to Swim and Educational Toys

I struggle to put the lessons from this one into practice as much as I should, but when I remember, the results are always better.

Realizing that what you do matters much more than what you say is both powerful and frightening. But as parents, it's important that we stay aware of that fact.

I spent a lot of time in the water growing up. Not so much lakes or rivers or the ocean. Mostly just the swimming pool. I wasn't exactly what you'd call a natural at it either, though I eventually did decently as a competitive swimmer in high school. No, my swimming career wasn't born of passion or potential; it was out of practicality.

The roots of it began with free community swim lessons. One summer, my mom discovered she could get cheap summer child-care courtesy of a fortuitous schedule of lessons.

She would drop me off at the indoor pool for beginner lessons from 8:00 - 9:00, followed by intermediate lessons from 9:00 - 10:00.

From 10:00 - 11:00, I'd walk the mile from the indoor pool in town to the outdoor pool, where another round of beginner lessons would go until noon.

Then in the afternoon, I'd get to stay at the pool to play for the rest of the day.

Did I mention I spent a lot of time in the water growing up?

As an adult, I have wondered why it's so hard for me to get a good tan when it was always so easy for me as a kid. Writing this down, suddenly it makes sense.

Now it's widely accepted that you have to pass the beginner class to take the intermediate one. And it's fairly reasonable to expect that most who are taking intermediate classes don't go back and take the beginner's class. Add in the twist that these were two-week classes offered multiple times over the summer, and you really start to wonder how she persuaded them to let me enroll in so many classes.

My mom wasn't afraid to put her persuasion skills to work. Like the time she took me to my future elementary school when I was four and sweetly asked the principal to put me in kindergarten a year early. "Mr. Johnson, he won't be any trouble." Then she'd look at me and say, "Tell the man you won't be any trouble!"

Mr. Johnson would smile and explain that the rules were the rules. Then Mom would counter, "He already knows how to read and count." Then she would look at me and say, "Count for the man!"

A few more rounds of exchanges went on as my mom's smile disappeared. Then Mr. Johnson's smile disappeared. I had already quit smiling way back when I had to promise not to be any trouble.

Eventually, her request was thoroughly denied to the point that she gave up. Though I don't quite remember the parting words, I'd place fair odds that it involved Mr. Johnson being instructed where he could place his rules. For the six years I went to school there, I did my best to never make eye contact with Mr. Johnson.

Now, if any of this sounds disparaging to my mom, I assure you that is not the intent. You raise 7 kids spread out 25 years apart and see if you don't want to rush the last one along a little, too.

Though unsuccessful with Mr. Johnson, her persuasion was no match for whoever ran the swim lessons. If there is another man on this earth with nine certificates for successfully passing pollywogs, I'd like to meet him.

Becoming a competitive swimmer was another matter of motherly practicality. When I was old enough to have an after-school activity, I had a long list of ideas: Boy Scouts, 4-H, baseball, drum lessons. I thought picking one was going to be pretty hard, but it turned out to be pretty simple. Mom picked for me.

"Your sister is on the swim team, and I'm not running all over town to different places and different practices. You are going to swim, too."

I wasn't happy. Not because I didn't like swimming, but because I didn't like not having the choice. The only one more unhappy with me was the aforementioned sister, who liked swimming but loved being away from me, her pesky, little brother. Having me around at every practice and meet took a good bit of shine off being on the swim team for her.

Now, my sister can be pretty persuasive, too. After a loud protest and some pouting didn't sway my mom—which never did—she came up with a plan. Joining the swim team required a tryout. Sister explained all I had to do was blow my tryout, and our problem would be solved. I thought she was a genius. An evil genius, but still a genius.

So, tryout day came, and Coach Eckhardt, smiling, spoke from behind his timeless mustache, wanting to see what I could do. So off

I went, swimming well enough not to drown and just good enough to make forward progress down the pool. With one eye on the coach and one eye on the Boy Scouts, my smile grew as his fell.

Coach broke the news to me of "maybe next year," and for a brief while, the plan looked like it worked. That was of course until Mom heard about the results.

In my mind, not knowing who to blame for sure, Mom twisted my ear in one hand and the coach's in the other and led us back to the pool for a re-tryout. Maybe it didn't happen that way, but what did happen was that it was explained to me that my options were to make the team or spend every day sitting at the pool, watching the team practice. I swam like I was escaping a shark.

With that, my swim career was born, and many more hours were logged in the pool after that.

So, when it was time for Ella to learn how to swim, I had all the necessary skills to teach her myself. No need for classes. I could offer her one-on-one instruction; it would be a bonding experience. It all made perfect sense, at least until we got to the pool and actually started trying it.

I'll spare you all the details. Details that you likely already suspect, including the pleading, the bargaining, the yelling, the attempts at tricking, the reasoning—the whatever the complete opposite of bonding was.

I can summarize it all by telling you that one day, after a solid hour of trying, I finally got Ella to put her face in the water. It was a hard-fought battle, but finally, I had a sign of forward progress. That false hope lasted less than a day, because when we went back the next day, she wouldn't put her face in the water again.

I succumbed to the lesson route, the first round of which we both learned a lot. Unfortunately, none of it had anything to do with swimming.

First, I opted for the four o'clock time slot because it had the most open slots. *Better teacher-to-student ratio*, I thought to myself as I out-smarted all of those nine a.m. parents.

What the morning parents knew that I later found out was that the indoor pool deck is a smooth 120 degrees in the afternoon. That's not a problem if you are actually in the pool; if, on the other hand, you are a parent on the deck, it is miserable.

Ella, on the other hand, learned a lesson—or if not a lesson, at least got practice—in the art of distraction.

"Okay, Ella. Let's try putting your face in the water," the teenage girl instructor would chirp.

Ella's response: "I really like your suit. It's so pretty. Where did you get it?"

Suddenly, the talk of swimming and blowing bubbles gave way to which Kohl's location had the better selection.

A few more weeks of swim lessons down the road, and I broke down and took her to the swim school in town. We showed up for the "free evaluation" where they "analyzed her skills" and "matched her with a personalized lesson plan." Going in, I was a skeptic; it all sounded a little too over the top to this nine-time pollywogger.

During a brief interview on deck, the school manager asked me what I wanted to accomplish. I confessed we needed to start from the ground up. "I'll be happy when we get her to put her head under the water."

"Oh!" He grinned. "That's easy!"

Skeptically, I looked at his swimsuit and tried to predict where he had bought it.

But sure enough, a couple of minutes later, the two of them were in the pool and within ten seconds, he had her head under the water. It wasn't even by force!

A minute later, she was bobbing under the water and out, over and over again.

I was close enough to hear how he pulled this off. It's not magic, but it was magically simple. I'd tell you now, except that one day, I hope to mesmerize another frustrated parent with the trick, and I don't want to ruin it should I get the chance to seem like a wizard.

Needless to say, I signed up on the spot, and she has made steady progress ever since, including now being on the swim team. When she started the team, her new coach counseled all of us parents. "Let me do the teaching and the coaching. Your job is to find something positive to say and pay for this."

My response to that? A handshake, a smile, and saying, "No takebacks."

This story of Ella's swim lessons came to mind after some house-cleaning in recent weeks. Housecleaning is really an understatement. What we have been doing is staging our house for showings so that we can sell it.

If you've been through this, you know the torment of doing things like packing away all your books and then, soon after, buying nicer-looking fake books to put in their place.

Just tonight, a couple of sweet middle-school girls came by the house raising money for the diabetes foundation. As I opened the door, one of them commented on our *for sale* sign in the yard. "Showings blow, don't they?" If the first rule of sales is relating to your customer, this young lady has a very bright future. Indeed, I wrote a donation check.

Headaches aside, in this process of getting our house properly staged, we had a lot of de-cluttering to do.

I am a hoarder.

There are no stacks of newspapers in my home teetering on collapse. There are just a few waiting to be read. We don't have forty cats running around. Just the one, and she sleeps most hours of the day. No odd collections, save a few junk drawers. My glove box is cluttered, but the name of the disorder behind that is laziness.

Still, I am a hoarder. I hoard memories.

The degree of my hoarding, like many adults, stepped up when I became a parent. The first school paper that came home from daycare was admired with great pride and hung on the refrigerator. It inspired thoughts of an elaborate system of photographing or scanning the everyday pieces and creating a filing system for the most cherished, whereby we could save all her schoolwork. It didn't take long before she started coming home with big stacks of papers on a daily basis, clearly showing the impracticalities of such a system.

Before long, a new system took place—find a way to throw away the mounds of paper without Ella seeing it. I'm thinking an enterprising investigator could do some research and trace back the whole idea of paper recycling to parents looking for a way to get rid of daily backpack loads of school papers.

Memory hoarding may sound innocuous, but in some ways, it is much more severe than other types of hoarding. Your run-of-the-mill hoarder may be content to put their things in stacks and take comfort in that they aren't going anywhere.

Memory hoarders have no such luxury. We have to go through our collection all the time to make sure everything is still there. The serious threats to a normal hoarded collection are the relatively slow laws of entropy or the ratings needs of a reality show. Memory hoarders are in a constant fight with something deteriorating much faster and against an opponent that cannot be defeated—the failings of human memory. The harder we grasp hold of the memories, the more we realize what is slipping away, and the more our anxiety goes up.

The war will be lost. I know this, yet I fight on, knowing the value of the battles I win along the way.

There are some things that make the battle easier—tangible things to which memories are attached. Things like photographs, videos, written stories, places, and clothes. All these things can be powerful memory aids. But I think a strong argument can be made for one category to lead them all: Toys.

Our home is overloaded with toys. Way too many of them. Still, you can pick any one of them at random, and it likely has a special story or several attached to it.

So, there we were, needing to de-clutter our home, which meant aggressively culling down everything. Including toys. These wonderful tangible links to so many memories of Ella and Colby.

I really shouldn't complain about this, because Usha and Ella did all the work sorting the toys into piles. Perhaps it was because we all knew I'd be lousy at it. Regardless, when I entered the picture, everything had been sorted into piles: the storage pile, the church pile, the trash pile, the goodwill pile, and the balance that we were keeping, already neatly put away.

My job was simply to take each pile to its destination. Much of it was bagged or boxed, so I was able to disengage from most of it. One toy that was too big to box and too big to bag was also one that was hardest for me to see go.

When Ella was one, for Christmas, she got a kitchen playset. At the time, we thought it would be a little big for her, but to our surprise, on Christmas Day, she took right to it. She grabbed the pans, put them on the burners, took a spoon in hand, and went to town with make-believe cooking.

The play kitchen became an instant favorite. She made us dish after dish of her own creations and took such joy in feeding us every one of them. Like a kitchen that is the heart of a home, Ella's kitchen became the heart of the playroom. Many tea parties were catered from that kitchen. Some days, it was a full-service restaurant, with the waitress's sass of a southern diner.

When Colby came along, she became an instant patron from the start. Ella would gleefully serve her little sister, and Colby happily watched her big sister, maybe not aware of what role she was playing but definitely aware of all the fun and love going on.

When Colby began standing, she found her way around the kitchen like a natural, too. Proudly, she would stir and tend to her pots, knowing exactly what to do with the lids and the spoons. It was so much fun watching her, and I was lucky enough to catch some of it on video.

I showed that video over and over, including to her Granny Detta, who was staying with us at the time. "Isn't it amazing what she just instinctually knows? She just knew what to do. I didn't have to teach her how at all!"

Detta delighted in the video, too. But she had a simple observation that I had just flat-out missed.

"Neil, you didn't have to teach her to use the toys. How many times have you cooked dinner with Colby on your hip, with her watching you stir your soups?"

And there it was.

What we strive to teach our kids so many times results in us pounding our heads against the wall in frustration. Meanwhile, what we do without a second thought, they absorb like a sponge.

That is both a heart-warming and heart-stopping thought.

There are things I hope Ella learns from watching me, but all too often, I'm afraid the things she sees me do should come with warnings about what not to do. But that isn't the way it works, is it?

And maybe, just maybe, when I wanted to teach Ella to swim, I should have just swum and let her do the rest.

If I can put those lessons into practice, the kitchen playset may be the best educational toy I've ever used. It will certainly be one that I won't forget.

CHAPTER 35

What They Don't Tell You About Swing Sets

This essay also appeared in The Oklahoman *newspaper and is a nice follow-up to the previous chapter about educational toys and lessons.*

There is something important they don't tell you when you buy one of those wooden swing sets for your kids. Buyers want to know how much it will cost, how long it will take to put up, how long it will last, and maybe a few questions about options. And that's usually all the conversation entails. But there is something else very important to keep in mind, and they aren't going to tell you.

One day, you will have to tear it down.

That may seem obvious, but I promise you that it is worth some thought. Don't worry; I'm here to help.

When it is time for the set to come down, tip number one is to get to it before the fire ants come out. They aren't going to be happy with your demolition, and they will exact some revenge. Or maybe those devil bugs sting just for fun. Either way, pick a day too cool for them to be out.

That leads into tip number two. You are going to be at least a decade older, or in my case, a decade and a half. Odds are strong that you aren't in the shape you were in when you put it up, and you are going to get a pretty good workout. You will welcome the cooler weather. It wouldn't hurt to do a little cardio in the weeks leading up to demo day. Just saying.

And the final tip when it comes to timing is don't wait until your little girl is packing up for college when you take it down. You may think you are ready for all that, but you are going to start thinking about ponytails swaying against the movement of the swing and singing silly songs while you used to push her, and those snot bubbles will catch you by surprise.

Okay, one more tip: Do it without an audience around for reasons listed in the previous tips.

My wife had been after me for well over a year to do something about our severely listing wooden play set. She is very attached to it, too, but not so attached that she was willing to watch it collapse on a kid.

A couple of weeks ago, a windstorm took off the roof of the swing set and pressed the issue. So earlier this week, I took her down with a mind full of memories and an embarrassing amount of hard breathing.

I say "took *her* down" because we named her the day she went up—Fort Chicky Chickee. We love a good nickname around here, and her raised platform looked like a fort, and she was ruled by girls.

Two girls, to be exact–Ella and Colby.

I can still picture Ella's surprised expression when she walked into the backyard and saw Fort Chicky Chickee for the first time. Colby was less impressed until she went down the slide for the first time. Then her expression quickly caught up with her big sister's.

Of course, the fort was home to all the "usual stuff"—sliding, swinging, sandboxing, and picnicking. Ella sang many verses to "El Cerrito Place" (the Charlie Robison version, not the Kenny Chesney version) while I pushed her on the swing. I loved hearing her little voice sing that song, and she loved me pushing her, so it was a win-win.

And Colby could make her mom slide down with her a hundred times with the irresistible combination of a sweet smile and insistent eyes.

Then there was the "special stuff" with things like decorating the fort with Christmas lights, modifying her with a special bridge, and using her as a viewing platform for fireworks.

And there was the "You never expected that stuff." I sat in the upper fort while on the phone with my mom discussing Colby's funeral. The two of us trying hard to console the other and failing miserably because, well, because it's not possible. But Fort Chicky Chickee offered some comfort, some temporary refuge from the larger world. She was a tiny space where things made sense if I could just keep from thinking about the world beyond her.

A couple of years later, we made the move to Oklahoma. Ella was getting older but would probably be young enough to play on a swing set for a couple of more years. Was it worthwhile to move it?

We spent a little time on the rational aspects of moving a wooden playset to a new home, but it didn't take long, and the emotional aspects took over. Fort Chicky Chickee would be relocated!

It's a good thing, too. We didn't know it when we moved, but we, of course, would end up adding another child to the family. And adding a boy meant it would no longer belong to two girls. So, the name of the fort was changed! Just kidding. It's still Fort Chicky Chickee because it–like our family–will always be indelibly marked by Ella and Colby.

An extra slide was added. The sandbox toys became more earth-moving machinery-focused. Physics experiments of objects being thrown from the top deck became normal. Brother and sister shared chocolate malts together. Grandparents didn't act their age. Wasps attacked and provided opportunities for boy and dad to show toughness. (Boy did better than dad.)

But icy cold winters and hot dry summers took their toll. Attempts were made to increase her longevity, like some boards being replaced and painted with lemon oil to revive her cedar and repel bugs. Bolts were tightened. Supplemental fasteners added. The set with a 3-year warranty lasted 15, but just barely.

Every swing set has its own stories. Those were just some of ours.

Buyers of new swing sets will soon be living out their own stories and creating their own memories. Those memories will flood your brain on the day you take that swing set down. The pieces will get hauled away, and the memories will be all that you have left–so make lots of good ones.

If you do, you'll be blessed with some well-earned snot bubbles of your own, and you won't want it any other way.

CHAPTER 36

Biochemistry and Prayer

What I lack in understanding, I try to fill with gratitude. In this case, for getting graded on the curve. I thought my days of counting on a curve would end after college. Turns out, they had only just begun.

B ack in college, my agricultural engineering degree plan required a particular biochemistry course. For those of you who don't know, biochemistry is the study of ... well ... I don't really know.

Going into the class, I knew I was starting at a disadvantage. The biochemistry course had an organic chemistry prerequisite, but that course was not in our degree plan. But six buddies and I figured that others had made it successfully through, so we could too.

We were so serious about doing well that we showed up on the first day of class, which we had generally considered optional. Actually, we considered all the class days optional, but particularly the first day.

By the end of that first class, I had seventeen pages of notes. I wrote down everything, and I understood none of it. Intimidated, I trudged on and thought it would all start clicking soon.

The daily page count of notes dwindled rapidly from seventeen to ten to two to no notes. Eventually, I was just doodling and eventually lost the spiral and was not even bothered by it being missing.

I have absolutely zero recollection of the first exam. And it's not just the years that have faded that memory. I mean, I could have walked out of that test, and someone could have asked me for the questions, and I wouldn't have been able to help them. If it had been written in Russian, it would not have affected my performance.

When the next test rolled around, our group of buddies was going to get serious about being ready for it. The plan was to meet at my house and figure this nonsense out, no matter how long it took. Out of the seven of us, only two showed up—and I lived there!

Thirty minutes in, we determined I wasn't helping my friend, and he wasn't helping me, and the textbook was no help either, so we took a study break.

It was a five-hour study break at a place called the Dry Bean Saloon, and all seven of us participated in that part. Like men destined for a firing squad, we found fortitude and courage to face our fate with whiskey shots. While I can't recall a single biochemistry term, I do recall my tab for that evening. Nine quajolotes, the Spanish word for wild turkeys, is what we refined gentlemen called shots of Wild Turkey because it sounded more exotic and less cheap.

The second exam went like the first. Or maybe totally different. I don't know.

As for the rest of the semester, we probably just skipped straight to the break part of studying and fumbled our way through to the end with sincerity but lacking any real understanding.

And when the final grades came out, I got a B.

Thank God for curves.

Now that whole endeavor may seem like a waste, and in many

ways it probably was. However,—and I don't know this to be true, but I like to think it is—I am sure our professor has several good belly laughs over some of our answers. We probably turned a dreaded night of grading tests into a humorous one. Probably put him in a good mood and made his wife happy. Heck, we could have unknowingly saved his marriage. Or perhaps we drove him to Wild Turkey, too.

But while I didn't learn about biochemistry, it was still a learning experience with lessons I carry today. One of those lessons relates to something you might be surprised by: prayer.

No, it's not from praying to pass a test I wasn't prepared for.

It's because prayer and biochemistry share a lot in common for me. I needed to take biochemistry, and I know I need prayer. I didn't have the prerequisites for biochemistry, and I have probably missed the prerequisites to understand prayer, too, so I fumble through them both.

One drove me to drink, and the other sometimes makes me miss quajolotes.

I believe in biochemistry. I believe in prayer. But I couldn't explain either.

Now, maybe your prayer world is all squared away. I hope it is. I know it is for some, just as some are fully competent with biochemistry. But let me offer just one example of why I find it difficult.

A year or so ago, I was listening to a Sunday sermon, and the preacher relayed a story from a recent trip to Israel. He had been leading a group on a tour of holy and historical places, and the ten-day trip was nearing its end.

One of the final stops was at a site popular with visitors to make prayers for healing. As the group gathered, one of the ladies asked them to pray for her knee, which had begun giving her pain on the trip. They did as she asked, and the next day, they all flew back to their homes in the States.

The preacher reported that a week later, he received an e-mail from the woman thanking him for the wonderful trip, and she closed by telling him the good news that her knee had healed. To which the preacher summed up the story by saying that God answers our prayers for healing.

Now, maybe that prayer in that place by those people made all the difference.

Or maybe a week of lots of walking tours had aggravated her knee, and being home for a week had given it time to rest and feel better.

I don't know, and it's not for me to say.

But I do know what those words from the sermon said to me.

They said, "Neil, we know you prayed hard, and you prayed sincerely for your daughter when she was sick. We know hundreds of others joined you in your prayers. But they didn't work because you didn't say them in the right place ... or with the right people ... or the right way. If you'd only have flown to this special place, your daughter would have lived."

Now, I don't believe that. And I am not telling you what to believe about it anymore than I am trying to tell you what to believe about biochemistry.

But when you share what you know—or what you think you know—about prayer, please know that your story of inspiration may be a story of sorrow to someone else.

So how do we navigate those tricky waters?

I don't know.

What I do know is that I will keep saying my prayers of gratitude. I will keep saying my prayers for others, not in hopes of changing

God but in changing me. And I will pray not only for the protection, health, and healing of others, not because I know what I am doing but because I know that God grades on a curve, too.

CHAPTER 37

Christmas Shopping with Colby

I wrote this leading up to our first Christmas after Colby died. It was done to preserve some special memories, but it holds lessons for me, too. First among those is how my children have helped me be a better man.

One thing is for sure: Christmas shopping will never be the same. And that's okay. Colby made her mark on me and that is the best present I could have ever asked for from her.

Got your helper with ya today?"

I don't know if moms get that question. But every time a dad is out running errands with a kid, the chances of hearing that question at least once run about sixty percent. If your list of stops includes a hardware store, a good downtown cafe, or a barbershop, it's pretty much a guaranteed lock that you'll hear it. Not even the oddsmakers in Vegas would touch that bet.

I certainly got asked it a lot when I was out with Colby. And I remember when going places with my dad, people would give me a look over and ask him the same question. The difference is that Colby really was a good helper. Last year's Christmas shopping made a good example of this.

Before we get to that trip, I should explain that Colby was always fun to take on any shopping trip. She loved the different sights, the music, the fountains, the snacks, and the adventure. She also loved the attention, almost as much as I did.

It wasn't hard for her to get attention. First of all, the curly red hair was a showstopper all on its own. She heard "look at that hair" so many times, I used to joke that for a while she thought that was her name. Colby never verbally answered thanks to compliments about her hair, but usually she would slightly lean her head down to one side, blink shyly, and sweetly smile. The only thing missing was blushing cheeks. It was quite a practiced pose, but it was a genuine one, and it elicited much awing and cooing from her admirers.

Another thing that always got attention was her size. Even at the age of 2, Colby wore clothes sized for a 9- to 12-month-old. Seeing her size, most strangers assumed that she was indeed about 9 or 12 months old and, in turn, were always amazed at all the things she was doing. "Walking already!" and "I can't believe she keeps those glasses on" and "Look at her go!"

The "look at her go" comments weren't about her running speed. Colby moved with a purpose. When she saw a display window with something of interest, she was off to inspect it. She was particularly fond of an elephant display we passed once. When it caught her eye, she made a beeline for it, moving her arm like an elephant's trunk in front of her face. Stars, balloons, fountains, animals, music, plants, statues, Starbucks—all sorts of things captured her attention. And when one did, she locked in. And Daddy sometimes followed, sometimes held hands, but never, ever led.

And when she stopped, it was with a purpose, too. Namely, to more closely inspect or enjoy the type of things mentioned above. There was a beauty in watching Colby in those moments. She didn't rush her enjoyment of what the rest of us might see as small or ordinary. She studied them, analyzing them for the joy they might contain, and whatever good she saw in them, she savored fully. Or until my patience ran out.

So, there was the walking and the stopping, but the real crowd-pleaser was when she was ready to be picked up. Usually, it was because her legs needed a little rest, and occasionally it was something up ahead that made her apprehensive, but whichever the cause, the routine was the same. She would stop, turn around, and look at me. Both arms would go straight up into the air, and her head would tilt down. Can such a bold command be presented so sweetly? Colby could, and her audience melted in appreciation.

I would pick her up, and she would snuggle her head against my chest in a hug-like fashion to say thanks, then look to get her bearings again and point to where she wanted to go. Pointing with a purpose. Always a purpose. Well, almost always. Sometimes when she had worn herself out, the snuggled head would just stay on my chest, and she'd contemplate a nap.

Not a lot of actual commerce took place on these trips. Usually, we never bought anything aside from a snack or lunch, some days both. I have fond memories of a lunch at Maggiano's where we found ourselves in the midst of a midday crowd of business diners. Well-suited patrons cringed at having a small child seated in such close proximity to them. I'm sure they had visions of spaghetti sauce being flung in their direction and having to ratchet their conversation volume up over the sounds of a noisy kid. Even the waitress was edgy. It was a high noon showdown at North Park Mall, the briefcases versus the diaper bag.

Colby had shunned the public high chair by this point. Though she still used her high chair at home, at restaurants she preferred booster seats, laps, or sometimes just standing if in a booth. That day, she stood, much to the chagrin of the people in the booth behind us, nervous that this better angle put them in the potential line of fire. We ordered—one order of spaghetti, two plates, please, and a side of soup, just in case Colby was in the mood. That day, she wasn't.

Then Colby did what she always did. She found something to play with, like stickers or colors, or my iPhone, and occupied herself until the food came. Then, she would eat, though often not as much as we would like, partially due to being pickier than her big sister. The biggest challenge was that once she was done eating, Colby didn't like waiting for me to finish; she wanted me to get busy playing again. But she didn't direct her impatience at anyone but me, and it wasn't with crying or fussing. It was with insistent gestures and irresistible smiles, which she never doubted the power of, and for good reason.

Lunch went as smoothly as is possible with a two-year-old, with only one real interruption. We had to do a diaper change right as the food arrived. Timing-wise, it wasn't such a bad thing, as it gave the food a chance to cool off a bit. Logistics-wise, we encountered one obstacle: The men's room at Maggiano's was lacking a changing table.

I briefly considered giving our neighboring tables something to talk about and changing her in the booth but instead opted for standing her on the sink in a counter-changing maneuver. It's not as hard as it sounds if you have a kid who will be still and listen, and Colby was good at that.

We did catch one guy by surprise, though. As he entered the door and saw us mid-change, he startled himself, backed up a few feet, and reread the "Men" sign on the door. I always loved it when someone did that. I find that thought process amusing. You can almost hear it out loud: "Hey, that's a bald guy with a baby and a diaper bag. Oh no! Clearly, I walked into the women's restroom by mistake!"

As lunch drew to a close, others leaving the restaurant would stop by the table. "Lovely daughter you have there," and "She is so well-behaved," and "Brought your helper with you today, I see." The waitress even brought another waitress by just to see her. "Look at that hair." And pose.

Such fun.

Yes, mall trips were always a fun way to spend time, but we could make them productive, too.

Last Christmas, I set out to do some gift-buying, and not only was Colby along for the trip, but she turned out to be a big help.

Stop number one was a little one-of-a-kind jewelry shop that is one of my go-to spots. They have a nice selection of the unique and unusual. A few things there are on the high end, but most of it is every-day-type items and reasonably priced. Plus, the lady gift wraps for me.

All the sparkly things were almost sensory overload for Colby. She didn't know which way to look at first.

Making one quick lap around, we circled back to the brooches. "We need to get Granny something from you girls. Which one do you think?" I said aloud, but mostly just talking to myself. Colby reached for an owl-shaped brooch, and the selection surprised me. Granny loves birds of all makes and models, but she is particularly fond of owls; that wasn't a bad idea at all. I picked it up, looked at it, and put it back, thinking we might come back to it.

"What else do you see?" I asked while looking at some other animals that might catch her eye. My fingers pointed over other options like elephants, giraffes, and brightly colored hummingbirds. Colby's finger pointed right back to the owl. Two minutes into the trip, and already one present down. *Good start*, I thought.

Next stop, earrings. We looked over the display from one of Usha's favorite designers, and I narrowed it down to two choices, but I couldn't decide which one I liked best. Holding the two options, I asked Colby, "Which one do you like?" She pointed to the set on the left. I played with them and mixed them around, putting her selection on the right side and asked her to pick again. She picked the same set. Two gifts down and in record time.

In the kids' jewelry section, I overruled Colby's choice, opting for a Hello Kitty bracelet for Ella. She didn't fuss at me, but she should have. Ella never did wear what I picked. I wish I could remember what Colby was recommending because I would try it this year.

From jewelry, we moved on to the Apple Store. I already had been thinking of getting Usha an iPod Touch, and Colby didn't have much to say as we looked at the display model while waiting for the wizard/genius/guru or whatever the heck Apple calls their sales guys. I think she recognized its similarity to my iPhone, but she was perplexed as to why it didn't have any pictures of her and Ella on it.

She wasn't much help in getting the iPod, but when we went to select a case, her decisiveness kicked right back in. The guru pointed to a section of several dozen cases and said, "Any of these will fit." Colby scanned from top to bottom and then reached for a reddish-maroon case. I gestured to several other options, and each time Colby pointed right back to her first pick. Who was I to argue? All done at the Apple Store, and we hadn't even been shopping for fifteen minutes yet.

It was time to get something for Daddy. I had a pair of dress shoes needing new laces, so we swung by the shoe store. I found a pair similar to mine, showed them to the saleslady (assuming shoe salespeople don't insist on being called geniuses), and told her my plight. "Oh look. You brought your little helper. And look at that pretty red hair." And pose.

Next thing you know, I was walking out of there with free shoelaces. And since Colby had, for all intents and purposes, paid for them, we later wrapped them and put them under the tree from her to me. That package evoked more curiosity from Usha than any other present ever has, but we managed to keep it a secret until Christmas Day.

On a roll, we decided to try our luck at the Body Shop, home of all sorts of smell-good lotions and potions. The women in those types of shops are always helpful to bewildered husbands, usually overly so. But walk in with a girl as cute as Colby, and the entire staff is at your beck and call. Selections made, we went to the register to pay. The lady offered one or two free small sample-sized products. Instead of me picking them up, Colby did, and she inspected them with a big smile. Another saleslady saw this and offered more samples, which elicited more smiles in return. This repeated until we had almost two dozen samples of lip balm, lotion, cream, and who knows what else.

Do you think there is any chance of that happening had I been shopping by myself? Me either.

All of this happened so fast that the nice lady at the jewelry shop hadn't had time to wrap the gifts yet. I was out of places to go, so off to Starbucks for a snack and chocolate milk. There we got lots of smiles from the employees, but no one offered anything for free.

We shared a cookie and drank our drinks, after which Colby took all our trash, one piece at a time, to the trash can. Each time I'd have to lift her up so she could reach high enough to throw it away, and each time she would giggle. A lady watched this back-and-forth travel between our table and the trash can. Once the table was clear, I began gathering up our backpack, and the lady leaned over and said, "Enjoy it while you can. They grow up so fast."

I remember thinking about how difficult it had been for Colby to grow and saying to myself, "If you only knew." Now, of course, I look back and think, *If I only knew.*

At the time, none of us knew what lay ahead. Now I am forced to accept that Christmas shopping will never be the same. Christmas will never be the same. Heck, going to Starbucks isn't even the same.

I'm not the same either. In some ways, Colby left me a better man than I ever would have been without her. The truth is she helped me in many ways far beyond the trivialities of Christmas shopping. And in many ways, I'm a broken and lesser man without her.

After all, no one could expect me to be as good without my little helper.

CHAPTER 38

Flirting and Rubbing
Up on Each Other

*This is another piece reminiscing about my younger days.
In it, I contemplate how long-ago interactions can stick
with you, and some thoughts parents can use to help their
kids benefit from those interactions.*

Right off the bat, I have a confession: The title of this piece is clickbaity. The flirting is innocent, and the rubbing purely metaphorical. Admitting that upfront is surely against all protocols of clickbait-writing, but what can I say? I struggle with both writing titles and adhering to rules.

A month ago, Alex and I went to see a stage production of *To Kill a Mockingbird*. I posted a couple of pictures on Facebook and was happy to see a comment from Lissa, a friend from high school. She invited us to visit a performance at her local theater.

My first reaction was that Alex would love that. My second reaction was that it would be great to see a friend I haven't seen in ... well, let's not do the math and just say it has been a while.

My next thought was how I would explain to Alex who this person was. I would say "friend from high school," and he would be perfectly content with that answer. If you call someone a friend, that's all Alex requires. Old friend. New friend. Close friend. Never-met-in-person friend. It doesn't matter to him. Friend covers it all, and he automatically adopts them as his friend, too, and loves them all the same.

But those thoughts were enough to get my mind wandering a little deeper.

Lissa was indeed a high school friend, but not a typical friend. For starters, she was two grades above me. We were both on the swim team together. Only rarely did we bump into each other outside of school, practice, and swim trips.

The gulf between a 14-year-old freshman boy and a 16-year-old junior girl is a lot wider than two years. I didn't know much, but I knew that much. Lissa probably knew that better than I, but she didn't act that way. The senior boys had taken me under their wings, and Lissa and her friend Betsy treated me like one of the gang right away.

Now, as best I remember, both Lissa and Betsy had steady boyfriends for the two years we went to school together. That posed no problem for me. I was barely beginning to get comfortable speaking to girls. No one—them or me—would have even considered me asking one of them out in the realm of possibility.

But that didn't stop me from trying to flirt with them.

I'm sure it started out by accident. I made them laugh at something, and that made me feel good. That got my confidence up, and I would make them laugh again. Then I would step it up and say something dumb or go too far, and instead of laughing with me, they would laugh AT me. Or, worse, ignore me.

And so it went—me trying different things to get a positive reaction from them and seeing what happened. I wasn't smart enough to recognize it as a learning experience; I just became addicted to positive reinforcement. Thinking about it, our new puppy and I aren't that much different.

I am sure the lessons would have been faster had I actually realized I was learning. Instead, I was in search of the giggle, the laugh, the slight eye raise, and the blush. And unknowingly, I was learning from the things that didn't work and especially learned from the chastising from Lissa and Betsy I would get when I went too far.

I learned that funny was good. Sincerity was required. And pickup lines out of *Playboy* were meant for finding hookups, not relationships.

It was about this time in my life that I got the nickname Dwight. We were at an away meet in Lubbock, and there was another team staying at our hotel. The senior guys wanted to chat up some girls, and they let me tag along with them under one condition—that I not participate in any actual chatting. Perhaps they had seen enough of my misfires to not risk it.

So, we all sat around a lobby table, and the other guys introduced themselves with made-up names, and then they introduced me, picking the name Dwight because I listened to lots of Dwight Yoakum.

"That's Dwight. He is cool. But he doesn't say much," one of them said to the girls, then he looked at me with eyes that said, "Don't say anything."

And I didn't. I just sat there trying to look mysterious and aloof. Trying hard to look aloof pretty much guarantees you don't look aloof. Not that it mattered; it was all for fun anyway, and the other guys had great fun painting stories onto the blank canvas that I was giving them.

Word got around to the rest of the team soon about my new name and the crazy stories they had told the girls from the other team about me, and from that point on, everyone on the team called me Dwight. Even the coach.

There is an idea known as the Butterfly Effect that surmises that a butterfly flapping its wings in the Southern Hemisphere could culminate in creating a hurricane in the North Atlantic. I know enough about computer modeling to know that the origin of this idea is more about the hubris and flaws in modeling weather data than anything, but I still wholeheartedly accept that seemingly small, insignificant things can ultimately have large effects.

In thinking about my friendship with Lissa, I can't say with absolute certainty that my life would have turned out differently without her. But it might have.

Those playful, but innocent, conversations with Lissa and Betsy certainly shaped the way I interacted with girls. You can't spend that much time with girls who are smart, beautiful, and have fun personalities without coming out of it more confident and better prepared. They may not be the only reason that I have usually dated above my league, but they are certainly due some of the credit.

My wife—my smart, beautiful, fun wife—will tell you that I was annoying the night we met. I've always countered that I must have been just the right amount of annoying, because we are still together after ... well, again, let's not do the math.

The compliments I give my wife and the flirting I do with her are all true, sincere, and well-deserved. But I am thankful for old friends who gave me the confidence to approach her the first time I saw her, and I was smitten. And I appreciate the early lessons I have carried in expressing my thoughts to her. I may not be suave, but I have come a long way since my Dwight days.

And while this story may seem to be about flirting, it's really not. It's about how we carry the interactions we have with others long after those interactions are over.

Scientists tell us that when we shake hands with another person, the bacteria that are transferred can change the microbiome on our skin. Sometimes the transfer can be small and sometimes quite significant and lasting. Either way, we leave that simple interaction a little different from the way we went into it.

Thinking about my friendship with Lissa got me thinking about all the other ways I have metaphorically rubbed up on others and how that has changed in me in ways I probably haven't given much thought to. Indeed, I had never connected any mental dots between Lissa and my marriage before, but with just a little bit of reminiscing and the benefit of hindsight, it seems obvious now.

And my first takeaway from that conclusion was the benefits of "rubbing up" on good people.

Which seems true enough and even worthwhile, but in practice, you quickly run into the question of "Who is a good person?"

Am I a good person? Sometimes.

Am I a bad person? Yes, sometimes, I am that, too.

So, I have wrestled with these thoughts for the past month. In fact, this is probably the sixth time I have attempted to put them in writing, troubled each time I attempted.

Then I finally realized the trick isn't in looking for good people to rub up against. The trick is to find the good in people you rub against.

Look for the good in others, learn from it, and carry those lessons with you. And when you get the chance, thank them for it. Both of you will walk away better from it.

Thanks, Lissa.

CHAPTER 39

The Forty-Year
Fishing Story

Someone once said a boy doesn't get to be a man with clean britches. The same can be said for overcoming disappointments. Disappointment is a powerful teacher and sheltering our kids from it does no long-term favors.

I n 1982, unbeknownst to him, Henry Fonda and I bonded.

That was the year *On Golden Pond* was released. I was ten, and the movie was really aimed at an older audience. But while much of the storyline was lost on me, I did relate to Fonda's eighty-year-old character, Norman.

First of all, both of us learned the term "suck face" as a colorful way to describe kissing. And then we both used the term to make my dad laugh, because a 10-year-old saying "suck face" is almost as funny as an 80-year-old saying it.

But where I really felt a kindred spirit with Norman was when it came to fishing. Norman was tormented by one particular trout he named Walter. My tormentors were several rainbow trout in Cement

Creek, Colorado. Norman caught Walter by the end of the summer. My quest took a bit longer.

Forty years, to be exact.

In 1982, my big sister Jennifer let me tag along with her family to Colorado for a summer getaway in the mountains. Prior to that trip, my travel experience had been almost exclusively limited to a sixty-mile radius from my home and an occasional trip to Fort Worth. My sole experience with mountains was when I could fake being sick and stay home from Sunday church to watch *Grizzly Adams* with my dad.

That all changed when they squeezed me into an already packed Mazda and pointed it five hundred miles to the Northwest.

In addition to Jennifer were her husband, Dan, and their two daughters, Whitney and Jessica.

For all this to make sense, I should probably include that Jennifer was my oldest sibling, and I am the youngest, with a twenty-five-year gap (as I mentioned earlier in the book).

The gap between Dan and me was twenty-eight years. That meant our relationship wasn't the "typical" brother-in-law type. Or at least I guess it wasn't. It was my normal, so I didn't know any better.

Is it typical for one brother-in-law to yell at the other one, "Quiet the hell down so I can get some sleep"?

Prior to that Colorado trip, that seemed to be the primary focal point of my relationship with Dan —being scared of awakening the wrath of that booming baritone voice. It would be entirely unfair to give the impression that these interactions were all there was in our relationship. In fact, it was a tiny fraction of the time. But when it did happen, it was memorable.

The real truth is that I found him fascinating. He was smart, well-informed, and had an opinion on everything. An opinion he was completely unafraid to share. Only as I got older did I realize his opinions were so strong and well-thought-out because he was always willing to offer them up to scrutiny. That's a lesson well worth pondering, but not really part of this story.

Sometimes Dan's demeanor could come across as cantankerous, but Dan had a jovial side that he let shine just as loudly. Thinking about now, I suppose one of the main qualities that made Dan such a special and unique character is that he was full-throated in whatever he was doing.

On the way to Colorado, that was certainly the case as he happily sang along with Merle Haggard about rainbow stew as he drove.

I do remember the drive being both long and interesting. The length I chalk up to the anticipation of being there. I couldn't wait to see it, because my imagination couldn't render what I might possibly see.

At the same time, it was incredibly interesting, seeing foothills and mountains for the first time. With one gaze, I could see more trees than the combined number of trees I had seen in my life up to that point. I remember the car zig-zagging up the mountains on narrow winding roads with steep drop-offs that were both frightening and exhilarating.

On one of those roads, as we neared an afternoon mountain shower, Dan rolled down the windows, inhaled deeply, and yelled, "Feel that mountain air!"

The air was shockingly fresh. But the real shock to my system was Dan's unbridled joy and enthusiasm. I am from a more reserved stock and not accustomed to such openness.

The cabin we stayed at was just outside of Crested Butte. Now, forty years can fade a lot of memories. Things often aren't what you remember.

In my head, downstairs there was a small living area to the left, a table and kitchen to the right, and the back left corner had a bedroom and a bath. A ladder in the living area led to an open loft with two beds.

Outside, there were a handful of similar cabins spaced out around us and a road that curved around back that made for easy exploring. But the main feature was a creek–Cement Creek–that flowed from right to left just twenty yards from the front door. And I don't mean a trickle. There was white water rushing over rocks and a dull rumble that meant you had to speak up to hear each other. Between our cabin and the creek was a rock fire ring and chairs for cooking and relaxing.

For a boy from the arid Texas Panhandle, that creek was mesmerizing. It was so foreign to me, I might as well have been walking on the moon.

It left such an impression on me that when my eight-year-old son, Alex, and I went looking for it last week, not only was I able to drive straight to it, it was all exactly as I remembered.

Well. Almost exactly.

The cabin was much smaller than I remembered. But the floor plan and the setting were just as it had been in my mind.

And one thing about the creek had changed. There was an area that we fished that was only about a quarter of a mile downstream from the cabin. It was where the road entered the property and crossed over the creek. That crossing is a large culvert now, and I am pretty certain it used to be a bridge.

What definitely changed is that when we were there in 1982, a beaver dam downstream from the crossing had created a large pool of calm, clear water that held rainbow trout easily visible from the banks. The beaver dam was gone, and with it the calm pool that was home to those trout. My trout. My Walters.

One of Dan's many interests was fishing. And we fished for trout every day we were in Colorado.

I had only a little fishing experience and even less "catching" experience. But I was undaunted. The fishing I had done was in the dirty, desperate waters of the Texas Panhandle. Who even knew if there were fish in those lakes, and if so, where they were?

Here at Cement Creek, you could see the fish! SEE them! Right there! *What could be easier*, I thought.

My first dose of reality came with my back cast when I stuck my lure in the branches behind me. Tree branches are much easier to avoid on the banks of Lake McClellan, Texas, than the forested streams of Colorado.

That was Dan's first dose of reality, too, though the lessons were slightly different. My lesson was how easy it was to get tangled up; his lesson was how hard it was to fish when he had to keep helping me untangle my line.

Limited back casts only made the next problem more acute—inaccurate forward casts. Prior to that day, my definition of a successful cast was chunking it out as far as it would go. Aiming just meant hitting the water. There was no such thing as too far, and being off track came with no penalty.

Small stream fishing is about tight targets, and the penalties are harsh. I had zero of these skills, and if you factor in a newly required abbreviated side cast, it was less than zero.

Quickly, three things happened. Dan switched my rig from a lure to a bobber and a hook. He made me responsible for untangling my own messes and keeping my hook baited. And he confined me to fishing an area of the pool away from where he was fishing–at least that was his theoretical hope.

There are two things that help your casting accuracy. Practice is certainly important, but nothing hones your skills and focus like having to untangle your own mistakes. By the time Dan had caught our limit on the first day, I had not hooked a single fish, but I greatly improved at putting the hook where I wanted it.

Day two would be much easier–I thought.

On the bright side, there was less tangling on the next day, but not zero. The total number of fish I caught was exactly the same–zero. Dan caught the limit.

Day three, Dan limited out again, but instead of heading back to the cabin, he indulged me and suggested we hike downstream to look for a better spot. There were no well-worn trails. We were mostly bushwhacking our way downstream, fighting our way through thick branches and steep terrain with our fishing gear.

At one point, the bank got really steep and high. A narrow footpath six inches wide was cut into the side. Below us was a fifteen-foot drop into the rocky creek below. Above us was an almost vertical sheer cliff wall that rose up another fifteen feet.

Ahead of us was a long and lean green snake, none of us looking to make way for the other. I remember Dan wielding his fishing rod like a fencing sword and me multi-tasking–trying to get out of the way, trying not to fall, and trying to watch what happened. Somehow, we negotiated past each other and onward we went.

Not much further, I either lost focus or embraced my awkwardness and took a misstep. Down I slid.

My right hand was gripping my fishing pole, as I was not going to let go of it and lose my chance at catching those "easy" trout. My left hand grabbed at whatever it could and found a tree root sticking out. The same tree root had just rubbed my left side raw and bleeding.

If you have ever seen one of those cartoons where a character is saved from a fall by a branch, that was me.

Dan, who had both hands full of fishing gear, was trying to balance all of that while standing on the ledge and reaching down to grab me. He managed to do it all, and while I don't remember what he had to say about it, I do know the next day he went lake fishing without me.

He soothed my dejection by taking me to a tackle shop that afternoon, where the owner sold us some salmon eggs that he assured us the trout loved and would catch me a fish.

That brings us to day five, the morning of which started with Dan reading to me from the paper. Some guy from Texas had just been arrested in the area for having over three hundred trout in his possession. So not only had I been watching Dan catch the limit every day while I had yet to land a fish, now I had to deal with the indignity that someone out there could catch them by the hundreds!

I thought about this a lot as I fished alone at the spot between the beaver dam and the road crossing with my jar of little red salmon eggs. The man from the bait shop was right about one thing; the trout loved them. He was entirely wrong about me catching a fish with them, though.

One by one, the trout stole the eggs off my hook right in front of my eyes. Never did I get a solid hook in one. I walked home with an empty bait jar and a heart full of disappointment.

Dan fished that afternoon, and when he brought home the fish for that evening's dinner, I watched him clean them. Their bellies were full of my red salmon egg bait!

I'm not sure if there was a day six. If there was, I didn't catch any fish that day either.

As we drove away and crossed the creek, I stared down for one last look at those "easy-to- catch" trout, wondering what it would have been like to catch one of them.

There was no one way for me to know it at the time, but I grew up a lot on that trip. The best evidence I have is that my relationship with Dan had evolved. My fishing prowess–or lack thereof–wasn't the catalyst. But I think he recognized my determination, my attempts, my willingness to learn, and my nascent steps toward independence.

From that trip on, he was willing to invest more time with me. Dan taught me chess, baseball, stocks, politics, business, responsibility, history, literature, and more.

And it wasn't a one-way street. He would ask my opinion on things. Sometimes he would find my answer interesting, and more often, he would force me to defend it, leaving it either stronger or changed.

Apart from Dan, that trip also gave me a lot of confidence: confidence to explore, to dream of the bigger world, and to keep trying in the face of failure. The value of those things greatly exceeded my diminished confidence in fishing.

I've thought about those fish–my Walters–many, many, many times over the years.

Like I mentioned earlier, Alex and I were in Colorado recently. One day, we headed out to find that place, that cabin, that creek, that spot, those Walters. I guess more accurately, the descendants of those Walters.

The beaver dam was gone, as was the pool I remembered. I had every intention of redeeming myself by catching a fish there, but it's probably for the best that it was now running rapids, as it is on private property.

So instead, Alex and I camped one valley over, along another mountain stream. Mid-day fishing brought several sticks, one lost lure, and a growing dread that I would leave disappointed.

It was also a new appreciation for Dan because I realized how much harder it is to fish when you are acting as a guide for a young boy.

But that evening, I spied some pocket water that looked promising and placed a perfect cast that let my lure drift right into it, and bam. I caught a beautiful brown trout.

Catching a fish would make all the difference–I thought.

I was wrong.

In his poem "If", Kipling tells us a man should be able to meet with triumph and disaster and treat both impostors the same (Kipling, lines 11–12). The triumph of my catch on this trip and the disaster of not when I was ten were both impostors. Holding that fish, I was elated, but also keenly aware that nothing had really changed.

What the trip was before, it still was.

Like Norman, I released my Walter, because it wasn't really about catching a fish. It was about knowing I could.

Even more so, it was about the experiences that Alex and I were having along the way. Forty years from now, who knows what he will remember, what lessons he will realize he learned.

And for whatever years I have left, who knows what I will learn, too. My recent lesson serves as a good example. Sure, if we never caught fish, we probably would not keep doing it. But it's still not about the fish.

It's the pursuit and what happens along the way.

CHAPTER 40

Bill

*Probably the best daddy example I ever had was my brother,
Bill. This was the speech I gave at his funeral in the church
that I grew up in.*

I've never been on this side of this particular pulpit before.

Forty-five years ago, I was in this church for the first time. The
pews didn't have cushions back then. The carpet was orange. I sat
right there in the second row next to my mom.

That clock back on the wall. That's new. I can tell because I used
to stare at the old one, begging it to tick faster.

Mom hoped one day I would grow up to be a preacher. Lucky
for the congregation here, that didn't happen.

Lucky for my mom and the rest of the congregation, her eldest
son, Bill Turner, would preach here many times.

I don't know that Bill aspired to preach. Probably not. But that
didn't matter; it needed to be done, and he stepped up.

Grass needed mowing. Bill stepped up.

Books need to be kept. Bill stepped up.

Something needed fixing. Bill stepped up.

The original preacher at this church would often end his sermons by asking us all to ask ourselves, "What kind of church would this church be if every member were just like me?"

Any church full of members like Bill Turner would be phenomenal.

Bill didn't just step up for church. He stepped up for friends, coworkers, neighbors–and of course, family.

We could spend a long, long time recounting those stories. And I hope you all spend time sharing some of your favorite ones. As for me, well, I had a hard time deciding what to say.

I could tell you about the time I "helped" him shingle his roof.

I could tell you about the time I "helped" him hang sheet rock.

However, I can't tell you about "helping" him build a bay window in his living room. He didn't tell me about that project until it was over. He may have had a lot of patience, but he wasn't a complete glutton for punishment.

I tested that patience a lot.

Back when Lake McClellan was an actual lake, Bill took me camping. I got lost in the night walking to the restroom, and he had to find me.

Bill took me to play golf, though he spent more time in the rough with me than getting to play himself. I lost a couple of hundred of his golf balls, at least.

Sometimes Bill and I were 42 partners. I was too busy being a cutup to pay attention to who was playing what. Bill knew what was in everyone's hand, 2 or 3 dominoes in.

Bill took me on a family vacation all the way to the Smoky Mountains, where he endured too much of me trying to be funny and too little of me showing appreciation.

Bill helped me fix my cars–and by help, I mean he did it and I watched.

He put up a basketball goal in his driveway, just so I could practice. I didn't make the team. I don't roof my own house or hang sheet rock. And it's best we don't discuss my golf game here in the Lord's House.

As a kid, when you grow up with a person like Bill always in your life, you don't know how rare it is. You don't understand how much you have to appreciate and how you should be soaking those lessons in.

I squandered a lot of good learning opportunities.

Nevertheless, I stand before you today a better man because of my brother, Bill.

I'm a better man than I would have been because he taught me a lesson too great to ignore. He didn't use words. He taught by example. He taught me about being a father ... a daddy. Bill is one of the all-time great daddies.

I've heard my whole life that Bill really wanted a son. You sure couldn't tell that from watching him adore his girls. He was a proud dad.

So, when I had girls, I had a great template to follow. Love them a lot, yell at them once in a while to keep them on their toes, be a good listener, and enjoy the journey.

And maybe the biggest key of all–play like a kid. If you saw the slideshow, you saw that Bill's biggest smiles were when he was playing with kids. And the kids loved it.

All kids. His kids, their kids, his siblings, their kids, strangers' kids– it didn't matter. Bill had a magic touch with kids.

So, when I had a boy, Bill gave me a toolkit for that, too. It's not way different than the girl template ... maybe less, letting them put ribbons in your hair and a little louder when you need to yell.

There is a popular phrase in parenting and child therapy circles these days. They say to "meet the child where they are." That phrase never made sense to me until I started writing this speech. That sure seems to describe Bill.

Maybe that isn't exactly what they mean; if it's not, it should be.

Bill, as a kid, I didn't fully appreciate just how rare and special you are. I certainly do now.

Thank you, brother. You will be missed.

CHAPTER 41

Parenting Lessons From a Whispering Cowboy

This story is about a different Bill, not my brother. And I don't just mean a different person. He was a different kind of person. Having left home at the age of nine to make his own way in this world, he had a hardness about him. But if you were willing to work hard, he made room for you. Every great once in a while, he might even share a laugh with you. When he did, you knew it was genuine.

It started when I was fifteen and had my hardship driver's license. The calls would come at 5:30 a.m.

You never knew when or how often. I'd answer with a hello, knowing he was the only one to call at that time.

"Working?" Bill would ask.

That's it. Just one word. What it meant was, "I have day work for you today if you are okay with skipping school. So, are you going to school or coming to work?"

Not once did I pick school.

Bill was part of a farming and ranching operation, and he lived a few miles away from us. There was always work to be done.

"I'm working. What are we doing today?"

"We start at 6:15. Be here at 6:00 if you want breakfast." Bill gave me the important information, and he ignored the rest.

As a teenager, I never ate breakfast. But on day work days, you never knew when lunch would be. There would be lunch for sure. You just didn't know when, so eating breakfast was a good idea. And if you got there right at 6:00, you could be sure breakfast would be half over.

There were actually a lot of things you didn't know when you showed up for work. You didn't know if you would be hauling hay, working cows, mending fence, or something else. You didn't know if you'd be done by noon or finishing up in the dark.

What you did know was that you would be paid fifty dollars. That was the rate whether the day was short or long and whether the work was easy or hard.

I did day work for others, too. They all planned ahead and worked pay out by the job or hour.

None of them let me skip school to do it, except my dad, who also waited until the morning to ask me and also had a set rate. His rate was $0 a day.

I still picked work over school every time.

I always like the simplicity of Bill's system, not that we ever discussed it or negotiated anything. It's just the way it was. We both knew what to expect. He trusted me to work hard, even if not always working smart. I trusted him to be a good boss. As far as I know, neither of us had any complaints.

By now, you have figured out Bill was a man of few words. Not only that, but his speaking voice was barely above that of a whisper. In the best situations, you had to strain a bit to hear him, or you'd miss it. And if you missed it, you missed it.

I only remember him repeating himself once.

Add in some engine noise or something, and it was a real challenge. Take hauling hay, for instance. Usually, Bill would be driving through the field, and the rest of us would be loading the trailer. One or two of us would be walking the field and tossing bales to someone on the trailer, stacking them.

We would rotate around from time to time, including Bill.

I'm not sure why Bill, being the boss who was paying us, would do some of the harder parts, too. Maybe he wanted to stretch his muscles, or show us that he still could do it, or probably show us that he could do it better.

A lot of things about Bill were just an enigma.

What I did know was that when I was the stacker, I didn't want Bill swapping out with me. The stacker communicates with the truck driver, telling him to slow, stop, or go. You want the trailer being loaded to match the pace with the guys throwing bales up there, so the stacker acts as sort of a traffic controller.

Bill spoke so dadgum quiet that hearing him say "hep" or "haw" was the hardest task of the entire day. Inevitably, I would be going when I should be stopping or stopped when I should be going.

I'm sure it was a frustrating experience for Bill, too. I was never the driver too often or for too long. Frustrations aside, it did teach us to try and focus on what was important and filter out the noise. We dang sure didn't seek out more noise, like attempting to play the radio.

Working cattle with Bill was better, though I knew a lot less about cattle than hauling hay. I was green then and even greener now. But when I wasn't sure what to do, I could look right at him for instructions. This exchange didn't take any words, so hearing wasn't an issue. I'd look at him, lost, and he would point with his eyes. From there, even if I were messing up, at least I'd be messing up in the right place.

My strongest memory of working with Bill actually came from a certain lunch. We had been working cows all morning on a ranch I had never been on, and to whom it belonged, I have no idea. Those were just more details that didn't matter.

It must have been around Skellytown, because we stopped at a cafe there for lunch. I ordered the chicken-fried steak and sat at the end of the table with a buddy of mine, through whom I had actually met Bill. We talked teenage boy stuff. The others were grown men and chatted with each other as we all waited for the food.

At some point, another set of men came into the cafe and sat. Bill, who was always quiet, got completely silent and stared intently at the table of other men. I had no idea what it meant, but it was noticeable—not just by me, but by everyone. We all kept talking, just quieter and with one eye on Bill.

The food came out, and we all started to eat. All of us except Bill. His napkin and silverware sat in their original spots; his plate was untouched. Paying no one else any mind, he stood from his chair and walked over to the other table.

I went motionless, my mashed potato loaded fork suddenly stopped frozen in space between my plate and my mouth.

My eyes were locked on Bill, and I assume everybody else's were, too. I wasn't looking at them, but it must have paused everyone's conversation because I could hear Bill speak to one of the men at the table. His volume was at the same quiet setting as usual.

"Stand up," Bill said.

"Bill, I don't want any trouble." His voice was a good bit louder than Bill's and a little shaky.

"Stand up"—that being the only time he repeated himself that I can ever remember.

"I'm not gonna..."

Bill grabbed a left handful of the man's shirt just below his neck and began lifting him to his feet, but his right hand punched him right back down into his seat. A second punch to his jaw put him out of his chair and sprawled him onto the floor face down.

Bill bent over and, with one hand on the man's belt and the other grabbing his collar, I knew that man was about to be thrown through the plate-glass window onto the main street. If the shirt had not torn, that very well may have happened.

Instead, Bill had to regrip, and about that same time, an older lady came storming out from the kitchen, swinging a broom, yelling, "Get out! Get out! All of you get out!"

She wasn't just aiming for Bill. She was clearing out all of us, and the broom was making contact as she went.

My mostly uneaten chicken-fried steak regained my attention, and I tried to time a few more fast bites as she circled wide of me. She may have been old, but she was quick, and I feel real confident saying that was not her first time to swing a broom at a man. I did manage to get out the door with a biscuit in hand.

To this day, I still eat fast when I sense tension at the table.

We were all on the sidewalk pretty quickly after that, hearts racing and chattering with excitement.

Well, not all of us. Bill made his way to the driver's door as calmly as if he had just collected his mail at the post office. He looked at my buddy and me and said, "Get in," with the tone as if he were already tired of waiting for us.

We got in the truck, looking at each other wide-eyed. Our heads were full of questions like who was that, what was it about, and were we going to stop for lunch somewhere else? But we dared not ask, so we just waited for the answers to come on their own. Turns out the only answer we got was to the last question, and that answer was no.

Later, we asked one of the other guys if he knew what it was all about. All he said was it's best to stay out of others' business. I took that as the punched fella had wrongly gotten into Bill's business. Later, I realized he could have been telling us to stay out of it. Then I decided whichever way he meant it, both meanings were probably right.

So, what did Bill teach me about parenting? Obviously, he did not pass along his brevity to me. He may have been a man of few words, but that lesson has yet to take hold.

I've been following several parenting groups for a while. A few are autism parent support groups. Then there are several schooling groups—homeschooling, road-schooling, public schooling, wild-schooling, unschooling, and probably a couple I can't remember now.

There are some good ideas and inspiration to be found in those groups. Sometimes there is the opportunity to be helpful to someone else. A few funny things get posted. And to be sure, most of it is a lot of nothing that is neither here nor there.

But one very common theme is asking how to handle criticism or disapproval from others. Or a closely related variation is coping with self-doubt stirred up by the opinions of others.

To be honest, it's a little painful to see. I don't care what path you take or choices you make; someone is going to think it's the wrong thing. And not just a tiny minority, but a healthy percentage won't agree with you.

I think about that pretty often, and for some reason, lately, I also thought of that old, whispering cowboy, Bill.

First of all, if you find something that works for you, don't worry so much about what others are doing or how they do it. Plenty of folks could point out flaws and potential problems with how he managed and paid us. Who cares? It worked for him and worked for us.

Second of all, there is a lot of noise out there. This is especially true in the realm of advice, which is often much more about validating the choices of the advice giver than it is about the edification of the receiver. If you can't tune out the noise, you are going to miss the whispers—those subtle signs that things are on track or advanced warnings that things may be swerving.

The communication you get from your kids and spouse may not be as loud and may even be unspoken, but its value far exceeds that of that one (or more) PTA parent telling everyone what she would do in your shoes.

And speaking of those busybody parents, we should all endeavor to do a better job of minding our own business. Sure, we are going to have opinions on the parenting we see going on around us.

We should pray for enough wisdom and humility to know that we know far less about others' full situations to pass judgment from a high horse. We may not be at risk of flying through a plate-glass window, but that doesn't mean we don't deserve it sometimes. Well, maybe not that, but at least a broom to the head.

Finally, I don't think Bill set out to teach me any of those things. Or maybe he did. Who knows? He was a little weird and a damn hard read.

But whatever I learned from Bill, I didn't learn from listening. I learned by watching.

If Bill were a bigger talker, I would have learned a lot less. Read that again. It may be the only valuable thing in this whole piece.

Our kids don't learn from our long lectures. I know this, yet I am still highly prone to delivering them. It's a hard habit for me to break.

Hopefully, I am giving them some better lessons by my actions.

And if nothing else, I hope they can see that I am trying to do just that, even if I am falling woefully short some days. Maybe most days.

But hey—at least I'm messing up in the right place.

CHAPTER 42

Surprise Canned Goods and Roadkill

My parents were children of the Great Depression. They would shake their heads at my lack of frugality, but their experiences did leave an indelible mark of admiration and gratitude in me.

If you had your pick, you would go grocery shopping with Dad instead of Mom.

But there was no picking. Life was chaotic, and whichever parent had the time to shop was the one who went. Dad would take me along "to help," which was code for getting me out of the house to give Mom a break. Mom would take me when there was nobody else to leave me at home with.

To be clear, I was always happy to go. Both my parents were good people, and in a time without iPads or on-demand kids' shows, the grocery store was exciting. Okay. Maybe not exciting. But it was something to do.

The reason Dad was the better pick is that he had a sweet tooth and a soft spot for kids. That meant you could always talk him into a dessert of some kind. Some Little Debbies, a box—yes, box—of ice cream, or a chocolate cake.

Mom's tooth was not as sweet, and though she loved her kids, soft was never an adjective she was burdened by. That's not to say she would never indulge us with sweet treats. They were just on her terms. Her terms did not include yielding to begging from a seven-year-old.

To understand the rest of this story, you need to know a couple of things.

Mom and Dad were both kids during the Great Depression, and that experience marked them for life. This was especially true of Mom, who grew up in Chicago. Dad grew up on a farm in Texas, and that had some built-in food advantages.

The other thing to know is that our household was of modest means; that is code for we were poor, at least from an income perspective.

That meant Mom was always trying to stretch a nickel into a dime. This was certainly the case at Frank's Grocery Store, where there were no Little Debbies to be had on her watch.

But she was creative and found other ways to make things fun. A classic was a wire bin on the canned food aisle that would hold the marked-down cans. These were cans that had lost their labels, and the contents were a mystery. They were also only 10 cents, as opposed to the usual 25 cents.

It was a heck of a deal. Mom was saving money, and she got to entertain me by letting me pick out which cans to put in our cart.

The first time I played the game was quick. All the cans looked the same, so I just grabbed a few and put them in the cart.

That night, she let me pick one of them to be a part of dinner. It all seemed pretty simple. We just needed to open it up and see what it would be. Corn? Carrots? New potatoes? Peas would be okay. Baked beans would be a home run. It's all fun, right? The surprise was the fun.

You know what's not fun? Beets.

You know what wasn't fun the next night? Spinach.

You know what none of the cans contained? Corn, carrots, new potatoes, baked beans, or even peas.

I have no doubt Mom got even more of her money's worth at our future stops at the markdown bin. I'm sure she was tickled watching me shake the cans next to my ear, trying to hear clues. Or counting the ridges on the cans, trying to compare them to the ones on the shelf with labels. Then, finally, holding it next to my chest and seeing which ones felt luckiest.

This memory came to mind on my own recent grocery shopping trip. As I went down the aisle, it occurred to me that I never see those markdown bins with unlabeled cans anymore. It's probably against the law to sell anything without a label, which led me to wonder what happens to all the cans that have labels that fall off.

You are probably ahead of me at this point, but the next thought was, man, Frank sure had a lot of labels fall off. Shortly after that, it washed over me.

"Labels that fell off" was code for moving old inventory that hadn't sold. You know what doesn't sell fast? Beets. Spinach. Collards. Waxed beans.

That Frank. He was good at marketing.

Mom had some natural marketing in her, too. She talked Frank into letting her take the old produce he was throwing out to feed to our animals. We'd get to park in the back and go through the big gray Rubbermaid barrel that had all the produce culled for the day.

Most places have made that illegal now, too.

The animals that we had varied over the years: rabbits, chickens, pigs, and cows, to name a few. Many of which were part of our food supply. We usually had an abundance of eggs, fresh milk, and homemade butter.

Then there was the year Dad took a liking to Cornish hens, and Mom did the math on how much they cost. The next thing you know, she ordered 200 Cornish hen chicks in the mail, and when they matured, we ended up eating them 3 times a week. Mom never had to worry about Dad spending extra on Cornish hens again.

But before those produce scraps ever got fed to the animals, Mom pulled out anything still fit for human consumption. A potato could have a bad spot, but the good part was going to go into hash.

There are plenty more stories involving frugality and food.

When my school had a canned food drive, I took it as an opportunity to unload some of those beets and spinach. Mom put a stop to that and swapped those cans out for corn and baked beans, along with a lecture about dignity and how to treat those less fortunate.

Then there were the surprise stops and excitement—true excitement—when Mom would let me pick out Hostess treats at the day-old bread store, which was more aptly named the "past the best by date store."

There was her advice when I left for college. It wasn't about grades or girls. It was "get a job in a restaurant and you won't go hungry."

She hated it when I told people the guinea hen roadkill story because she felt like I was picking on her; I tell it now out of admiration.

Dad and I were putting a roof on the hay barn when an oil field truck came barreling down our road. Mom kept a flock of guinea hens, and that truck clipped one and killed it. My mom happened to see it and walked out to the road, looked at it, then looked over both shoulders to see if anybody was watching. She didn't think to look up high, so she didn't see us on the hay barn.

"What's she doing?" I asked Dad.

"Working on dinner, and if you are smart, you'll be quiet about it."

I didn't follow his advice, and that night when she served roasted guinea, I protested, telling her I knew where she got it, and I wasn't going to eat it. After dinner, she said fine, but she wasn't cooking anything again until the guinea was all gone.

Microwaved leftover guinea ain't too bad.

When I was very young, frugality was my normal. I didn't think anything of it. As I got to my teenage years, I bristled at it, feeling "less than" because of it. In my young adult years, I took false pride in it, thinking I had overcome some real adversity.

Now I have found admiration in it.

Mom's frugality is what let her squirrel away money to do some special things. Things like driving all the way to Amarillo to buy me a black forest cake for my birthday. Or take me to a Benihana's Japanese Steakhouse when I was eleven, where I learned to use chopsticks. Or let me buy a frozen duck so that I could try to make duck à l'orange.

It was a disaster. But that didn't stop her from letting me experiment with other things in the kitchen.

But these memories also fill me with another emotion: Gratitude.

I never went hungry. I never worried about not having food. Sometimes we ate things I didn't care for, but I was never too long between things I loved or special treats. And she gave me an appreciation for trying new foods.

Maybe when you read through this, you were surprised by some things. Maybe you could relate. Maybe you had it worse.

But if we are just comparing our experiences with each other, we are missing so much context.

We are the luckiest people in all of human existence. We eat better and live better than the richest kings and queens of history of even 150 years ago.

It's humbling and worth spending some time thinking about and appreciating the things that got us here. The fastest route to losing our way is to lose our gratitude.

I guess there were some good surprises in those unlabeled cans after all.

CHAPTER 43

Oprah and Pineapples

This story was written well before the last chapter, but it makes sense to include it here.

Oprah has added stress to my life. I am not alone. Men everywhere can relate.

The particular instance that I am referring to is from circa 2005. As a part of some Oprah show that my mom was watching, some lady shared a story about how she asked all her kids to write her a letter. The letter was to say one thing the child really liked or admired about their mom. The idea was that the lady would keep them in a special–froophy, no doubt–box, and she could read them whenever the whimsy hit her.

After seeing this show, Mom decided that was what she wanted for Christmas. She wanted each of us to write her a letter that she could keep in a special box, and the subject of the letter was supposed to be one thing we liked about her.

There was one major problem with this. I like doing nice things for people, but I don't like being told to do nice things. So, I didn't write it.

Then a year went by, and I thought about writing it again, but I wasn't sure what one thing I should pick, and I was still a little sideways about being told what to do. Add being stubborn to my list of many flaws. Mom would agree, but she would concede that I came by it honestly.

Then another year went by, and I kept thinking, *I need to do that someday.*

Another year or two of good intentions went by with no results to show for it.

Then in 2010, I sat down and wrote this letter. I didn't play by the rules, and I didn't pick just one thing I liked about her. Instead, I shared a story that represented a common theme throughout my childhood and how those things stuck with me.

Here is that letter.

Pineapples

When I was in the first grade, most days, I ate school lunches. But some days, you made my lunch, and it wasn't unusual for you to pack something a little extra special. One of those days, you packed a small blue-and-white Thermos with cold, fresh pineapple in my lunchbox.

I remember that you had cubed it, lightly sugared it to make sure it was sweet, and chilled it the night before in the refrigerator. At the time, I am sure I was completely unaware of the trouble you went to in even getting a fresh pineapple. I'm sure I still don't fully know, but I have my guesses. It probably involved you skipping buying something you wanted or finding a way to earn a few extra dollars somewhere. One way or another, some sacrifice was involved because you wanted to make my day a little extra special with some fresh pineapple.

When lunchtime came around, the first thing I did was take out that Thermos and try and open it up. But I couldn't. The screw lid was too tight for me. So, I got up from my table and took it over to Mrs. Swope and asked her for help.

When she opened it for me, she looked at what was inside and said, "Wow. Whoever did all this for you sure went to a lot of trouble. She must think you are pretty special."

I never eat pineapple without thinking of that day.

And I never forget Mrs. Swope's words when I think about all you have done for me.

Thank you for the pineapple and for the countless other things you did for me, just like it.

Love,
*Neil**

---

* Mom passed away a couple of years later. She was eighty-seven. And even if Oprah hadn't made my life harder, I'm sure Mom knew how much her kids loved her. But it's nice to know that when she had those moments of doubt, she had a box of letters to remind her.

CHAPTER 44

They Don't Write Love Songs About People Like Us

Like most social media users, my posts about my life tend to be positive stories. Complaining doesn't seem helpful, and I am cautious to never give my kids the impression that they are anything less than a blessing to me. Even losing Colby, as painful as that was, the time I had with her was worth it many times over.

Still, there is a reality to being a special needs family. Omitting that is an injustice to what they go through, and so many of them have challenges far greater than I do. This piece was written in hopes of acknowledging that and honoring them.

I've been back in the woodshop recently. I enjoy it. It gives me a creative outlet, and it is fulfilling when I get to see a project completed. Perhaps best of all, there are periods of uninterrupted time to ponder.

I play music while I am working. I'm normally a podcast kind of guy, but shop noise makes that too hard. Instead, I just put the music on random. Some songs get drowned out; some don't.

A few days ago, the songs that made it through were just one love song after another. There was new love, rekindled love, newfound appreciation love, complicated love, jealous love, taking a risk love, uncertain love, coming undone love, come back love, growing old together love … all kinds of love, it seemed.

But somewhere in the mindless droning of the sander, something occurred to me. They don't write love songs about people like us.

That is not saying that some of the love songs don't resonate with the emotions and thoughts I have about my wife, both now and over the years. It's not hard for me to remember those heart-fluttering, thrilling, and scary early days. And I still daydream of ways of making her smile and someday seeing her eyes sparkle in the Paris spring.

Those things apply. Those things are important. But those things don't tell the whole story. They don't tell our story.

See, our story involves three wonderful and deeply cherished children who happen to have some special circumstances. The youngest has autism. The middle child passed away from a rare genetic condition. And the oldest has had to cope with the impact of those things on her and on our family.

Which brings us back to music. It's one thing to sing about how heavenly love feels. Where are the songs about when your autistic child is hours deep into a meltdown, you are lost at what to do next, frustrated, tired, and scared, wondering if things will ever get better?

There is a moment when the rest of life's juggling has crashed to the floor, and all you feel is failure. Then your spouse places a hand on your back, and that simple act gives you the courage to go on one more minute. Then one more. Then, sometime in the next 10 to 120 minutes, things take a turn for the better, and slowly, you start picking up the pieces.

I am not knocking that "lying here next to you feels like heaven" feeling. But feeling in love in those times is easy. Living out your love when things feel like they are going to hell—now that is something special.

The relationship stresses are immense. Date nights are rare. Getaway weekends are mythical lore. Heck, a short, uninterrupted conversation seems an impossibility most times. Yet, acknowledging that runs the real risk of guilt and misinterpretation.

We had some unwelcome practice before our youngest was born. As I mentioned, we lost a child. She was two, and it was crushing. But our eldest gave us a reason to carry on, and many times she actually did the carrying. It was both remarkable and, at the same time, incredibly unfair to her, which is a story for another time.

They don't write love songs about picking out music together for your daughter's funeral. There aren't catchy lyrics about the trust and confidence it takes in your relationship to give your spouse space to grieve. Nobody sings about the tearful hugs you give each other when hanging that empty Christmas stocking. A kiss under the lights of the Eiffel Tower would be sweet, but it can't touch the level of love it takes to get through the tragedy of child death.

If that were the sum total of woodshop thoughts from that day, all of this would have stayed between me and the sander.

But something else happened on that day. I had shared some stories about being a stay-at-home dad and adventure-schooling Alex. I got some comments about how wonderful our situation is and how lucky I am. Let me assure you, it is and I am. I am blessed with an incredible wife, great children, and circumstances that allow us to put a high priority on things we think need a high priority.

I truly can't ask for more, and I want no one to feel sorry for me.

But we are far from the only family with these types of challenges. Many have far bigger challenges. I had the realization that when I share the great stuff, with little mention of the hard stuff, I'm being unfair to those parents. My incomplete portrayal of how things are should not discount the real problems that they battle every day.

Sometimes I see a mom or dad at their wits' end, and I know the positive stories I share aren't inspiring at that point. They probably feel like another brick stacked on them as they try to tread water.

I can't take away the relationship challenges that special needs families face. I certainly can't write a love song to celebrate them. After all, there are not a lot of great rhyming words for autism or bereaved.

But I decided I could share these thoughts and hope that someone out there feels a little less alone. Or, better yet, that those around them understand a little better.

Maybe I could even find something helpful to end this story with…

There is a story about a young woman asking her grandmother about the secret to a long marriage. The grandmother puts it wisely and succinctly: "We never hated each other on the same day."

I will not allow myself the hubris to pontificate on long marriages, but I will unashamedly steal the crux of that wisdom to share a secret about our marriage so far. We have never fallen apart at the same time. When one of us is crashing, the other is rescuing.

Now someone ask Blake Shelton to put a tune to that.

CHAPTER 45

What Wild Kids, My Dad, Ducks, & Pinto Beans on a Cold Day Have in Common

It wasn't until I put this book together that I realized how much I write about food. But this really isn't about food; it's about community.

This is a story about a favorite restaurant of mine. It's known for serving home-cooking, but my fondness for it goes beyond just the cooking part. It provides other feelings of home, too. But before I explain any further, let me set the stage with another story.

One table away from us at lunch today sat a family with two young boys. Over the course of the meal, I could hear the familiar sounds of keeping young children entertained at a sit-down restaurant. This included a mix of some admonitions, some adoration, some instructions, and some giggles.

Near the end of the meal, when the kid's boredom was at its highest and the parents' patience at its lowest, the mom said, "Stop that.

We are at a restaurant," which was soon followed by the sound of a tipping glass and spilling water.

The exasperated dad declared half-wistfully, half-apologetically to those nearby, "I knew we should have gone to McDonald's."

Maybe it's because I have walked in his water-soaked shoes, but he certainly did not owe me an apology. To the contrary, I had been eavesdropping on their table banter off and on and had been appreciating it for the memories it brought to mind and in admiration for what the parents were teaching their kids.

But when your kids are throwing rice by tiny fistfuls, nobody ever comes up to and says, "I really admire what you are doing here." Instead, you get the look from one cranky person, and suddenly it feels like the whole restaurant is giving you the evil eye. Sometimes you get the preemptive evil eye just when walking into a restaurant with a kid!

It's not always that way, of course. I have been complimented on my girls' behavior at a restaurant. An older lady approached our table with a vexed look that didn't match the kindness of the words she had to say. In a somewhat hushed tone, she said, "I just had to tell you how well-behaved your girls are."

I was a little surprised by the comment but thanked her. As she turned to walk away, the vexed expression explained itself when she fussed a whole lot louder, "I wish more kids knew how to behave when they go out to eat."

Thinking back, her actions were probably a whole lot less about saying something nice about Colby and Ella than making a point to some other patrons who had not met her standards. But either way, the lady was missing the point. Kids don't magically know how to behave in a restaurant, nor can you teach them at home.

They learn by doing, and you go through a lot of screams, spills, and fork-catapulted peas before you get your first compliment from a stranger on their good behavior. And even after that, there are still plenty of talks about what is appropriate for a restaurant, pleas to "stop that," and embarrassment that the whole restaurant is looking at you.

For the record, I'm still waiting for the second compliment on the restaurant behavior of my offspring. Some days, it is clearly much further away than others.

I'm sure you are wondering what all of this has to do with one of my favorite restaurants, which I began this story with. Well, I'll tell you.

Sometimes you just want to go eat at a comfortable place. For the exasperated dad, it was McDonald's. For me, it's a place with certain home-like qualities. It's going to eat at Mrs. Donna's Cafe, better known to the rest of the area as Old Timer's Restaurant on the square in downtown Rockwall.

Mrs. Donna is the owner and cook at Old Timer's. Once Ella was old enough to talk, she began calling it Mrs. Donna's Cafe, and around our house, the name stuck.

My first trip to Old Timer's was well before I had kids. It was a cold March day in 2001, and we had just moved to Rowlett. I drove the bridge across the angry lake and into Rockwall looking for a new place to try for lunch, and Highway 66 put me right on the square where Old Timer's caught my eye.

I don't know what I was in the mood for that day or what I was seeking, but once I saw the place, I thought to myself, *That is my dad's kind of restaurant.* I had lost my dad about five weeks prior, and I knew I had to give this place a shot. I thought I was going in for food, but what I found was comfort.

Now, don't get me wrong. The food was great. I still remember ordering the pinto beans. Mrs. Donna's pinto beans are good any-time, but especially on a cold day like that one.

But the place was truly like my dad's choice diners, right down to the waitresses who worked with a friendly sass that they ratcheted up or down to fit the temperament of their various regulars. And even though I wasn't a regular yet, I felt comfortable right away.

I thought a lot about my dad that day. I still do when I eat there. I think about the different places we had stopped for lunch and the stories that went along with them. I recalled my fascination with a cafe a hundred miles from home, knowing my dad by name. About how he knew what he wanted to order without looking at the menu. Even about some of the talks we had about how to behave in a restaurant.

I did become a regular and, over the years, carried many people along with me to eat there. Some liked it a lot; some left wondering why I had made such a fuss over it. That's okay, as I'm getting old enough to realize it's alright that people like different things.

My mom liked it. Moms always worry about their sons eating enough and the things they approve of, so she was always pleased with what she saw there. One day, while my mom was staying with us, I had a dentist appointment, and she wanted to tag along to get out of the house. We had breakfast at Old Timer's, and I left her on the square to shop at the antiques stores and quilt shop while I went to the dentist.

When my appointment was over, I went back to the square and found her still at Old Timer's, sitting in a booth, reading a book. It turns out none of the shops were open that early, and she had nowhere else to go but back to the restaurant. Going in to get her, Mrs. Donna must have felt sorry for my abandoned-looking mom.

She wagged her finger at me and said, "You can come here and you can bring your mom here, but you have to take her with you when you go!" I started to explain, but quickly saw it was going nowhere, especially with my mom laughing with glee at getting taken to task by someone else. Thirty-some-odd years old, and I was still apparently in need of learning proper restaurant behavior.

Along the way, Ella entered our lives, and three and a half years later, Colby, too. Each one of them going from carriers, to laps, to high chairs, to booster seats in the booths of Old Timer's. The waitresses and Mrs. Donna regularly checking on them, offering compliments and praise. I remember the girls getting a lot of attention there, but I don't ever recall being self-conscious about their cries or the occasional fit. I credit that to Mrs. Donna herself and for the community atmosphere she creates there. You don't feel among strangers there; you feel among neighbors and friends.

Ella is a big fan of Mrs. Donna and her cafe, as you can tell by her renaming of it. The two hit it off early, largely in part to some natural grandmother qualities Mrs. Donna has about her. Over the years, it hasn't hurt that, on occasion, Mrs. Donna will break out some ice cream and serve it to Ella for an impromptu dessert. She would ask, "If it was okay with Dad," as she scooped and slid the bowl over to Ella, but it was one of those times you didn't dare say no. You wouldn't want to anyway because of the joy they both shared in turning an ordinary moment into a special one.

But it's the memories of Colby there that are the sweetest for me. It was in Mrs. Donna's that Colby first used a booster seat. From that moment on, having made up her mind that she was a big girl, I don't think she ever sat in a high chair at a restaurant again.

Of course, she wasn't big in size at all. Which meant she could sit on the table itself, and at times she did that, too. Not exactly restaurant manners, but never a problem at Mrs. Donna's.

During this time, Colby was really getting her legs going and test-
ing her independence, and Old Timer's was a great place for that. She
would explore the stool seats at the counter and walk to the other
side of the restaurant to stare at the cars on the street from the large
plate-glass window.

Mrs. Donna and the patrons let her have the run of the place, all
watching her with looks of encouragement rather than judgment.

Then, Colby would come back to the booth, grab my hand, and
beckon me to follow her. She would lead me to the front door, where
she would reach for me to pick her up. I would, and then she would
point to the mounted duck and say to me, "Ack! Ack!"

Her expectant smile would wait for me to reply, "Quack! Quack!"
when it would transform into a smile of delight.

Then she would point with a little "that way" gesture to the pictures of ducks a little further down the wall, where the ack, ack,
quack, quack and corresponding smiles would repeat. Then to the
next. We'd make it back to our regular booth, and I would sit down,
only to have her grab my hand and start all over.

Any other place and I would have felt too silly to keep it up. At
Old Timer's, I would have felt too silly not to do it again and again.
Everyone saw it, and everyone saw her joy. Of course, it should be
done. We weren't taking away enjoyment from anyone's meal. They
were enjoying watching her smile and work her charm on her daddy.

When the food came, we would sit down to eat. Some days, Colby
ate a lot. Some days, none at all. Every time she would be done before
me and looking for something to do. The ack, ack, quack, quack
game isn't friendly with eating, so I would always attempt to give her
something to play with at the booth. Almost always, her attention
turned to playing with the little square packets of jellies and butter.

She would take them out of the bowl and then put them back in the bowl. She would stack them up and knock them over. She would line them up in train-like fashion, and sometimes she would organize them in a manner that made sense to her, even if I never caught on. Colby played with them much like her big sister did and probably like countless other kids before them.

By the time I finished eating, things in the kitchen had usually slowed, and Mrs. Donna would come out to visit. She would marvel at the new things Colby was doing and ask how things were going. She knew we were facing medical issues, but like us, she didn't have a good handle on what all they were.

When Colby started wearing glasses, Mrs. Donna would share stories of her own grandkids wearing glasses. When she saw the uncertainty in my eyes or the worry in my voice, she would find words to encourage us but not gloss things over. Most of all, she cared, and it showed.

When we lost Colby, as you would expect, the hurt was immense. What you might not expect is the many flashes of "Oh no, how are we handling such and such" moments that you have to deal with. The old common adage that babies don't come with instruction manuals is a lie. Bookstore shelves are filled with them, countless websites dedicated to them, and the hospital sends you home with pages more too.

What you don't get an instruction manual for is dealing with the death of a child. There are no checklists or what to expect guides. So, as your heart is shattered and your mind is reeling, you keep bumping into these "I didn't think about that" revelations, and you scramble to figure out how to deal with it.

One of those moments was "How do we tell Mrs. Donna?" My shattered heart hurt just a bit more to think about that.

A mutual friend delivered the news for us. I am not sure how or what was said.

What I do know is that I spent some time worrying about what would be said the next time I saw her. I was dreading that moment, not because of anything either of us had done but because I knew that sharing that grief together for the first time would be hard, and I didn't know what to say.

Well, it was hard, but I didn't have to worry about what to say. Mrs. Donna gave us a huge, understanding hug and said the only thing that needed to be said: "I'm sorry."

Ella and I had breakfast at Mrs. Donna's a couple of days ago, and they told us that Mrs. Donna was going to retire today. I think I heard them say she had been working there for twenty-six years. That is 26 years at 7 days a week, with very, very few days closed for holidays or vacations. Her retirement is well-earned, and I hope she enjoys every minute of it.

While I wish her nothing but the best, I hope she knows we will miss her. I hope she knows she has touched a lot of lives and provided a lot of memories. I hope she knows how much we enjoyed her restaurant and how good it made us feel to be there. I hope she knows how much I appreciate those memories of Colby there and that I will miss those ducks on the wall. I hope she knows how much it means to me that someday, somewhere, Ella will find a restaurant that brings her memories of her daddy, and she recalls some special moments she had with me at Mrs. Donna's Cafe.

CHAPTER 46

Adventures Beyond My Comfort Zone

We parents put a lot of pressure on ourselves about teaching our children. It turns out our children are pretty good teachers, too.

This story was written in December of 2010 when Ella was six, and Cheryl Taylor is the pastor in the story.

If you know me, you know that I approach new experiences with some degree of trepidation. And if you don't know me, you don't have to be around me long to figure that out.

I like knowing what to expect. I like knowing what will be expected of me. But despite all of that, I don't confine myself exclusively to my comfort zone. I've found that on those occasions when I push my bounds, it often results in something to be thankful for: a good story, a lesson learned, a hearty laugh, or the like.

One of those occasions was one night last September. Our church held a special service dedicated to wholeness and healing, centered almost entirely around prayer—a time to lift ourselves, our needs, and the needs of others up to God. It was held separately from our normal service, and both its format and tone were different. Not better, not worse, just different.

I attended but reluctantly so, never having been to this type of thing. Ella went with me, knowing it wasn't a regular service, but with far less apprehension than I had. This service had no bells, no choir, and no children's time. In fact, if memory serves, Ella was the only kid there.

But none of that seemed to bother her. She had on her normal going-to-church-smile, content to be surrounded by people who loved her no matter the circumstances.

As the service began, we all filed into the sanctuary, the rest of us with serious faces surrounding Ella's smiling face. The smile got even bigger as she saw the front row open and asked if we could sit there. It was one of those smiles that you don't even consider denying. Off to the front we went, just right of center.

It's been a few months, so I don't remember the exact order of things. I know our pastor welcomed us and introduced what we would be doing and why. We sang together, prayed together, and listened together about the importance of prayer.

The next part I remember well. Our pastor invited us to think about our own prayers and offer them up to God in a variety of ways. We could pray them from where we sat; we could light a candle; we could share them with a pastor; we could say our prayer with a stone that we placed in the baptismal font and take another's stone symbolizing their prayer; we could contemplate our prayers in front of a painting, or any combination we felt moved to do.

These options weren't offered up to make our prayers more potent.

They were just ways to freshen our perspective on prayer and engage with it in a somewhat tangible way. Not better, not worse, just different.

As these prayer options were being explained, Ella's smile perked up a notch again. She leaned over to me and, in an excited and loud whisper, asked, "We can pray for whatever we want?"

My mind immediately presumed all the things that Ella was thinking about praying for. I was sure her mind was filling with thoughts of puppies, toys, candy, and new clothes. Looking to head this off at the pass, I asked her, "What are you going to pray for?"

Her eyes were brightly lit, and her smile whispered back, "Colby. I am going to pray for Colby."

Those words filled me with equal parts shame and pride. I was so proud of her for her thoughts and so ashamed of me for mine.

My skeptical look changed to a smile, and I told her, "Ella, you are such a good big sister and so sweet. You can always pray for Colby." But I wanted to reassure her, too, so I added, "But she isn't sick anymore. She is in Heaven, and she is okay."

Her face let me know she was processing this, and her eyes lit up again with another idea. "And I'm going to pray for Mommy, because I know she hurts."

One of the great joys in parenting is when our children surprise us. This time, Ella had done it twice in under a minute. I find her level of maturity and compassion amazing.

The accompanying lesson was delivered in those same moments, but it took some time longer for it to sink in. Usually, I approach prayer with timidity and solemnity. Ella takes another attitude toward prayer, one of excitement and an inherent understanding of how special it is. You can almost hear her saying, "I can say whatever I want to God and He listens to me! He always listens!"

Imagine how special that must make her feel. Ella loves to be listened to and for people to take her seriously. Her parents, teachers, family, and friends play the role of her audience, but even at our best, it's inconsistent. But through prayer, she gets to talk to God anytime she wants about whatever she wants.

Ella clearly sees the ability to pray as a treasure, and she embraces it.

And don't we all want to be listened to?

I've never been able to fully wrap my head around prayer, but I suppose I had always looked at it as an obligation, a duty you were supposed to do. I still wrestle with questions about prayer, but Ella helped me see it in a different way, a better way—as a blessing and an opportunity.

CHAPTER 47

All Saints Day

Another story about six-year-old Ella at church.

Today was All Saints Day, and it was the focus of our church's services. For those, like me, who didn't grow up with All Saints Day, I should explain. On November 1st of each year, some Christian denominations honor all the saints in Heaven. In our ceremony, a bell was rung for each member of the congregation that had passed away since the last All Saints Day.

Our pastor and choir did a wonderful job, the lessons were good, and worship was beautiful, as we knew it all would be. Still, Usha and I had been dreading this day. We knew at some point in the service, Colby's name would be called, and the bell would ring for her, and that it would be a difficult moment.

In anticipation of that moment, we had told Ella what would take place beforehand. We wanted to let her know that she may feel sad because she misses her sister, or happy to hear Colby remembered, or maybe even both. We told her that Mommy and Daddy might cry, and we wanted her to be ready just in case.

Her response was just in the vein that everyone has come to expect from Ella. She said, "Don't worry, I'll sit between you and Mommy," letting us know she would be there to take care of us.

And that's exactly what she did.

Turns out, I shouldn't have been worried about the moment the bell rang. I should have been worried about the whole service because I started sniffling about a quarter of the way in. I thought I was hiding it pretty well until Usha slipped me a Kleenex, at which point I knew at least she was on to me. The Kleenex was quickly followed by gentle pats of Ella's hand.

Not too many minutes later, I noticed Usha dipping into the tissues, too. And Ella went to work patting her, too.

And so it went, back and forth. Ella trying to pat and hug us both. Later in the day, she would tell me her arms weren't long enough to hug us both properly at the same time! Six-year-old arms aside, I assure you she was doing a great job.

The bell tolled for Colby and many others. The tears ran steadily, and the tissues ran out. So, Usha leaned over to Ella and asked her to step out to the fellowship hall to get some more tissues. Off she went, a girl on a mission.

A few moments later, the doors opened and she returned to the sanctuary. Her face was full of confidence and pride, and in her hands were so many tissues, it looked like she was carrying pom poms!

It must have been most of a box. In those moments when we couldn't even comprehend being able to stop crying, we—and all of those around us—suddenly had smiles on our faces.

Classic Ella. When she sets out to help, she means to do it in a big way.

And that's exactly what she did.

CHAPTER 48

Millie

The lessons I explore in this essay didn't come from a person. The teacher was a horse.

I recently had the pleasure of crafting a cutting board for the Oklahoma Quarter Horse Youth Association, which gave me some time in the shop to reminisce. Sanding gives you lots of time to think.

1983 was a dry year in the Texas Panhandle. I guess it's never really what you would call wet there, so drier than normal is probably a better way of phrasing it. That meant hay was scarce and expensive, which meant people were thinning their livestock holdings. It was that summer that my mom and dad traded a beat-up old truck worth about $600 for a 5-year-old Quarter Horse mare. Her registered name was Golden Millie Rose. We just called her Millie, and she was my first horse.

Millie was what they called green-broke. That meant you could ride her, but she didn't care for it and would regularly make sure you knew how she felt. And I was a green rider, which meant I wanted to ride but didn't know what the hell I was doing. It was a match made in affordability.

I became obsessed with all things horses. I would draw them. Read about them. Daydream about them. Brush Millie. Feed Millie. And when hounded, teased, and scolded sufficiently, I would nervously try to ride her. Horses can sense when you are scared, and that suited Millie just fine because we both knew who was boss.

Part of that obsession meant that I read over her AQHA registration papers over and over again. Mom paid the fee to have her registered in my name, and that was pretty cool for a boy who seldom had name-brand anything. It listed all the important details about Millie–her grandfather was Hollywood Gold, who I'd later learn was famous and from the esteemed 6666 Ranch. It listed her other lineage and her birthday. And it listed her color as sorrel, which I thought was some fancy word for brown–brown being the color she most closely resembled from the standard eight pack of crayons.

I wasn't the only one with a sudden enthusiasm for horses. My mom was quite excited about Millie, too, and was less afraid of riding Millie than I was. The problem was that Dad forbid Mom from riding her. Whatever his reasons for doing so, the reason he voiced was that it was too dangerous for Mom. That didn't make Mom happy, and it sure didn't make me feel less nervous about riding Millie myself.

For those who know my mom, Winnie, you know that you only told her she couldn't do something at your own peril. Dad said she couldn't ride Millie, so Mom said, "Ok"… and she quietly went out and bought her own horse. She rented a stall a few down from where we were keeping Millie and kept her horse, Fancy, there. She didn't tell any of us for a month or so.

One day, she took me to feed Millie, and Dad wasn't with us. I saw her scooping grain and feeding what I thought was someone else's horse and asked what was going on. She replied with a question of her own, "What do you think of this horse?"

"It's okay, I guess. But not as good as Millie."

"Well," she said in an offended tone, "she is mine. Don't tell your father."

I was shocked. I was thrilled. I was scared of Dad's reaction. And I thought it was hilarious. Millie knew who was boss. Winnie was boss, too.

Mom didn't just have a horse: she had a saddle and all the tack and had been riding Fancy every day for weeks.

I was worried about how I was going to keep it a secret. Mom must have been, too, because she told Dad that night. I've blocked the memory of that night, but Mom didn't. She relished telling how she surprised us all. And like the old adage about being careful what you wish for, Dad was more careful about telling Mom what she couldn't do.

A minor but confounding surprise for me in that whole ordeal was that Fancy was also listed as a sorrel, but she most definitely appeared to be a different color to me. She was much redder in color. How they could both be called sorrel didn't make sense to me.

Now that Mom was riding, it meant I was riding more because she didn't like riding by herself. And that is when my path to horsemanship began in earnest.

That doesn't mean it was smooth. Not at all. There is a small chunk missing from my right ear where Millie bit me to prove it.

Millie made me cuss, cry, and want to quit, but I didn't. I trudged along, and gradually I would experience moments of accomplishment and joy. Those little confidence-boosters kept me coming back for more.

Quarter Horses are known for their versatility, and Millie was no exception. I tried everything with her. The list included parades, trail rides, play day events, pushing cows, shooting arrows off her, camping trips, roping tame dairy calves, doing tricks, trying to make her a jumper (which was only successful at creek crossings because she hated water), and any other skill I saw at a horse show or read in a magazine.

When we got other horses, she made a good lead horse for training them. As I got older, I could trust her to let my girlfriends ride her or even the younger siblings of my girlfriends. She somehow knew she needed to be more patient and less stubborn than usual.

Millie was a fast horse. Probably the fastest I ever rode. Dad said she could trot faster than other horses could lope. Her lope was Harley Davidson-smooth. And when she ran, it was thundering exhilaration.

As time went on, Millie seldom bucked, unless she was asked to carry two riders. She hated that and would not stand for it. When she did buck, it was more of a mild warning and never too serious. We even got to the point where I could ride her without any tack at all. No saddle, bridle, halter, or even rope.

I truly loved that horse. And I truly believe with all my heart that she ... tolerated me.

That may be too harsh. Maybe at times she loved me back, especially when I didn't ask too much of her or when I brought her watermelon. But for the most part, she just did her best to tolerate me trying to be a cowboy, or an Indian, or a show-off. Tolerating was good with me, though. I could accept that.

That doesn't mean she didn't take a few jabs here and there.

Millie's classic move was to step on my foot and then lean into me hard and knock me down. It was no accident; she knew exactly what she was doing.

She also knew exactly what she was doing if I let her get too close to a tree. Lots of horses will walk under a branch slightly above their head and, not accounting for your height as a rider, run you into a branch. Millie accounted for me, all right. She would raise her head up to bend the branch way forward, and about the time when I was where the branch should be, she would duck her head, and the branch would snap back and whack me in the gut, chest, or face.

That may sound ornery, and I guess it is. But friends do that kind of stuff with each other. Heck, she helped me do that kind of stuff with some of my friends, where we would make a game out of trying to pull each other off their horses or have yucca pod fights while riding (think snowball fights with heavier, harder ammo).

And Millie was my friend. And my teacher. And my coworker. And my babysitter. And a roommate through part of college.

I often marvel at how much time and money we put into horses when I was growing up. And it was money we didn't really have. The more rational and fiscally responsible decision would have been not to do it at all.

But in my recent reminiscing, I think about how different I would have been without those horses and especially Millie. I am a better man because of that horse. I'm not claiming greatness or even goodness, but I am definitely better than I would have been without her. And that makes me grateful for the sacrifices my parents made for Millie and me.

The story could end there, but I have a little more to add.

Because of how important Millie was to me, I wanted the board I am making for the Oklahoma Quarter Horse Youth Association to be named after her. I had some beautiful Oklahoma black walnut that reminded me of Millie's color, so rather than a charcuterie board, I made an end-grain cutting board with it.

In writing up the description, I realized it was going to horse people, and I'd better figure out my confusion about what sorrel really
means. They would know, and I wanted to make sure the description made sense.

So I found a group that specializes in horse color genetics and
posed the question to them with an old picture of Millie attached.
They explained to me that Millie was more accurately a chestnut,
but some might call her a sorrel, and that the mixing of those terms
can be a regional thing. Furthermore, they explained that whether
she was called sorrel or chestnut really didn't matter because technically, she was red.

And for the first time in thirty-eight years, I finally realized my
"brown" horse was really a redhead.

Suddenly, my fondness for redheads had a known root cause–
Millie. And of course, that fondness goes beyond just hair color. No
doubt independence, strong will, sometimes orneriness, determination, outspokenness, spiritedness, and high standards all play a part,
too. Best of all, my redheaded wife and daughters don't just tolerate
me: they love me back, too.

So, Millie, thank you. Not only for making me a better man,
but also for helping guide me to my girls, who have taken up where
you left off.

CHAPTER 49

Playing Hooky

As previous chapters attest, I was no stranger to playing hooky. If there were a hall of fame for such a thing, I would have a gold jacket and bronze bust with a unanimous vote. And while I now have to admit I greatly overindulged and missed out on many things, you will never convince me that sometimes playing hooky is the best choice of all.

The first thing you have to understand about what the Arboretum meant to Colby is that Colby loved being outside.

Love it like walking down the stairs at 5:30 in the morning and pointing to the front door, asking to go outside. And when that didn't work, pointing to the back door and trying again. Love it like playing outside in the evening until she falls asleep leaning on a toy. Sunshine, rain, snow, wind–oh how she loved the wind in her hair—hot, cold, bundle her up or strip her down, just let her go outside kind of love.

The Dallas Arboretum is a great place for any child. For a child who loves being outside like Colby did, it's a place of fairy-tale-like magic.

The joy of an Arboretum-day experience began in the parking lot. Getting out of the car, Colby would always have a huge smile of excitement and anticipation. It was glorious to take in, but it was best not to dawdle. If it took too long to set up the stroller and square away the backpack, that wonderful smile would be put on pause long enough to protest the delay. Either way, once we started walking toward the entrance, the full smile would be on display.

Speaking of the stroller and the backpack, the two of them spent a lot of time together. Since Colby could walk, she wanted nothing to do with riding in the stroller at the Arboretum, so most of the time, the backpack rode in her seat. It's not that she didn't like riding in her stroller. At home, there were times we would take two-hour walks with her in the stroller. But at the Arboretum, Colby relied exclusively on two modes of transportation: she either wanted to walk or be carried.

For a long time, the shunning of the stroller confused me, but I finally figured it out. When Colby was at the Arboretum, she liked looking in all directions. There is so much to see, and she didn't want to miss any of it. Being in the stroller was like having blinders on her, where she could only look straight ahead. Even more objectionable for her, in the stroller, she was at the mercy of the driver in terms of direction and speed. If she was walking or being carried, she could look any direction she wanted, indicate where she wanted to go, and most importantly, where she wanted to stop and soak it in.

And soak it in she did. The trees, the seasonal displays, the spitting frogs, the squirrels, the birds, the koi, and the animal statues all captured her attention. It was fertile ground for playing with her sister and hamming it up with Mom and Dad. She even liked sharing the Arboretum with strangers because she did a little people-watching, too. And of course, she liked it when people stopped to compliment her curly red hair. But of all the many things she loved at the

Arboretum, there was one particular time that left her in total awe—the Dallas Blooms Festival.

The Arboretum is wonderful to visit any time of the year. Nature's beauty may change with the calendar, but it's always there in some form, and the Arboretum does an excellent job of showcasing it. Most of Colby's visits to the Arboretum as a toddler were during the summer, fall, and winter, and there was no shortage of beauty for her to enjoy. This was what she knew of the Arboretum, and she loved it.

One particular Wednesday in April, Colby normally would have gone with me to a board meeting for a local civic organization. But on that Thursday, she was scheduled for a pre-surgery exam, to be followed by surgery on Friday. Knowing a couple of stressful days lay ahead, we decided to play hooky and go to the Arboretum for a day of relaxing fun.

Of course, early April and the Arboretum mean Dallas Blooms: 500,000 blooming tulips and daffodils, 3,000 azaleas, and 80,000 pansies surrounded 1 little red-haired girl who was experiencing the Arboretum she loved in an entirely new, completely spectacular way.

Picture this scene. Here is Colby, who loves flowers—all flowers. She took delight in the lowliest dandelion or tiniest blue clover. She loved flowers so much that she had invented her own sign language for them, pushing her fist through her other closed hand and opening up her palm as if her fingers were the blooming petals. And here she was standing on a brick pathway surrounded by thousands of blooming tulips in every direction.

She stood still at first in complete amazement, not smiling but with her jaw dropped. She did her sign for flower, then turned thirty degrees and did it again, then again and again and again. For the next several minutes, she did nothing but turn in slow circles, signing "flower." Her expression morphed from disbelief to belief to a boundless smile born of pure delight.

Yes, we played hooky that day and with absolutely no remorse. We spent it at a place where men and women toil with God's paintbrushes to transform a sixty-six-acre canvas into an ever-changing, always beautiful interactive work of living art. A place so beautiful, it commands your attention and eschews the normal distractions of modern life. A place where kids can be kids and parents can bask in their creation. A place where memories are cast so that we may carry them in our hearts, even when time pulls on us like a riptide, dragging us where we don't want to go.

In May, our beloved Colby passed away at the tender age of two. If there is a blessing in our tragedy, it's that she had such a wonderful spirit and uplifting personality that she gave us a treasure chest of blessed memories.

As you can tell, the Arboretum holds a special place in many of those memories. For that reason, we were deeply touched when the people of Samuel Jackson, Inc. created a memorial fund benefitting the Dallas Arboretum in honor of Colby. When we found out that the fund had already exceeded $22,000, we were both touched and overwhelmed.

We are so pleased that Colby inspired such a large donation to the Children's Adventure Garden at the Dallas Arboretum and delighted in knowing that it will help provide additional memories for untold numbers of children of all ages.

We hope that some of those memories involve you and your family, even if it means playing hooky one day.

CHAPTER 50

Meeting Colby's Petting Zoo

*Colby had a life insurance policy, not huge but not incon-
sequential. We wanted to use it in a way that honored her,
and a dear friend, Cindy Skidmore, suggested that something honoring Colby should be done at a place she loved—
the Dallas Arboretum.*

*That policy, combined with generous donations from, Sam-
uel Jackson, Incorporated, funded a special feature in the
children's area being constructed at the time—Colby's Petting Zoo. This is the story of our first visit to the completed project.*

The Dallas Arboretum is 74 acres. The Children's Adventure Garden is 8 acres of that. Nestled near the entrance of that garden,
tucked up against a wall behind a playhouse and taking up just about
thirty square feet is Colby's Petting Zoo. Just like Colby, some wonderful things come in small sizes.

Our first time to see Colby's Petting Zoo, we walked timidly
around the First Adventures section, almost as if we were expecting

it to jump out at us and say "boo," but it didn't. In fact, we almost looped that entire section before we found it.

When we finally laid eyes on it, we eased closer to it, trying to soak it in and reconcile it with expectations we had formed only from hearing the concept, but never seeing actual plans or its progress during construction. The volunteer working that section approached us and, noting our interest, began telling us about the petting zoo.

"This is one of my favorite parts of the whole garden. Here, kids are allowed to touch the plants, feel them on their fingers, and smell the scents they leave behind on their skin." This much we knew, but she had no idea who we were or what our connection was to this space. Thankfully, she didn't stop there.

"One little girl was here, and she was so shy. I pointed her over here to the petting zoo, and she began exploring. She became fascinated. Her shyness faded away, and she delighted in touching and examining all the plants."

I have no idea what the girl she was talking about actually looked like, but in my head, she had red curly hair and glasses. The story could not have been sweeter to my ears. We told the lady how much we appreciated hearing it and went on to explain why, introducing ourselves and showing her and the other volunteers a picture of Colby.

At this point, the garden was about an hour from being officially open, so after a healthy amount of time admiring Colby's Petting Zoo, taking pictures, and simultaneously grinning and stifling tears, we decided to see some more of the children's garden before the crowd showed up.

We didn't manage to see it all, but what we did see was incredible. It's garnered the attention of all the local media and many national outlets, including *the New York Times*, *USA Today*, and *National*

Geographic. All the attention is well-deserved, but the true beauty of the garden isn't that it is getting rave reviews from the press. It was built for the kids, and you can pick any bench, take a seat, and soak in the magic, watching children of all ages explore, play, learn, and engage with nature.

As the crowd increased, we eased our way back toward Colby's Petting Zoo for another look before we left. Seeing the First Adventure section gave us a whole new appreciation for the petting zoo.

This time, the First Adventure area was full of children. A dozen feet from the petting zoo, little boys fenced with fake asparagus and dug into the earth with play shovels in the same manner they would use a sword to slay a dragon.

The displays were built for the full spectrum of rambunctiousness, and they were certainly being put to the test. The goals of hands-on displays and happy children were both being fully met. Watching the unbridled energy at play was something to behold–I still smile thinking about it.

Yet Colby's Petting Zoo sat there unoccupied for the moment, content to wait for the next child who wanted to take a different approach to their exploring—a child like Colby.

Usha likes to tell stories about how Colby loved to play with tags on her toys. She would feel the satin between her fingers, examine the loop and how it attached, and most fascinating was the patience with what she did. It wasn't just tags that captured her attention–it was the leaves on a tree, blocks shaped like animals, an ordinary rock, and certainly the plants at the Arboretum.

Of course, before the petting zoo, the plants were just there to enjoy with your eyes. Now, the petting zoo gives the opportunity to get up close, actually touch them, and make them easier to smell.

It's a good thing that the petting zoo didn't have a crowd of kids around it. The kids that it attracts need time to quietly enjoy and explore. Such an experience should be unrushed and savored. I have no doubt that is how Colby would have approached it. And I have no doubt countless other kids will, too.

Someday, Colby's little brother will have the opportunity to visit Colby's Petting Zoo. Maybe it will captivate his attention. Maybe he will rather slay imaginary dragons. Either is okay with me. There are different kinds of kid personalities, and they need different outlets. The designers of the Children's Garden did a masterful job recognizing and addressing this simple but often overlooked fact.

And I am so glad that we had the opportunity to honor Colby by providing a space for kids who want to explore the way she did.

Small, but overflowing with treasure.

Providing the opportunity to fully live in and enjoy the moment. Unhurried by distractions.

A teacher of lessons, even to the unintentional student.

Witness to the wonders and blessings from God.

We knew the petting zoo was a perfect tribute to Colby from the first time we heard of it–we just didn't know how perfect.

CHAPTER 51

Chickens

This story was from when Ella was five and was written a month or so before Colby had passed. When I found it on an old hard drive amongst some notes, I realized my essay writing pre-dated the therapy writing path I eventually found myself taking. I suppose that even then, I was trying to find ways to hang onto precious memories.

Ella has always been a good eater. She is good about trying new things and eats a wide variety of fruits, veggies, and meats–and desserts of course! The meat aspect of her diet has always been interesting to me, because I was never completely sure if she made the connection between live animals and what's on her plate.

Last fall, she started requesting "fish with eyeballs" whenever we had fish, which was her term for whole fish. She even tried the eyeball–but only once! So based on that, I was pretty sure she understood that at one time, that fish was once alive, but she never asked about it. And other meats don't look like their source. Beef and pork aren't even animal names.

I've never wanted to try to hide that we eat animals, but I also didn't want to suddenly have to start doing battle with a protesting PETA prodigy at mealtime.

In January and February, our Aunt Bhavna visited from India. Bhavna is a vegetarian, so that made some dinner conversations with Ella interesting, including Ella's response when Bhavna was beckoning her to visit India. Ella, waving a fork of porkchop in the air, announced, "Hello! I eat meat!"

But even with this, there were still no pointed questions from Ella about how animals become tasty.

So last week, during a trip to IKEA, something happened where I thought things were about to come to a head. There was a stack of whole cow hides for sale, and she asked, "Daddy, why do they have so many cow skins?"

Completely caught off guard, I answered, "Well, I guess the cows were done with them."

I didn't think that would fend her off, and much to the delight of an old grandfatherly type who was observing all this, it didn't. She followed up with the simplest, yet often hardest query.

"Why?"

She was looking at the hides. The old man was looking at me with a look that said he suddenly didn't mind that his wife dragged him out shopping. And me? I was looking around for a lifesaver.

"Look, Ella. A lamp that looks like a flower" was all it took, and she was off running ahead. As we moved on, I glanced back at the old man just to let him know this wasn't my first rodeo, and feeling a little guilty, I had ruined his only fun for the day.

A few days later, we were on our way to the zoo when we passed a semi-truck load of live chickens on a "field trip" to Pilgrim's Pride. I was wondering if Ella would notice, and she did.

"Daddy, chickens!" was followed by a thoughtful pause. "Where are they going?"

"Hmmm. Maybe to another farm?"

She let my answer stand. I had no idea that later at the zoo, she would relieve me of my anxiety by letting me know she fully understood the concept of meat coming from animals.

We were touring the farm animal section, and Ella spotted a group of chickens.

"Daddy, chickens!"

"Yep," I mumbled.

"Those chickens are big!"

"Mmm-huh."

"We eat chickens," she said very matter-of-factly.

Eureka! "That's right! We do eat chickens!" I responded excitedly and at least a couple of levels too loudly. It was plenty loud enough for the nearby mothers to hear—without the benefit of any of the prior context, mind you.

As those nearby moms clutched their children and shot me looks filled with expletives, Ella chastised me, too.

"Daddy!!!" she whispered loudly. "Don't say that so loud! They will hear you, and it will hurt their feelings."

"Sorry," I said, feigning regret, but inside I was heartily laughing.

I didn't have the guts to make eye contact with the moms as we moved on. Though the whole topic was suddenly no big deal for me, I'm sure we caused a few hard questions and interesting conversations for some others.

That one was for you, Old IKEA Man.

CHAPTER 52

Burying the Hatchet with Charles Dickens ... Sort Of

This was written in the year following Colby's passing. Being an earlier essay, it may seem odd to find it placed here in the latter part of the book, but it was a deliberate decision. Sometimes you don't know how far you have come until you look back.

Since this was written, I have readjusted to the typical norms of answering "How are you?"

But recently, I crossed paths with another dad who had lost his daughter just a few months before. Reflexively, I started with "How are you?" and I could see his mind doing the calculus of whether I meant hello or if I meant "How are you coping?" His blue screen flickered, and I thought, I feel you, brother.

It's a question we all get asked every day of our lives from the time we can talk. We all ask it about as much as it's asked of us. You'd think with all that practice, it would be an easy one to answer, and, until recently, it always has been. But these days, when someone asks, "How are you?" my mind races to form an answer while my expression races toward deer in the headlights.

On occasion, the result is the equivalent of giving someone the blue screen of death on a computer—the freeze-up lasts long enough that the whole conversation has to be rebooted.

It's not that I mind the question. It's always touching when someone is expressing concern for us, and, at times, it's surprising who is doing the asking. That makes the pressure to give a good answer even higher, and with it, the probability of a blue screen goes up, too.

What makes the question difficult to handle is, well, it's hard. First, I have to figure out if it's the normal pleasantries we all engage in or if it's being asked out of concern for our grieving. Then, if it's out of concern, a decision has to be made if the questioner is just signaling concern, or do they really want an answer. If they really want an answer, thought must be given to just how deep an explanation they want and how much they can handle.

Once processed down to this level, I begin searching for the way to summarize and convey, which leads me to ask myself, "How AM I doing?" and then I feel the fuse pop—blue screen.

If you have asked me how I am doing and received the blue screen, I apologize, but don't worry. Blue screens aren't painful, and you didn't send me to the edge of a breakdown. There were simply processing conflicts in my brain; it froze up and locked out my tongue. Most folks recognize this and bring me back up in safe mode with talk about the weather or sports. Attempts at reinstalling the driver with questions about Ella or Usha are usually successful, too.

If all else fails, try a universal recovery disk, otherwise known as a cookie. And by cookie, I mean the real thing, not computer lingo.

So, it's with the kind folks who wonder how I am doing in mind that I am writing this. I usually convey thoughts better when I am writing anyway, and this way I don't have to guess at how much you want to know. You can read as much or as little as you want. And if you are reading this on your computer and get a blue screen, that one isn't my fault.

. . .

Charles Dickens lowered my high school GPA. Okay, that may not be entirely accurate, but bolder claims have been made on shakier ground.

In my high school career, I was not a fan of assigned novels. Of all the assigned books, I suppose I probably read only one from beginning to end. Most of the time, I relied on a mix of the usual get-me-by tactics of *Cliff's Notes*, movie adaptations, and whatever I gleaned from class lectures. More than once, I took the book they handed out, put it in my locker where it stayed untouched until it was time to turn it in; at least I always returned them in good shape.

As a senior, perhaps looking ahead to the challenges of college or tired of the stress of winging it, I made a mental commitment to actually read the books. It was a short-lived attempt that ended with the first book Mrs. Burton assigned, Charles Dickens' *A Tale of Two Cities*.

This time, I did open the book and read the opening line. "It was the best of times, it was the worst of times..." Well, I tried.

I can't say precisely what my thought process was at that point, but it was something very close to, if this Dickens fella can't figure out whether or not someone is having a good time, I'm not going to read 544 pages watching him try to figure it out. And with that, the book went back into the safe confines of my locker. I went back to winging it and got the grades—ok, *earned* the grades you'd expect from that strategy.

So, it's with a touch of irony and perhaps a hint of karma that these days, when someone asks me how I am coping with the loss of my daughter Colby, I think of Dickens's famous opening line. I am now a believer that great times and terrible times can share the same calendar day. In fact, sometimes they are only separated by mere moments.

One of the best of times—walking Ella to school in the morning. In those twelve minutes, the only distraction to our conversation is the care put into avoiding getting run over. It's a brief escape away from the world of phones, television, radio, and chores. These conversations run all over the place, but together they form a window into her marvelous mind. I get to hear her creativity, her hopes, her worries, her questions, and the uniquely Ella perspective. And sometimes we just act silly. When we get to the door, I send her off with a wish and a kiss. And with that, times change.

One of the worst of times—the walk home. It's a time many would cherish, and I suppose I do, too, in an odd way. It's peaceful and quiet. It should be an ideal time for letting your mind drift in whatever direction mental tides take it. But my mind does not drift. It races to the deepest parts of the thoughts that are ever present, but usually forced to compete with the normal distractions of life.

In these 4,096 feet between the school door and an empty home, the absence of typical distractions is oxygen to a fire. My mind burns with the loss of Colby. Walking against the flow of school-bound foot traffic, I pass strollers and sets of siblings that punctuate the pain with thoughts of what could have been. What should have been. Tears are common, but I fight them back, waiting until I walk through our door, expecting to collapse on the floor like a runner after a marathon.

But I don't collapse.

Usually.

I often wonder if there is some neighbor along the way, watching and puzzled by this daily routine. It must be quite a sight. A near-bald, near-forty-year-old man walking with his daughter, with smiling skips, happy hops, and silly songs—only to return a short time later, with a pained expression and watery eyes. What explanation have they settled on to satisfy their curiosity?

Maybe they wonder why I put myself through something that upsets me. Maybe you are wondering the same thing. The answer to that is a simple one: It's worth it.

The best of times—knowing that both my wife and our relationship have a strength that I could have never imagined. Every marriage faces tests. We have had other tests, and we will face more in the future. Of all of these, I pray that the test of losing Colby is the hardest. Of course, we did not want this test, but still, even unwanted tests let you know where you stand.

I know I am blessed with a wife who has been there for me in every way possible. Often, she knows my thoughts with just a look, and even if she is sharing the pain at that moment, she is quick with a reassuring squeeze of hands or a Kleenex if need be. She listens to my struggles, even the repeated ones, the irrational ones, and the small ones. And when I don't want to talk, she gives me a knowing hug and space to just be sad without further explanation. She knows what I am going through better than anyone, and my hope is to show her my appreciation and love by providing her with reciprocal strength and support.

The worst of times—carrying the weight of unspeakable things impossible to share with anyone, compounded by the fear that those who have given me so much support feel slighted or betrayed by these

omissions. I know many others face similar circumstances to our tragedy. None of them is more fortunate than I in having an incredible
support network. But there are some things that cannot be unheard
once they are said. Things that have no power to heal and that cannot be explained.

My family and friends have given me so much in this difficult
time. I hope that they can allow me this one small thing and trust
me to protect them from things best left unsaid.

The best of times—stumbling across a cherished memory. Every
memory is cherished, including the difficult times. But when a photo,
place, or person triggers a memory about Colby's spirit, it's like finding a priceless stone.

The worst of times—those times when my brain rebels against the
constant pressure to cling to every memory. Times like when I am
drifting off to sleep, and I bolt up at the sound of cries over a baby
monitor. It's not until my feet hit the floor that reality slaps me fully
awake to a silent room.

The best of times and the worst of times—dreaming. Occasionally, I get lucky and dream of Colby at play and laughing. Sometimes the dreams go deeper, and things happen like I am watching
her play in her high chair, I turn to get something, and when I turn
back, she is gone.

Most often, the dreams are of those final days in the hospital and
reliving them in such detail is an emotional hurricane. You may be
surprised that all these dreams are the best of times, because I get to
hear her laugh, caress her hair, or kiss her face. Dream or not, that
feels good.

Dreams end. I wake up. Reality sets in. Best turns to worst. It's a
debatable worst, though. I'm not sure which is worse, waking up or

the nights I don't dream about Colby, because those leave me feeling cheated.

The best of times and the worst of times—Father's Day. The worst of that day is just as you would imagine. Every day has its difficulties. Special days carry special challenges. This past Father's Day, I was surrounded by lots of love and support, but the one thing I wanted the most no one could give me. I spent most of the day with forced smiles for Ella or with my head down, just hoping for it to pass quickly.

But in the middle of it, I shared a once-in-a-lifetime moment with my girls. All my girls. Ella and I were baptized that day, Usha was by our side, and the baptismal water was mixed with the water saved from Colby's baptism. The one thing I wanted most, no one could give me, but I ended that day feeling closer and more strongly bonded to my daughters and wife. And that made it the best Father's Day ever, even if it was the worst one, too.

So, Mr. Dickens, I concede the point of our debate. Sort of.

Looking back, I can point out the "best" and "worst" of times. I can even understand that the two feed off of each other. The bad makes it easier to fully appreciate the good. The good, making the bad cut deeper.

But life is predominantly made up of time in between the extreme ups and downs. It's adjusting to a world that is a bit wobblier on its axis. It's unsettling and challenging, but not impossible. It's contemplating my degree of craziness and fighting off the temptation of giving in to it. It's draining, but it's not uncommon.

It's knowing that I'm a different person but trying to figure out what all that means. It's an odd sensation of being on the verge of tears but feeling peaceful about it. It's learning to accept a constant heartache but taking care not to ignore it.

Mostly, it's the ordinary activities of everyday life—trips to the store, mowing the lawn, washing dishes, and projects for work. Sprinkled throughout the day are both twinges of hurt and occasional moments when it physically feels like a hay hook has pulled my heart from my chest. But there are also sprinkles of both simple pleasures and uproarious laughter.

So maybe it's not truly the best of times and the worst of times. It's just times.

Of course, when someone asks me how I am doing, that's a longer answer than they want to hear or I want to give. So, it boils down to this.

When it's the worst of times, I appreciate and welcome your compassion. But I invite you to share in my happiness, too, because even broken-hearted, I still experience the best of times. As devastating as losing Colby has been, the blessings she gave were greater. If I had only the option of replaying everything exactly as it happened or never having had Colby at all, I would go through all the pain again because it was and is most definitely worth it.

CHAPTER 53

Libraries are For Laughing

Years after this was written, Alex was born and attended library story time near our new home. He was one of the rambunctious kids, not harmful or destructive, but living his fun out loud in voice and movement. A lady chided, "He is ruining it for everyone!"

Don't worry, lady. Libraries are for laughing.

B*ump-bump.*
    Sometimes you know where you are by sight.
Bump-bump. Giggle.
Sometimes you know where you are by sound.
Bump-bump. Giggle, squeal, giggle.
Colby knew she was at the Rockwall County Library by feel. The speed bumps in the parking lot always tipped her off that she had arrived at one of her favorite places.

And if the laughter after rolling over each bump wasn't enough evidence that she was happy to be there, try showing up before the library opened and getting her to wait in the car. Trying to keep her waiting in her car seat for ten minutes would be like trying to keep a racehorse in a starting gate for ten minutes. You could probably do it, but it would be one of the longest and toughest ten minutes in your life.

I never lasted anywhere near ten minutes. In fact, I quickly learned just to park the car, get her unstrapped, and go to the front door where Colby could pace back and forth until the doors unlocked, opening the way to stories, exploration, play, and fun.

I don't remember Colby's first visit to the library. Ironically, she probably spent the whole time sleeping in her car seat carrier while big sister, Ella, was picking out books. Soon, Colby was big enough to look at books, too. I don't remember the details of those early visits, but I do remember enjoying watching her grow to like the library. The details I do remember clearly are when she began to love the library.

In March of 2010, I reluctantly decided to try out the story time program with Colby. I say reluctantly because I suspected I might be the only dad in the group, and I had some concerns about intruding into a mom's group.

Colby and I showed up early, as usual, and made our way to the story time room where we waited, both unsure of what to expect. My suspicions were correct. That particular day, I was the only dad. But I quickly realized that my concerns were unfounded and that it was silly to have them in the first place. Going anywhere with Colby was easy. Her curly red hair, beautiful face, and cute personality always got all the attention. All the moms there were warm and welcoming to sweet Colby and, by extension, me.

While I was settling in and feeling better, Colby was still wide-eyed and wondering what to expect. There we were. Me sitting on the floor, her sitting on my lap, and the room filling up around us with other kids–some rambunctious, some quiet. Colby had plenty to look at but remained uncertain as to what we were doing there.

Then walked in Ms. Andrea, who began passing out bells to shake and talking about songs we were about to sing. Colby timidly took her set of bells in her hand and studied what the other kids were doing with theirs. The singing started, and the bell-shaking joined along. Colby saw some kids shaking their bells, but rather than shaking hers, she handed them to me, wanting me to shake them for her.

The singing was followed by the story. Ms. Andrea read from a large book with pictures easily seen by all. This particular story involved animals and animal sounds–always a favorite of Colby's, so it captured her full attention. Quiet up to that point, she began roaring with the lion and snapping her arms together for the crocodile. So engrossed in the story, she even left the safety zone of my lap, getting to her feet for a better look at the book.

When the story was over, her smile was big, but her clapping was cut short as she quickly began signing "more" as she saw the book being put away. Soon afterward, buckets of toys were brought out, and free play began. But rather than going to the toys, Colby made her way to the front of the room where the book was, wanting it to be read again. So, we did.

She did eventually play with the toys, and the time flew by for both of us. We enjoyed it so much that we went to another story time session the next day. With that visit and each one after, Colby grew more and more comfortable. She began shaking her own bells, first with one set and later working up to a set in each hand. She loved exploring the room and its decorated walls. She developed a preference for her favorite toys–toy animals, of course, and puzzles that she insisted on doing herself.

And while she was enjoying all those things, I was enjoying watching Colby. Watching her excitement and curiosity. Watching her confidence grow. Watching her discover. Watching her interact with other kids. Watching her have fun.

All my life, I had thought of libraries as solemn collections of books and places to be quiet. Colby showed me a library is much more than that. It's a place to stretch your wings, to learn, to grow, and to enjoy. Libraries are for laughing!

Each minute we spent there left a satisfaction of being filled to the fullest. Not a second wasted. Not an uncherished moment.

After Colby passed away, I found myself again reluctant to go there, unsure of the pain of facing the abrupt end of these precious story time adventures. But once again, thank goodness for her big sister, Ella. Knowing I couldn't deny her the joy of the library gave me the strength to go back there.

Was there pain? Certainly.

But there were also treasured reminders that lifted my heart. The speed bumps in the parking lot. The "grass" tiles on the bathroom floor that had made Colby step cautiously as she walked across. The frogs on the carpet that had caused her to ribbit and jump. The adult-sized rocker that she insisted on sitting in, which made her look so small but made her feel so big. The librarians who loved her and to whom I will always be grateful for providing such a wonderful place and programs to share with my daughters.

Just as my previous reluctant trip had ended, so did this one. I left feeling closer to my daughters, appreciating them more, and with invaluable memories.

Who knew that a building full of books could do all of that?

CHAPTER 54

School Buses in Big Sur— Thoughts on Easter

As mentioned earlier, we have incorporated road-school-ing trips into Alex's education. These are extended trips, camping across the States, and doing our curriculum as we travel. I am amazed at the richness and opportunities it has allowed us to infuse his learning, and my learning, too.

I want to say we cruised Highway 1 from Monterey to Big Sur and back, but cruising is the wrong verb; it implies smooth movement. This was anything but as we pulled over more than a dozen times in the 30-mile journey down and almost as many times on the return trip, too.

The entire round-trip took us over three hours and would have taken us all day had it not been raining. Even with the rain, it was still stunning. Steep, but grazable, lush green hillsides sloping into the rocky Pacific coastline. Every pull-off had visitors like us, holding up their phone cameras like us, trying to capture an image to do the landscape justice like us, and failing... like us.

At some point, you realize the best thing to do is just bask in the view, let it wash over you, and soak it in.

As we were working our way back north, we crossed paths with a school bus. I couldn't help but wonder what the kid on the bus, who had lived his life going up and down this road, thought of it all–the scenery and those of us visiting it.

Did he look upon it with wonder and appreciation? Or was it all so ordinary to him that he had become numb to it all long ago?

I started thinking about this school bus again today, on Easter. I realized that I am the boy on the bus.

The story of the cross began hitting my ears before I understood words. I've heard and read of the miracle of resurrection all my days. I've always carried the blessing of forgiveness of my lengthy and growing list of sins.

And if I am honest, most of the time I am mostly numb to it all. Yes, it is there, and I am aware and grateful, but the stunning glory of it all has become "ordinary."

When I do contemplate it, my words and thoughts are inadequate—like the phone camera that can't capture Big Sur.

And that has me thankful for both Easter and the boy on the bus.

Today, I am thankful for the occasion to celebrate and the reminder that even if I cannot comprehend it or describe it, I can bask in it as it washes over me.

Happy Easter.

CHAPTER 55

Dibs, Giggles, and Quacks

My essays have looked at parenting from many angles: a son, brother, dad, husband, and more. This one offers thoughts as a child of God.

We aren't very good at planning in advance. On the very rare date night, Usha and I typically pick a restaurant on our way into town. It has happened that we start thinking about spring break plans on the first day of spring break. And Ella has had more than one birthday party, a full month past her actual birthday. That's just a few examples, and trust me, there could be plenty more.

May 11, 2014, was an exception. Though the actual date wasn't selected for quite some time later, the planning for it began 20 months in advance. Few people knew it, but at that time, our plans to move to Oklahoma were taking shape. Simultaneously and coincidentally, our plans for another baby were starting to get serious, and few people knew of that either.

One person who knew of both was our pastor, Cheryl.

In the midst of Cheryl's support and counsel on these matters, she expertly walked the line of being sad to see us go, happy for what the future held for us, and just the right amount of concern that we were prepared for these choices. Cheryl is a smart lady.

Having good, trusted counsel is priceless. They think about things that you haven't and help you consider things from perspectives you may have overlooked. That was true in this case, too. In thoughtfully analyzing the confluence of these two decisions, she also came to realize that if these two events did in fact take place, our baby would be born in Oklahoma. That caused her to make a declaration.

"You are bringing that baby back here to Rockwall to be baptized. I call dibs."

I have heard the theory that there are actually eleven commandments. They didn't all fit on the front of the tablets, and the eleventh one, etched on the back, never received proper recognition because, let's face it, stone tablets are kinda of a pain to flip over and see if there is anything there.

I'm pretty sure that eleventh commandment is "Thou shalt honor thy pastor's dibs."

Eleventh commandment or not, Cheryl had no reason to worry. Dibs or not, we wouldn't have it any other way. Cheryl had not been a passive observer in our journey with Colby. She lived it with us: late nights, early mornings, hope, joy, laughter, tears, heartache, and all. She puts that love and passion into everything she does. Having her perform the baptism ceremony, a ceremony that at the time we could only hope would be needed, would truly be an honor and blessing to us.

As things turned out, we were blessed with baby number three, Alex, and the baptism ceremony would be on. It would take place in Rockwall, and Pastor Cheryl would do the ceremony. Cheryl even suggested the perfect date. Ella and I had been baptized on Father's

Day a few years before. Cheryl felt it only right that Usha have one of her kids baptized on Mother's Day, and when she suggested it, we jumped at the chance.

So, for twenty months, I had contemplated a future baptism day, and for three months before the actual day, I even knew when it would take place. That's a lot of time to think things over and think about what will happen … how you will feel … what that day and moment will be like. Despite having all that time to think about it, I suppose I only did superficially. I knew it would be emotionally charged, but I didn't give thought to what all that would mean. I didn't think exactly what that day would be. At least I didn't until the night before.

As Usha and I got ready for bed on Mother's Day Eve, I suddenly became quite worried. "Tomorrow is going to be hard," I said to Usha, not even able to get that simple sentence out without my voice cracking.

Usha is a smart lady, too.

When my voice starts cracking, more talking isn't what I need in that moment. We hugged. We nodded to acknowledge what was said. And we took in deep breaths to gird ourselves up for another trip through the highs and lows of a grieving parent.

I'm a quintessential worrier and well-practiced in the art of tossing and turning all night, letting those worries chase away sleep. But the human brain has some unique abilities. As I lay my head on my pillow, heavy with worries and sadness, my brain knew these thoughts were too much to bear in that moment, and it went into self-preservation mode. I quickly fell asleep.

Alex was in our room that night, as we were staying at my brother's house in his guest room. Maybe I heard him cooing in his sleep.

Maybe the thoughts I carried into my sleep lingered on. Maybe there is another explanation. Whichever the case, that night I dreamed of Colby and Alex.

I dreamed I was standing in a backyard with lush, soft grass. Then a little kid ran right past me. He was wearing a duck costume. The lower half was rounded like a duck's body, and the duck's tail stuck out behind him. His legs were covered in normal clothes, but he had two decorative webbed feet covering his shoes. He had arms bent in half to makeshift wings that he flapped as he ran, and his head was covered with a costume duck head that left his face exposed. And the face was Alex.

I was startled, then delighted to see Alex running. He had a huge smile on his face.

Then I was startled even more. There was a second duck costume coming my way, and inside it was Colby, her smile just as big and glorious.

Neither Alex nor Colby looked up at me or acknowledged my presence in any way. The two of them ran in circles, either racing each other or chasing each other. In my dream, I stood there confused and happy, trying to make sense of it all, watching them play together and listening to a mix of quacks and giggles.

When I woke up, I felt much the same way—confused and happy.

Dreams of Colby are always bittersweet. It's euphoric to see her again, like no drug could ever match. And waking up delivers a crash in proportion to the power such a drug would have. Still, I'd make that trade anytime—a metaphor of sorts of her life.

This dream carried an extra sting. It was a reminder that Colby and Alex would never play together. It was a reminder that Colby would not be there with us for Alex's baptism.

Recently, I told a friend that one of the hardest things to cope with was that not a day goes by that I don't think to myself, *Today would have been better if Colby were here.* Some days are worse off than others because of her absence.

It was with these things in mind that I began the Sunday morning drive from Plano to Rockwall. Usha and Ella were in the backseat, keeping Alex entertained. I sat in the front, happy to be alone in my struggle to stifle my tears.

It was a battle I would lose.

The closer we got to Rockwall, the more the emotions grew out of control. I thought about the dream. I thought about sitting in the front pew during her memorial service. I thought about the tree planted in her memory and the brick that bears her name in the church garden. Mostly, I thought back to what it was like to watch Usha carry her into the sanctuary and her reaction to hearing the organ played. Her arms would lift up with joy, and she would unleash the full force of her smile.

I pulled into the church parking lot with eyes welled up, snot dripping, and true heartache. Truly, my chest felt as if it were being crushed, and my stomach had stabbing pains. I was no longer worried about how I would get through the day. I wondered if I would get through that moment.

We may have had different reasons for needing it, but we all took a collective deep breath and stepped out of the car.

As we began walking in, the friendly waves began from across the parking lot. As we entered, hugs began flowing freely. Babies were handed back and forth. Greetings and stories began being exchanged. And despite having been gone for over a year, it immediately felt like home.

Recalling this now, I still struggle for the right adjective to describe the transformation that took place between 9:40 and 9:41. Magical seems a cop-out. Miraculous seems too exclusive. I don't know the right word. But I can tell you that at 9:40, I was a broken man, unsure if I could stand. At 9:41, I was at peace. Everything felt right. So right that I didn't even realize how quickly things had changed until later in the day when I was thinking about how rough the day had begun and yet how wonderful it turned out to be.

I want to make something perfectly clear. It's not that at 9:41 I had forgotten about Colby. In fact, I visited the Colby tree several times that day. She was on my mind the entirety of the time. But the heartache of the present was trumped by the joy of things to come. Alex and Colby will play together. That realization soaked me through in appreciation for God's blessings and the celebration of Alex's baptism surrounded by people who not only have the motto "feel the love, be the love," but who live it out.

And another realization hit. I have heard my entire life about Jesus making the broken whole again, but I don't know that I ever really comprehended it. On that day, I experienced what I think it must be like. I was broken, and then I was surrounded by and wrapped in the arms of unconditional love, and I was transformed.

That church is the most caring, loving, and supportive church I have ever known. That is yet another reason I am glad to have had Alex baptized there. But as remarkable as that love is, I know a greater love still exists for all of us. A love that has a lasting and eternal transformation for all of us—emphasis on "all."

As the day faded, it certainly didn't take long to get back to the realities of this world, with the familiar grief of missing sweet Colby, dealing with disparaging Facebook remarks from family about having Alex baptized, and the other trials of life we all face in various forms.

No, my experience that day didn't yield a permanent and eternal transformation. But it gave me a glimmer of what that must be like. I will carry that with me always and find comfort in it. And for all who participated in that day, either in person or in spirit, I hope this story gives you a glimmer of my appreciation for you.

CHAPTER 56

Ode to an Odometer

And why not an essay from the car's point of view? This one is one of my favorites. Writing it, I discovered not only can you load up a vehicle with actual cargo, its inanimate nature makes it perfect for loading up with emotional baggage, too.

Like most newly expecting couples, we made the requisite first two purchases. The first one was a camcorder. The second one was a vehicle more suited to hauling around an 8-pound baby and the 600 pounds of accessories and supplies that go with it. The camcorder model we bought was obsolete within two months of buying it, and I suppose the whole camcorder concept is fairly antiquated as well. The car we purchased, however, has 200,000 miles on her and is sitting in the garage with tires still warm from running kids all over town.

Her name is Bluebell. Or maybe Blue Belle. I have never really given much thought to how to spell it until just now. She didn't come with that name, of course. It didn't come until years later when Ella got to the stage of naming things. Being a blue Toyota Highlander, the name seemed to fit, even if it wasn't high on the imagination scale.

Ella still names things, and the creativity has dialed up over the years. Usha's Volvo's name is Fishlegs, for instance.

When we got Bluebell, she only had a couple of dozen miles on her. I think back to the three of us leaving the lot—Bluebell, Usha, and me—and how shiny new, unscratched, and naive we all were embarking down the parenthood road. Neither she nor we could have predicted the journeys and adventures the next years would bring. None of us were expecting the highs to be so high and the lows to be so low.

In this fast-changing world, it's an interesting mental exercise to think about how the world and our lives have changed when looked at from the point of view of a car. Consider that Bluebell has factory-installed cassette players and ashtrays. When last did you hold a cassette in your hand?

More than one guest has asked to connect their music via Bluetooth. Nope.

Befuddled, they follow up with "I guess I can plug it in if you have a cable." Nope. No cable and no place to plug one in. However, I have a Wheels on the Bus CD if you'd rather not listen to the radio station.

She is missing all of today's popular add-ons. No hands-free phone, no onboard navigation, no DVD player, no backup cameras, no auto-lift gate, no heated seats, and no cooled seats, either.

But she is still the fanciest car I have ever owned. I suppose that's not too high a bar, as most of the others were just lucky if they had matching hubcaps.

It's not just technology that has changed. When we bought Bluebell, we were still newly enough married to go parking on a date night. Heck, we still had date nights. I also had hair, was two pants sizes smaller, and could have a drink without getting sleepy. *Note to self: Those might be clues about why we don't go parking anymore.*

All in all, and certainly by comparison to me, Bluebell has held up well. Despite her age and miles, she still gets me where I need to go ... and sometimes in a hurry.

A couple of years ago, I was a few hundred miles away from home and out to dinner with dear friends in Lamesa, Texas. Just after we sat down, my phone began ringing. Caller ID said it was Usha's phone, and I figured it was Ella trying to reach me, so I ignored it with plans to call her back later.

She called again. And again. So, I excused myself, stepped outside, and returned the call, worried it might be Usha, and it might be an emergency.

When I called back, sure enough, it was Ella with a "Hey, Dad!"

I was cross with her for not having better phone manners than to repeatedly dial over and over.

"Ella, you can't call like that unless it's an emergency!"

"Well, there are about eight nurses and two doctors in here. I think this counts."

Usha was in the emergency room, and though things turned out well, at the time, things were very serious and quite worrisome.

Dinner ended, and Bluebell flew down some back highways at more than a hundred mph. The old girl still had it, and though I hope to never have cause to test it again, I have little doubt she would be capable.

She has never left me stranded by the side of the road. Sure, there was that blowout 12 miles outside of Pampa on a 12-degree, 50-mph wind day after Thanksgiving. Not fun conditions to change a tire, especially when accessing the spare meant unloading the back of the luggage and bags of Christmas shopping. Not a car passed by for ten minutes, but as soon as one bag of presents blew onto the highway, it got plowed over by a BMW speeding its way back to the Metroplex. Not even the rubber Gumby survived. If you didn't get a Christmas present from me in 2007 and you were expecting one, now you know why.

But you can't hold Bluebell accountable for me not checking the tire pressure before setting out on a seven-hour drive. So, she gets a pass, and I paid the price for my mistake with the challenge of changing a tire with numb fingers and frozen air-blasted eyeballs.

Writing this, I also recall at least twice returning to her at the airport parking after extended trips, only to find her battery drained. I'm still convinced she has a slow, undiscovered voltage drain on her battery. It went undiagnosed and then neglected for so long because she gets very few days off.

The only real problem she has had over the years is a persistent air conditioner problem. The number of times her compressor or blower has been replaced is surely in double digits. More than once, it has failed in the middle of summer, and more than once, I have sworn that was the last straw. Many of the repairs were covered by warranty, and even after the ones that weren't, as soon as the air was blowing cold again, the idea of car-shopping suddenly would lose appeal.

Lately, I have been giving more thought to replacing her. Lately meaning talking about it off and on over the last few years. Truth be told, I haven't really been in any hurry for another car. I think I just talk about it, because I know one day it will be inevitable.

The thing is I have never been prone to sentimentality over vehicles. Maybe it's because of having cars with mismatched hubcaps and always being excited about something nicer. But that is probably just a small part of it. After all, there are some really nice cars and features these days.

The more likely reason is that I have never been a parent without her. The crayon marks, the kid throw-up, the roll down your window diaper blow-outs. And the pull over the car because a kid said something so funny, you have to belly laugh. The sing-alongs with funny words. The serious conversations about boys, or why kids at school can be mean, or Santa Claus. My mind reels with other examples, but it all fits under the umbrella of quality time you get with kids in the car that doesn't happen any place else: no phones, computers, or TVs to distract.

If that needs further explanation, it can be boiled down to this. Bluebell has been with us to drive all three kids home from the hospital after each one was born. That includes driving at 12.5 mph with Ella because of the new dad overcautiousness. (I would have had the hazards on, too, if Usha had let me.) And in addition to that weighty responsibility of delivering our kids safely home for the first time, once she had to carry me home from the hospital when I had to leave a child behind.

The highest of highs. The lowest of lows. She has seen a lot. More than we ever could have imagined on her purchase day.

To this day, Bluebell knows secrets no others do. She knows I like a good road trip, and that isn't a secret to many. But what has been a secret until now is that she also knows that if I am on a road trip by myself, two hours is the most I can go before crying. Two hours without the distractions of phones, TVs, or computers, and my mind has too much time to think and too many memories of things I miss, and I hit a limit.

Someday, I'll be breaking in another car. She will have to learn that secret and the others. She won't have the full history and won't understand. But that's okay. She'll make her own memories. And maybe she will get a name even cooler than Fishlegs.

CHAPTER 57

Me and Mr. C

This is another story from my youth that came back to me years later with lessons preparing for the time when my daughter Ella would start dating. It appears here because it is a great lead into the closing chapter.

The twenty years referenced in the opening line have now grown to thirty-five years, and the lessons have only grown more important to me.

Earlier today, I had occasion to think about Mr. C, a man I last saw more than twenty years ago. Even though our paths haven't crossed in that time, I still think about him now and again. More specifically, I think about one particular story that has not only stuck with me, but that has come to have a deeper meaning to me now that I am a dad.

It was a warm workday afternoon, probably early fall because there was still plenty of daylight after school to be working outside. I had been doing something with the horses, either putting up tack after a ride or stacking hay. The road we lived on got some traffic, but not so much that you didn't look up every time to see who was driving by. So, when I heard the sound of tires rolling on caliche, I looked up and saw Mr. C's truck passing by.

If I remember correctly, Mr. C worked in the oilfield, checking on pumps and wells all over the countryside or something along those lines. Whatever it was, he didn't have a regular route by my house that I was aware of, so although I easily recognized his truck, it did catch me by surprise. I waved. He saw me and waved back. Then he did something I completely didn't expect. He stopped.

Not only did he stop, he backed up and pulled into our driveway. I started walking over from the direction of the tack shed, which wasn't far away but enough steps to try and contemplate what was happening. As I got closer, I was expecting his window to roll down for a quick exchange. The window didn't lower.

Instead, Mr. C turned off the engine, got out of his truck with a smile, and another wave. He stepped to the back of his truck, let down the tailgate, sat down, and happily said, "Have a seat."

A little more background will help you better understand what was going on. I knew Mr. C because he has a daughter a little younger than me. I met her in high school, and we had some classes together, hung out some, and had even been on a few dates here and there. In the course of all of that, I had met Mr. C a few times and had talked to him a little, but nothing that led me to expect an impromptu invitation to sit down and visit.

But that is exactly what we did. He asked me about school, about the horses, and whatever else it is that two guys getting to know each other talk about. He didn't have any hidden agendas, unsolicited advice, nor was he asking anything of me.

We just talked.

At the time, I remember feeling a mix of surprise and honor that he took the time to visit with me that day. Looking back and having experienced the eagerness to get home after a long day of work makes me appreciate what he did even more. I'm sure Mr. C was looking forward to getting home and to whatever plans were waiting for him there, but instead, he spent thirty unplanned minutes with me, never appearing hurried or uninterested. And now that I am a dad, that story has come to mean even more to me.

Being the daddy of two daughters, I've spent a fair amount of time thinking ahead to the "boyfriend" and "friends with boys" years. I suppose it's natural for us dads to look back at our own experiences and, when we are done wincing, try to learn from them. In my dating years, I met my share of girls' dads and experienced different styles of approaches. Some were good, and some were bad. Let me spend a minute on the bad ones, first.

There were the stereotypical threatening dads. These are the ones we all start off thinking we are going to be when it's our turn—the tough guys who make it a point to be cleaning a gun or recounting prison stories when they meet the boy. These guys love telling their buddies how they put the fear of God into some kid, when the reality is the kid is laughing with his buddies about what the dad did. I didn't meet a lot of these dads, but there were a few. (To that dad carrying a baseball bat, I wonder if you ever figured out how badly that backfired on you.)

There were the dads who wanted to make sure I knew my place, the ones who wanted to make it clear I wasn't good enough for their daughters, the ones who tried too hard to act like my buddy, and the ones who tried to embarrass me or make me uncomfortable. Some of the most interesting times came from the ones wanting to test my judgment, my intelligence, or both.

For you dads who have found success with those methods, you need to do what works for you. But when these things were tried on me, they all suffered from the same flaw. I was either in high school or not far removed from it, so I faced attempts at intimidation or undermining my confidence practically every day. You weren't discouraging me from doing anything. You were issuing me a challenge, or at least that's how I saw it.

Whatever trouble I avoided and whatever smart choices I made had a lot less to do with your approach to me and a lot more to do with how well you raised your daughter in those years leading up to our date. I was fortunate to have dated girls who had both strong confidence and better sense than I did. Those are the things that get the credit for responsible behavior. The girls get the credit for that, and so do you for your role in building that foundation. Without that foundation, your baseball bats mean very little.

Of course, I met plenty of dads who took good approaches, too. I'm no expert, and I'm sure I will make plenty of mistakes along the way. But I hope to make use of what some of those men taught me about being a dad. The lessons aren't revolutionary, but that doesn't mean they are all easy to do. I hope to love my daughter in such a way that she never doubts it, build her confidence so that she doesn't doubt herself, and give her opportunities to grow my trust in her.

And when I meet the boys she hangs out with or dates, I hope to remember the lesson from Mr. C and the fear he left me with the day of our visit on his tailgate—the fear of losing his respect.

Get better, Mr. C. And when you do, take good care of yourself. I know our paths aren't likely to cross again, but I also know that whoever's path you do cross will likely be left better off for the experience.

CHAPTER 58

On Being Happy

When I began piecing this book together, I had ninety some-odd essays and stories to cull through. Then I had to sort out which order to put them in. Picking which ones to open with was tough. Deciding which one to close with was much easier.

The single biggest impact on my fatherhood journey has been my wife. Like so many times in real life, Usha finds herself at the end of the list. But her place in this collection isn't an afterthought; it's a purposeful prominence. It's closing with my most important lesson.

This essay was written before Alex, but its message applies to him, too. Maybe doubly so.

I talk about my girls a lot. Some may claim they are all I talk about, and truthfully, I couldn't put up much of an argument. But one of them doesn't get mentioned nearly as much and certainly does not receive all the credit she deserves.

She is the last to get a hug from me, and when she does, she usually has to share it. Our conversations are seldom completed without interruption, and on the rare occasions we get to have time alone,
she mostly hears me tell stories about my other girls. Yes, I'm talking about my wife, Usha. And though I don't tell her often enough,
she is the best thing that has ever happened to me.

One otherwise ordinary January night in San Diego, an extraordinary thing happened. A boy from the Texas Panhandle, me, met
a girl from Trinidad, her. Geographically speaking, the odds of that
happening are probably on the order of the lottery. Long odds aside,
that night became the biggest defining moment in my life, when
somehow, despite a tendency to be shy, I convinced her that it was
a good idea to see each other again. And so, we did.

I left San Diego intrigued. A month later, I drove from Lubbock
to College Station, and we had our first date. I drove home from that
weekend with my heart noticeably beating and my mind wondering what special things lay ahead. As many wonderful hopes I carried with me, reality has played out even better.

A few years later, we married. Like many, our vows promised for
better or worse, in sickness or in health, and for richer or poorer.
We've seen all of that and in ways we couldn't have imagined.

Another thing I never would have predicted is that it would be
the challenging times that brought us closer. The easy times are great,
at times incredible. But it's the difficult times when you fully appreciate how strong your marriage is. When I've needed support, Usha
has been there for me in a way that only a loving spouse could. Just
as important, she welcomes my consoling when she needs support.

Life consists of the ups and downs and everything in between.
Usha makes my life richer. From the little things like introducing me

to mangos to the big things like helping me be a better father. She chuckles at my silly jokes and puts up with my awful ones. Her smile fixes most anything, and her laugh heals everything else. At times, she is too hard on herself, but not incessantly so. She can be quick to temper, but she is just as quick to apologize when needed. She is smart. She is beautiful. She is my wife, and I am a better person for it.

But alas, this story isn't for Usha, either. This is a story for Ella.

Ella, I do my best to teach you everything I can. I know some of the strongest lessons I impart are not by what I say, but by the examples of what I do. This is one of the greatest lessons I can share and one of the keys to happiness in life. Marry well.

Pick someone kind and loving. Pick someone who is better at finding the good in you than pointing out your flaws. Pick someone who inspires you to do great things. Pick someone strong enough to handle life's bumps and fun-loving enough to enjoy life's pleasures. Pick someone who strengthens your relationship with God. Pick someone who values you as much as you value them. Pick someone intelligent and enjoy the way they help your mind grow—and make sure they appreciate that you grow their mind, too.

Marry well and never forget that you did. Cherish all the blessings that come with it, and your life will be better for it.

Neil Turner's childhood was awash with influence from his story-telling parents and his older siblings' love of writing. In high school, he earned extra money by writing papers for other students. Since any applicable statute of limitations has long since expired, he would like to note that he remains mildly bitter about getting B's on his own papers while the ones he did for others received A's.

Later jobs included day work on local farms and ranches, fry cook, a bakery, and a butcher shop. Professionally, he worked as an engineer, a field not especially known for writing. But Neil found ways to employ his writing skills throughout his career.

After the loss of his daughter, he turned to writing to help process his grief and, in doing so, embraced the beauty and humor in parenthood. That led to this book, in which Neil shares personal lessons and observations from his unusual fatherhood journey, hoping it will enrich readers' own parenting journeys.

Neil resides in Oklahoma with his wife. Together they have three children. Neil homeschools their youngest child, Alex, who has autism. They share their adventures on various social media platforms, and if you would like to follow along, you can find more information and the links at www.OkieSchool.org.

www.ingramcontent.com/pod-product-compliance
Lightning Source LLC
Chambersburg PA
CBHW021213130626
46554CB00004B/1201